REFRESHING GRAMMAR

JAMES BURL HOGINS

Acquisition Editor / W. Philip Gerould
Project Editor / Geoffrey T. Garvey
Copy Editor / Andrea Coens
Text and Cover Design / James Buddenbaum
Production Director / Arthur Kuntz
Composition / Hagle and Company

Library of Congress Cataloging in Publication Data

Hogins, James Burl.
  Refreshing grammar.

  Includes index.
  1. English language—Grammar—1950-   I. Title.
PE1112.H625 1985   428.2   84-14006
ISBN 0-574-22095-X

Printed in the United States of America.

10 9 8 7 6 5 4 3 2 1

CONTENTS

PREFACE

Years ago, when I first started teaching in college, I wanted to write a book about the grammar needed to give a person confidence and to succeed with the writing that college and a job demand. But most of all I wanted to begin the book with the sentence, "Anything you can take a picture of is a noun." And the second chapter would have started, "Whatever an airplaine can do to a cloud is a preposition—over, under, between, through, and so on." Those sentences didn't survive, but the purpose for that book did survive and remains the same as that for my earlier dream: I want whatever I write about refreshing grammar and usage to be truly useful.

When the traffic ruins a sunny morning, when assignments, overtime, or a roommate invades our tranquility, or when the sight of cigarette butts, an overdue bill, plastic milk cartons, and unwashed dishes add more strife to our lives, we yearn to find calm, quiet, and invigorating surroundings. I, like you, experience the need for freshness, for unruffled times and places.

Persons who read a great deal as a function of their jobs—managers, editors, teachers—experience a similar desire for fresh, clear writing. That wish is similar to the desire for pleasant mental and physical surroundings. A refreshing sentence, a refreshing paragraph, and finally a refreshing composition add to the reader's understanding and appreciation just as a walk in the park makes the day go better. Good sentences that are clear, refreshing, and mature are truly worth striving for.

No one method or set of exercises will teach you how to write good, clear sentences. But you can begin. If you genuinely desire to write well and to communicate clearly, then you can succeed. Begin by acknowledging that a clear sentence, free of errors, is better than a muddled one and that an interesting phrase is better to read than a worn out one. And then you can begin.

Chapter 1 shows you how the sentence works, shows you by example how to find the basic sentence elements. As with each of the ten chapters, the first one ends with a review test of the material just studied. Chapters 2 and 3 involve you with the various classes of words. Practice is offered so that you will feel comfortable with the use of coordinating conjunctions and the like.

The next two chapters, 4 and 5, deal with subordination, a function of sentence construction that will allow you enormous variety in your writing. Chapters 6, 7, and 8 address the most common problems that college writers have. The exercises are geared so that you can practice editing incorrect sentences until you gain enough skill and confidence to write your own correct sentences with ease. Chapter 9 urges you to learn how to write interesting, refreshing sentences. Then Chapter 10, the last one, deals with punctuation, mechanics, and spelling.

No one could have had better help and encouragement while doing the hard work of writing than I have had. Marie Way worked hard and creatively for me on the exercises and on the readability of the text. Someday she too will know the satisfaction of seeing published words. Aenea, my classics-major daughter, helped me through some depressing times and always made me proud of her. Jon, my guitar-playing, fishing-buddy son, never failed to make being a writer and father worthwhile. Flora did all the rest—typed, ran errands, smiled, and offered the right words, strokes, and help just when something was needed. And SRA, from Mike Crisp to Phil Gerould to Geoffrey Garvey, has been good to me.

And to my very special friends at Mesa—Dick, Don, Art, and Hugh— I owe on-going gratitude for the good times. But especially to Con McAuliffe, Emil Hurtik, and Bob Yarber, who truly know, do I offer my promise to see the world as it is, reality-fabrication kits, and all.

J. Burl Hogins
Mesa College
June 4, 1984

SENTENCES

A good sentence offers delight and information to both the writer and the reader, delight because a moment's drabness has been broken, and information because something useful has been shared. A good sentence centers a writer's thoughts; a good sentence commands the reader's attention. At the heart of all great writing stands the sentence. Words make up the sentence, but words alone do not convey meaning; sentences do that. The words "dollars to want a you give I million" suggest gibberish until we arrange them into a sentence: "I want to give you a million dollars."

Learning to write a clear, meaningful sentence rewards the person who learns the task well with a lifelong tool, one that's both useful and satisfying. Perhaps you have heard about the sculptor, Michelangelo, who was asked how he could sculpt such masterpieces as the statues of David and Moses. He answered that he simply took a huge chunk of marble and chipped away everything that was not David or Moses. Our vocabularies are chunks of marble waiting to be shaped into our own creations. Few of us will be famous authors, but each of us can chip away at excess words and poor ideas until we have powerful sentences.

GRAMMAR AND THE MESSAGE

Grammar is only one block in the construction of the whole **message** which also includes purpose, audience, the words chosen, the writer's personality, the methods used to advance the thought, the rules of the language in operation, and everything that makes writing work. The whole message is the L.A. Raiders winning the Super Bowl, a team of climbers reaching the top of Mt. Everest, or Karpov winning at chess. The Raiders don't just score, the climbers don't just reach the top, and Karpov doesn't just win; planning, practice, effort, and error all go into the building of the final achievement. The totality equals the message.

The procedures or rules by which the climbers climb and the Raiders and Karpov play are the *grammar* of their *message*. A great pass in football works only when the ball is caught inbounds. A great word works only when it is in the correct position. To know definitions of verbs and nouns but not to know the procedures or rules to use them effectively helps neither the writer nor the reader. The grammar that you learn here is limited to the information you need to express your thoughts correctly. In the end, your use of grammar allows you to shape the message of your thoughts. Just as athletes, mountain climbers, and chess players learn basics first, so too must the writer learn a few grammatical concepts.

BASIC SENTENCE ELEMENTS ✓

1. Ice melts.
2. The warming ice melts.
3. The spring's warming ice melts quickly.
4. The early spring's warming ice melts quickly with the noonday sun.

A simple two-word sentence can expand until the sentence says exactly what we want it to say. Regardless of how much we add to the basic elements, we can see that the core of the sentence remains *ice melts*.

Every sentence possesses basic or core elements.

1. Doors open.
2. The doors open at noon.
3. The doors to the concert hall open at noon.
4. The concert hall's doors open promptly at noon.
5. Although the Stones do not appear until 7:00, the concert hall's doors open promptly at noon for the fans.

Principal Subject and Principal Verb ✓

All sentences build around two central elements: the **principal subject** and the **principal verb**. *Ice* is clearly the subject in each of the first examples, and *melts* remains the verb even in the expanded examples. The second set of examples has two words that form the core of the sentence: *doors* and *open*.

Even if we separate the subject from its verb, the two continue to cement the other words together and give them purpose.

1. Plants droop.
2. Plants that lack water droop.
3. House plants that lack water droop like tired birds.
4. When the air gets especially dry, house plants that lack water droop like tired birds.

The subject and verb may have groups of words before, between, or after them, yet the two of them remain the only necessary parts of the English sentence.

1. The horses stomped.
2. The horses stomped their feet.
3. After stopping, the horses, breathing heavily, stomped their feet.
4. After stopping in the snowy woods, the horses, breathing heavily, stomped their feet, reminding the driver of the miles to go before they could sleep.

This last sentence, filled with several word groups, maintains *horses* and *stomped* as the principal subject and verb.

Each group of words punctuated as a sentence must contain at least one principal subject and one principal verb.

The reason each sentence needs a principal subject and verb is that other subjects and verbs may be present; however, these other subjects and verbs will never be the main or principal ones. What the others do will be explained in later sections.

You already know two other requirements of every sentence, which are requirements of convention, not grammar:

1. Every sentence begins with a capital letter.
2. Every sentence ends with a period, a question mark, or, very rarely, with an exclamation mark.

Exercise 1 Underline the principal **subject** and the principal **verb** in the following sentences.   *1 – 10 do it or all*

1. The clouds float softly over the beach.

2. Books help those who use them.

3. The stars shine brightest during the darkest night.

4. The President of Egypt stood up just before he was murdered.

5. Exercise strengthens one's muscles and one's spirit.

6. Nero, who did not care about his people, fiddled as Rome burned.

7. The fruit on the outer limbs ripens first.

8. The grammarians, who are harmless, differed on nearly everything.

9. At the zoo, the lions roared all night.

10. Eight o'clock classes nearly always dragged.

11. The dog caught the Frisbee® in the air.

12. Some dogs almost always prefer a ball to a Frisbee.®

13. All successful writers begin by reading everything possible.

14. At the appointed hour, Denise called Sue.

15. The young man read the billboards.

16. The startled horse bolted at the reflection.

17. During the spring break, the students played volleyball at the beach.

18. The sun glistened on their sun-tanned bodies.

19. After a happy reunion, the young couple parted company.

20. Every morning before work, they jogged together in the park.

21. Dogs often travel far when looking for their masters.

22. Susan paced the floor waiting for her test results.

23. Nobody wanted to see him lose.

24. The old man finally crossed the street.

25. The grunion usually spawn between May and July.

26. The bars in Kansas always close on Sunday.

27. The young woman enthusiastically delivered her speech.

28. Through the sun-drenched valley, the deer bounded out of sight.

29. The second phase of the project finally began.

30. People came from all over the country to hear the concert.

Fragments

If a group of words does not contain a principal subject and a principal verb, then the group of words called a **fragment** is not a sentence. A fragment lacks independence; it cannot stand alone as a sentence. Several mistakes can cause a fragment, but the main thing to remember is that every group of words punctuated as a sentence must have a principal subject and verb. Notice these fragments.

> Coming home too soon.
> After the exciting game was over.
> If you wanted to go.
> A kickoff return in the first quarter.

Each of these fragments lacks something, and that something is a sense of completeness. You will have the opportunities later to explore this problem of fragments. For now, distinguish between a complete sentence and a fragment.

Exercise 2 Identify the following as a **complete sentence** (a) or as an incomplete sentence or **fragment** (b). You will return to this section later.

a = Complete Sentence   b = Fragment

_b_ 1. Leaving the television on all afternoon. ✓

_____

_b_ 2. Because the books looked out of place.

_____

_a_ 3. The government must respond to the people. (Preposition)

_____

_a_ 4. Hoping to improve her image with the women.

_____

_b_   5. Carol never knew the meaning of stopping too soon.

_b_   6. With the floppy disk in place.

_b_   7. Where the moon does not shine.

_b_   8. To buy a pair of hose.

_b_   9. Discouraged by his lack of progress during the game.

_a_   10. Have a chocolate and sit down.

_b_   11. In just one or two minutes.

_b_   12. To lose everything in a fire.

_b_   13. While we waited in the rain and snow.

_a_   14. If I go, I shall return.

_a_   15. Denise kept her word when she could.

_b_   16. Painting the overhead light.

_b_   17. If I should want a new car.

_a_   18. Because the old tower nearly blew down.

When is dependence clause

_b_ 19. Unless Mr. Shade climbs that tree.

_a_ 20. They lasted only four weeks in Europe.

Correcting Fragments More often than not, the fragment that troubles students can be attached to the sentence before it in the passage or to the sentence after it. Look at item 1 in Exercise 2:

> Leaving the television on all afternoon.

Look how easily this fragment can become an appropriate part of the sentence that follows it:

> Leaving the television on all afternoon, I caused the tube to burn out.

Notice how the fragment *After the game* can be added to a sentence:

> We bought junk food after the game.

For practice, go back to Exercise 2 and write a sentence either before or after the fragments to make them complete sentences.

Exercise 3 Sentence Building Learning sentence elements allows you to construct clear, meaningful sentences confidently, knowing that you control the words, not the other way around. Use the following example to get started. Then finish the ten sets, asking yourself when you've finished each set, "Does that sentence say just what I want it to say?"

Pick one A – J

Example of sentence building:

1. Time flies.
2. Time flies when I'm late.
3. Although some of my days drag, time flies when I'm late.
4. Although some of my classes drag, time flies when I'm late to class.

Begin with a simple, two-word sentence, then complete the four sentences, building more interesting, detailed statements as you go.

A. 1. Artists _____

   2. _____

   3. _____

   4. _____

B. 1. Whales _____

   2. _____

   3. _____

   4. _____

C. 1. Water _____

   2. _____

   3. _____

   4. _____

D. 1. Volcanoes _____

   2. _____

   3. _____

   4. _____

E. 1. Politicians _____

   2. _____

   3. _____

   4. _____

F. 1. _____ sinks.

   2. _____

   3. _____

   4. _____

G. 1. _____ creep.

   2. _____

   3. _____

   4. _____

H. 1. _____ burns.

   2. _____

   3. _____

   4. the Victim   had severe burns _____

I. 1. _____*light*_____ flashes.

2. _the red blue & yellow light of police car flashes_

3. _____

4. _____

J. 1. _____ rages.

2. _____

3. _____

4. _____

Action and Linking Verbs

An almost endless variety of definitions could be offered for subjects and verbs. You may recall from discussions in other classes that a **subject** is a noun or pronoun and that a **verb** is an action or state-of-being word. If you recall such a definition, don't feel it's being contradicted here—it isn't. This explanation discusses the same idea but in a different way that you may find easier to understand.

One kind of verb expresses physical or mental **action** (*talk, drive, study, think*).

The other kind of verb expresses a **state of being** or a **condition** (*is, am, seems, appears*) by **linking** the subject of the sentence with another word in the sentence.

Action Verb An action verb may or may not be followed by a direct object (a noun or pronoun that receives the action).

> The men sang all night long.

Sang is an action verb but is not followed by a direct object.

> The men sang songs all night.

Sang is still an action verb, but this time it is followed by a direct object, *songs*.

Linking Verb A linking verb **links** the subject with either an adjective or a noun that follows the linking verb.

> My instructor was interesting.

Was links the subject, *instructor*, to a describing word, *interesting*. (This describing word is called an adjective.)

> My instructor was a rugby player.

Was links the subject, *instructor*, to another noun, *player*.

The most frequently used linking verbs are worth memorizing: *is, am, are, was, were, been, become, seem, appear, grew, look, smell, taste, sound,* and *feel.*

If you are in doubt about a linking verb, try substituting the word *seem* for the verb that you aren't sure about.
   If *seem* fits, the verb is linking.

   The roses appeared wilted.
   The roses seemed wilted.

The verb *appeared* is linking.

Subjects and Verbs

The subject is **who** or **what** the sentence is about. You can find the subject of a sentence by asking the verb "who?" or "what?"

   The workers built the bridge.

"Who" or "what" built the bridge? The answer, "workers," is the subject of the sentence.

   Our cats climb on the furniture.

Remember, to identify the subject, ask "Who or what climb on the furniture?" The answer points you to the correct answer, the subject, "cats." The subject of a sentence, then, is who or what the sentence is about.

You can identify the subject of a sentence by asking the verb *who* or *what*.

   My brother invented all kinds of gadgets.

Who invented all kinds of gadgets? The answer, "my brother" is the subject of the sentence.

If you cannot identify the verb in a sentence, try this: **add the word yesterday, today, or tomorrow** to the front of the sentence. The word inside the sentence that changes as a result of one of the added words is the verb.

   The men ran the entire race in the rain.
   (Tomorrow) the men will run the entire race in the rain.

The word that changed, *ran*, is the verb.

   Shirley seems unusually happy.
   (Yesterday) Shirley seemed unusually happy.

The word that changed, *seems*, is the verb.

You may have to try all three words, *yesterday*, *today*, and *tomorrow*, before you find the one that makes a word change, but when you do find a changed word, then that word is the verb.

To identify the verb in a sentence, add the word yesterday, today, or tomorrow to the sentence. The word that changes as a result of adding one of those words is the verb.

Exercise 4 Label the verb as an **action** verb or as a **linking** verb. ~~1 - 15 do it~~

Example:

		Verb	Label
A.	We bought warm jackets.	bought	action
B.	The birds were lovely in the morning light.	were	linking

		Verb	Label
1.	The gun is under the pillow.	is	link
2.	The soccer team played every Saturday.	play	action
3.	Again and again, nations threaten each other.	threaten	act
4.	The instructor was always fair.	was	link
5.	Our horse always seemed friendly.	alway	link
6.	Tina was the sweetest person in the room.	was	L
7.	Old books make great gifts.	make	A
8.	Viking, our dog, barked all the time.	barked	A
9.	Elephants haul huge logs in the forests of India.	haul	A
10.	*Patton* became a classic movie almost overnight.		L
11.	Video games are a favorite national pastime.		L
12.	Many people enjoy owning a motor home.		A
13.	Phil decided not to go to school.		A
14.	Together they went to the 7-Eleven.		A
15.	Lately, he was all she thought about.	was	L
16.	For some reason, Kym is the nicest person when angry.		
17.	Mike, Ellen's husband, teases her constantly.		
18.	Her courage served as an inspiration to everyone.		

19. Ingrid studied all night for the biology test.   _____ _____

20. Those persons truly enjoy writing and reading.   _____ _____

21. That '67 Corvette is my personal car.   _____ _____

22. Chip saw *Star Wars* twenty-two times.   _____ _____

23. Snow skiing looks harder than water skiing.   _____ _____

24. The pioneers did their laundry in streams.   _____ _____

25. Julie sunburned her nose.   _____ _____

26. The Mustang is Matt's favorite sportscar.   _____ _____

27. The winners waited on the platform.   _____ _____

28. Over twenty million people watched the Super Bowl.   _____ _____

29. Our neighbors were unusually helpful.   _____ _____

30. Rugby is a brutal sport.   _____ _____

31. The spoiled child was unhappy with his new toy.   _____ _____

32. The athletes conditioned themselves for the race.   _____ _____

33. Jon Buel, my brother, loves chocolate mousse.   _____ _____

34. Mr. Greenberg reprimanded the class for being tardy.   _____ _____

35. Michael biked 100 miles as a part of the triathlon.   _____ _____

36. The old vase wobbled unsteadily on the shelf.   _____ _____

37. The ocean waves crashed violently on the shore.   _____ _____

38. Vicious dogs often appear friendly.   _____ _____

39. My sister sleeps with ten teddy bears on her bed.   _____ _____

40. The cat pounced suddenly on the toy mouse.   _____ _____

Now for practice, go back over Exercise 4 and find the **subject** of each
sentence by asking the verb *who* or *what*.

The Complete Subject

The **subject** of almost all sentences is the **one word** that the sentence is about. (Once in a great while a sentence may have a two-word simple subject: *To win* was his only goal.) However, the **complete subject** is the one word that the sentence is about **plus** all the words that combine or aid or describe the one-word subject.

Example:

complete subject

The new micro-thin remote control unit allows you to control the sound from across the room.

The one-word subject is *unit*. The **complete subject** always includes the simple subject.

The Predicate

The **verb** of a sentence is either the action word that tells what the subject does, or the linking word that tells what the subject is, was, or seems to be. However, the **predicate** is the verb **plus** all the words that combine or aid or describe the verb. In the example above, the verb is *allows*, while the predicate is *allows* plus all the words following *allows*. Every word in a sentence belongs either to the complete subject or to the predicate.

Study these examples, looking at the **complete subject** and the **predicate**.

complete subject   predicate

    subject   verb

Avery Fisher   developed the first high-fidelity sound system.

complete subject   predicate

        subject   verb

Attempting to stay on top, Fisher   made over twenty-eight innovations.

The two words that make a sentence work are:

1. **The principal subject (also called the simple subject) and**
2. **The principal verb (often just called the verb).**

These two basic elements are both contained in larger elements in most sentences:

The principal subject is found within the complete subject; the principal verb is found within the predicate.

Exercise 5 Identify the **principal subject**, the **complete subject**, the **principal verb**, and the **predicate** using boxes as shown above.

1. A digital timer lets you record from a radio.
2. A separate preamplifier gives you more precise control with less distortion.
3. This component represents the best design.
4. You can have an automatic scan for the strongest signal.
5. Almost every complete system sounds excellent to someone.
6. Sensor controls provide fingertip control of sound levels.
7. Virtually everyone dreams of owning a stereo at one time or another.
8. The best test of a stereo system is to hear it in your own house.
9. Huge waves crashed along the shoreline during the storm.
10. Strong winds drove the water higher, almost to the sidewalk.
11. More than 2,000 people crowded in to watch the game.
12. At the ranch, the bees swarmed around their hive.
13. The empty box bounced off the truck and onto the road.
14. The tired '54 Chevy stalled on the freeway.
15. The man finally had the tape deck installed in his car.
16. Philosophy always interested her.
17. The young woman apparently had spring fever.
18. Last week he called to see if we were going.
19. The captain left for the galley.
20. Watching the sunset on the beach makes me feel peaceful.   20 — 30
21. Instead of heeding her mother's words, Irene plunged into the water.
22. Meryl Streep was on television last night.
23. People from all over the world flock to Hollywood.
24. As an extra on the set, I earned sixty dollars.
25. Laura's new watch has fourteen functions.

26. The new Ferrari cruises at sixty miles per hour in first gear.

27. My cousin constantly tells me his problems.

28. The physicist astounded the audience with his views.

29. We built a house for the mockingbirds.

30. Once a year my younger brother goes to Disneyland.

Exercise 6   Sentence Building Build the following sentences into more sophisticated statements by adding words to make a complete subject around the simple subject and to make a predicate around the verbs.

                         subject   verb

Example: The man limped.

             complete subject   predicate

                        subject   verb

The ragged and dirty old man   limped along the broken pavement.

1. _____ thief crawled _____ .

2. _____ grass grows _____ .

3. _____ water poured _____ .

4. _____ smoke curls _____ .

5. _____ music sounds _____ .

6. _____ leaves rustle _____ .

7. _____ birds flew _____ .

8. _____ car stalled _____ .

9. _____ thunder boomed _____ .

10. _____ lion crouched _____ .

COMPOUNDING

So far, we've discussed simple sentences. If we compound our wishes, we add to them; if we compound our beliefs, we add to them. Thus, in a sentence, if we **compound** the subject, we add to it, thus ending up with more than one subject:

> *Carl* and *Don* liked cultural enrichment.

The words *Carl* and *Don* serve as the compound subject of the verb *liked*. We can also compound a verb, ending up with more than one:

> Dick *collected* and *repaired* old watches.

The words *collected* and *repaired* serve as the compound verb of the subject *Dick*. Sentences themselves can be compounded:

> *Laura saw the movie*, but *she found it boring*.

The two simple sentences *Laura saw the movie* and *She found it boring* are joined together to form a compound sentence.

The fundamental compounded elements are:

1. **subject**   The *birds* and *fish* need feeding.
2. **verb**   The old truck *rattled* and *shook*.
3. **sentence**   *We played well*, and *we won the game*.

Compounding, then, is a technique of adding to the basic, the core, sentence, without the worrisome task of writing two or more boring sentences.

Compound Subjects and Verbs

Actually, we can compound any sentence element. The reasons for compounding include: (1) more options for the writer, (2) greater sentence variety, and (3) more interesting writing.

When two or more subjects, united by a connecting word(s), have the same verb(s), the subjects are <u>compound</u>.
   And when two or more verbs, connected in like manner, have the same subject(s), the verbs are <u>compound</u>.

Even though a sentence has a compound subject and a compound verb, it remains a simple sentence because you can still divide the sentence into one complete subject and one complete predicate.

> The Rhine and Rhone rise in Switzerland and flow toward the sea.

> Hawks and eagles soar and look for hours at a time.

Exercise 7 Fill in the blank with an additional subject, making a compound subject.

1. Time and _____ wait for no one.

2. Washington and _____ fought for American independence.

3. Fashion and _____ intrigued the teenagers.

4. The _____ and seasons seemed like old friends.

5. The _____ and storks danced a mating ritual.

6. Louis and _____ celebrated their first wedding anniversary yesterday.

7. His zest for life and his _____ for knowledge brought him tremendous satisfaction.

8. The innocence and _____ of children are always refreshing.

9. When finished with their work, the young woman and _____ left for the park.

10. _____ and jazz are my favorite kinds of music.

Exercise 8 Fill in the blank with an additional verb, making a compound verb.

1. Wild birds _____ and fluttered in our yard.

2. The swollen river _____ and raged.

3. The flag was thrown to the crowd and _____ .

4. Our piano sounds good but _____ worn.

5. Some music can soothe your anxiety and _____ your emotions.

6. The eager boy, intent on hoeing his garden, weeded and then _____ the rows of cabbage.

7. She ran into the dark night and _____ with all her strength.

8. The puppy _____ and chewed the old sock.

9. Don Quixote tilted at windmills and _____ young maidens in distress.

10. The child laughed gleefully and _____ down the hill to meet her friend.

Now add an appropriate **subject** or **verb**.

11. India and _____ are two of the oldest countries in the world.

12. Swimming and _____ helped Brenda lose ten pounds.

13. Venison and _____ taste somewhat similar.

14. Toyotas and _____ cost less and _____ longer than big cars.

15. Blue and _____ look terrible together.

16. Carl and his _____ testified and _____ against the thief.

17. A smile and a _____ can brighten and _____ my day.

18. Fast cars and _____ were Ed's life.

19. *E.T.* and _____ became instant box-office hits.

20. Magicians and _____ thrilled and _____ Irene to no end.

Compound Sentences

Sometimes a writer needs two sentences that are closely linked; the **compound sentence** fulfills this need.

Here is a compound sentence written by former President Carter to describe some special moments he had fishing for trout.

> About eight o'clock the cloud of mayflies began dipping to the water's surface for the females to deposit their eggs, and trout began to rise regularly to take the floating insects.

The simple sentences are connected by *and*; they are intimately connected in thought. First the natural bait appears, then the trout begin to feed. This blending of ideas is ideal for the compound sentence.

Two **options for combining two sentences** are especially important for you to learn thoroughly: (1) a comma plus a coordinating conjunction (, and, but, or, nor, for, so, yet) or (2) a semicolon (;).

Example: 1. The birds flew away, and they never came back.
2. The deer appeared cautious; they hardly moved at all.

A compound sentence is formed:

1. **By connecting two or more simple sentences with a comma plus a coordinating conjunction—*and, but, or, nor, for, so, yet*—**
2. **Or with a semicolon (;).**

Here are further examples of well-written compound sentences.

1. There were no stocked fish in this area, but there was a heavy population of wild brown trout in the rich limestone stream.

   Notice how smoothly the sentences flow, one into the next. This smoothness, and thus reader interest, would be broken if the author had stopped one sentence with a period and had begun a new sentence.

2. On my last four casts I caught and released three fish, so I went back to get my wife and three sons out to share the promising fishing.

Here the author uses a compound verb *caught and released* plus a compound sentence (joined with a comma plus *so*). Thus, the use of compound sentences makes for excellent writing.

Be careful that you don't confuse a compound verb joined by *and* with a compound sentence joined by a comma plus *and*.

1. **compound verb**   The weather rattled my teeth and shook my skin.
2. **compound sentence**   The weather rattled my teeth, and it shook my skin.

Exercise 9 Label the compound elements as **compound subjects** (a), **compound verbs** (b), or **compound sentences** (c).

_____ 1. The weather was good, but everything else was wrong.

_____ 2. I found it very difficult to strip off line when casting, and I broke my leader twice when large fish made stray runs downstream.

_____ 3. The trees, grass, and snags reached out for the bait on every cast.

_____ 4. The fish were feeding voraciously, but they were not looking for me.

_____ 5. I finally gave up and waited for the others.

_____ 6. The next day was Sunday, and after my sad experience everyone was convinced that I needed to go to church.

_____ 7. He and I had a long tug-of-war as I waded closer and closer to the pile of debris.

_____ 8. Within a half hour she, Chip, and I had caught brook trout weighing over two pounds.

_____ 9. Rosalynn and I climbed the steep and rocky slope above our cottage so that we could enjoy the view and see the thick pink and white laurel blossoms growing near the top of the mountain.

_____ 10. On my second cast, around and under a deep bank, I caught a 17-inch wild brown beauty, and from there on I could not miss.

_____ 11. He loved her from the moment of the boardinghouse fire, but they never saw one another again.

_____ 12. He maneuvered for position and made his move in the timely fashion of a great driver.

_____ 13. She negotiated for months, and then she demanded a raise.

_____ 14. Their similarities far outweigh their differences; they should get along better.

_____ 15. Jean was a brilliant chemist and was an excellent artist.

_____ 16. He yelled at life and scoffed at death.

_____ 17. The beaches on the Solomon Islands and the beaches on Maui are similar.

_____ 18. We refused to be beaten by his threats and denied him the satisfaction of harassing us.

_____ 19. I have no wife, and I have no family, yet my life is filled with contentment.

_____ 20. His bold attack worked, and his careful planning promised new success.

Exercise 10 Add either a **comma** (plus a coordinating conjunction—*and, but, or, nor, for, so, yet*) or a **semicolon**, and combine these two simple sentences.

1. The boys played hard. They tired from all the running.

2. The flight for Las Vegas was scheduled to depart in one hour. She quickly finished packing her suitcase.

3. He didn't want to sell the house. He simply had no choice.

4. It was a small fire, one that was quickly contained. People soon resumed their usual activities.

5. Every week he got his paycheck. He put half of it in the bank instead of spending it on frivolity.

6. Because of the Santa Ana winds, the clouds are almost gone. It is a fine day for going to the mountains.

7. They spent the entire weekend reviewing briefs. By Monday morning they were ready to close the deal.

8. Faust was tempted. He persisted in responding to the spiritual aspects of life.

9. Forming a study group, the students studied the material. They were well prepared for the test.

10. Ivan Ilyich sought the purpose for his dying. The solution escaped him until he reviewed his life.

11. The crowd went wild as he ran home. The visitors still won the game.

12. Lee spent the night with Sue Ann last night. They hardly spoke this morning.

13. Her father never told her that she was adopted. He always was a secretive man.

14. Bill's new book was a best-seller within weeks. He had never shown much promise before this book.

15. Our cat had her litter in the old boat house. Her kittens were out of my brother's reach.

Exercise 11   Sentence Building Build one good sentence from each group of sentences. The sentence itself may be compounded, or it may have compound verbs or subjects.

Example: An able man was chosen.
A prudent man was chosen.
An honorable man was chosen.
An able, prudent, and honorable man was chosen.

1. A. Pure water possesses no color.
 B. Pure water possesses no taste.
 C. Pure water possesses no smell.

 D. _____

2. A. Cicero was the greatest speaker of his age.
 B. Demosthenes was the greatest speaker of his age.
 C. John Kennedy was the greatest speaker of his age.

 D. _____

3. A. Bert addressed the actors.
 B. Bert related to the actors.
 C. Bert encouraged the actors.

 D. _____

4. A. The pioneers crossed plains in wagons.
 B. The pioneers crossed the rivers in barges.
 C. The pioneers crossed the mountains with determination.

 D. _____

5. A. The barn in the background was red with white trim.
   B. The flowers in the foreground were red with a white border.

   C. _____

6. A. Gardening is ignored in this country.
   B. Gardening is loved in England.

   C. _____

7. A. Kelly thinks cabbage is beautiful in a garden.
   B. Saundra thinks roses are beautiful in a garden.

   C. _____

8. A. The Coogans loved indoor gardening.
   B. The Newmans loved outdoor gardening.

   C. _____

9. A. Some members demanded word processors.
   B. Some members demanded microcomputers.
   C. Some members demanded cable TV.

   D. _____

10. A. They call it the king of trains.
    B. They call it the train of kings.

    C. _____

11. A. The Orient Express begins in London.
    B. The Orient Express ends in Istanbul.

    C. _____

12. A. Students are taught a practical orientation.
    B. Students are cautious learners.
    C. Students are efficiency-minded.

    D. _____

Exercise 12 In the following paragraphs, underline the **verbs** with two lines, and underline the **subjects** with one line.

An Unexplained Disaster

Many find it hard to believe, but one of the outright worst disasters came mysteriously and left in the same manner. The year was 1918; the month was March, and the place was a large American Army base at Fort Riley, Kansas.

A few men came down with a fever, aching muscles, sore throats, and other cold-like symptoms. But they did not have a cold. Within a few weeks more and more men became sick. Then the disease began to spread. First it spread across the United States, then to ships at sea, then to other countries. France, Germany, Italy, England, Russia, Spain, India, and finally China were all hit hard. Spain suffered especially, with tens of thousands of persons dying.

Doctors all over the world were baffled by this killer disease. They could find no specific reason for its worldwide spread. Before it had run its course, the epidemic had killed over 21,000,000 persons. India lost over 12,000,000 while the U.S. lost over 500,000.

The end of 1918 saw two worldwide killers stopped: World War I and the killer influenza epidemic. World War I stopped with a treaty; the other merely went away. We don't know where the influenza came from, nor does anyone know where it went. The influenza simply stopped killing people.

REVIEW TEST

I. Principal Subject

Choose the letter that corresponds to the principal subject.

_____ 1. John inherited his father's house.
　　　　　　　a　　　b　　　c　d　　　e

_____ 2. The ball game bored the entire crowd.
　　　　　　　　a　　　　b　　　　c　　　d

_____ 3. I am sure the invitation was sent.
　　　　　　　a b　c　　　　d　　　　e

_____ 4. The deer jumped over the fence.
　　　　　　　　a　　b　　　c　　　d

· _____ 5. When the water boiled, we made tea.
　　　　　　　　a　　　　　　b　c　d

II. Principal Verb

Choose the letter that corresponds to the principal verb.

_____ 6. The crowd jeered the band on the field.
　　　　　　　　a　　b　　　c　　　d

_____ 7. The killer whale was nearly extinct.
　　　　　　　　a　　b　　c　　　d

_____ 8. I felt the wind in my face.
　　　　　　　a b　　c　　　d

_____ 9. I liked the hard courses the best.
　　　　　　　a b　　c　　d　　　e

_____ 10. The cow and calf stood near the road.
　　　　　　　　a　　b　　c　　d　　e

III. Fragments

Identify the following as a **complete sentence** (a) or as a **fragment** (b).

_____ 11. After the storm had passed.

_____ 12. Roland makes a good amplifier.

_____ 13. Fender is the name of a famous guitar.

_____ 14. When he plays well.

_____ 15. John becomes involved in his band.

_____ 16. She detests going to nightclubs.

_____ 17. Although she does go on occasion.

_____ 18. Every year at this time.

_____ 19. Dick and Mel had argued and disagreed for years.

_____ 20. The Student Center offered word processing to us.

IV. Action and Linking Verbs

Choose "a" if the verb in italics is an **action verb**, "b" if it is a **linking verb**.

_____ 21. I *drove* the old car to work last week.

_____ 22. Hunting *is* a tiring sport.

_____ 23. I *am* the fifth of five sons.

_____ 24. The water *froze* last night.

_____ 25. The argument *wrestled* with some old myths.

V. Complete Subjects

Choose the letter of the **complete subject**.

_____ 26. All of the recent players on that team voted not to go on strike.
                                    a   b

_____ 27. One person's treasure is another's white elephant.
                        a   b

_____ 28. Television prevents some people from going out.
                a   b

_____ 29. Many parents know too little when they begin.
                a   b

_____ 30. All their clothes were stolen from the trees.
                    a   b

VI. Predicates

Choose the letter of the **predicate**.

_____ 31. I do not drink coffee or tea.
            a   b

_____ 32. The cancellation clause in the contract caused grief.
                            a   b

_____ 33. The record on the stereo made me want to dance.
                        a   b

_____ 34. Barb wanted to do what was right.
            a   b

_____ 35. Those new digital clocks are fascinating.
                        a   b

VII. Compounding

Select the correct letter for the words in italics.

    a = Compound Subject
    b = Compound Verb
    c = Compound Sentence
    d = None of the above

_____ 36. Brett and John Henry are *two of my favorite characters.*

_____ 37. Every other year we *hiked and camped* in the Rockies.

_____ 38. *That water and that bridge* are going to meet, soon.

_____ 39. *We won; they lost.*

_____ 40. *After we were stranded, we decided to sit and wait.*

_____ 41. *Old clocks and old watches* are comforting to wonder about.

_____ 42. The book's red cover *didn't indicate or suggest* its subject.

_____ 43. The Apple® computer *kept track of the recipes and printed the news.*

_____ 44. *Each plate had the old man's picture on it; each cup had his picture painted on the side.*

_____ 45. *The temperature gets over 100 degrees, and Bob's social life suffers.*

VIII. Subject and Verb

Choose the words that are the subject and verb of the sentence.

_____ 46. After the dance, Jane invited all the girls to her house.
   a. dance, Jane   c. girls, invited
   b. Jane, invited   d. Jane, to her house

_____ 47. Everybody on the team thought the same thing.
   a. everybody, thought   c. thought, thing
   b. team, thought   d. same, thing

_____ 48. The pictures tilted toward the right.
   a. pictures, tilted   c. pictures, toward the right
   b. pictures, toward   d. tilted, right

_____ 49. Bonnie's body movements are like those of a dancer.
   a. body, dancer   c. like, dancer
   b. movements, like   d. movements, are

_____ 50. In spite of Sue's wanting to watch TV, her brother made her wash dishes.
   a. Sue's, watch   c. brother, made
   b. brother, wash   d. her, wash

CHAPTER 2

CLASSES OF WORDS: NOUNS, PRONOUNS, AND VERBS

When we go to the grocery store, we know that the items we want will be arranged by kinds of foods: frozen, canned, fresh vegetables, milk, eggs, and the like. Consider how difficult shopping would be if no classification system were used. We might find the peanut butter next to the cabbage or the mushrooms in with the cheese. But someone has arranged and classified all the groceries into a pattern that allows us to shop without much difficulty.

Coaches classify individuals in a given sport the same way. In football, the function of the player classifies him as a tackle, linebacker, quarterback, and so on.

In English, grammarians classify words by the job they perform. These classes are called **parts of speech** or **classes of words**.

NOUNS

We find that many words are names. These we place in one class and call them **nouns**.

The naming of persons and things and ideas and emotions and places occupies much of our time when we are very small, when we are learning the language.

Persons	Things	Ideas
President Kennedy	clouds	democracy
Ms. Chenault	wood	nationalism
José Garcia	ships	trust
Emil Hurtik	computers	bravery

Emotions	Places	Activities
anger	town	smiling
love	New York	talking
sadness	India	loving
exaltation	backyard	flying

These words, as well as tens of thousands of others, all perform the same function—they name. As you already know, they are called nouns.

A noun is the name of anything or anyone.

Such simple expressions as *cork floats* and *ships sink* are sentences, and the nouns *cork* and *ships* are the subjects. You will find that every subject is a noun or some word or words used for a noun.

Nouns often appear in sentences not merely as the subject. In the following examples, the nouns are in italics. Notice that in every instance they name something or someone.

> In the early *morning*, the *campsite* came alive with stirring, yawning *bodies*. As the first to stir, the *ranger* gathered *sticks* and *leaves* for the *fire*. Then the young *recruits* made their *way* to the small *fire pit*, reaching out toward the *warmth*.

Exercise 1 Underline the nouns in the following sentences.

1. The artist draws with his eyes, not with his hands.

2. The worst thing a person can do with words is to surrender to the words.

3. The backbone of science is logic and experiment.

4. The image stayed in her mind for days.

5. The students became expert guides, helping the tired and feeble folks

    from their water-soaked abodes.

6. While cats can be finicky eaters, even the most demanding cat likes fish.

7. Mechanically inclined since childhood, Tom can fix anything from

    appliances to cars.

8. The plants are losing their leaves for lack of sunlight and water.

9. Exercise makes a person feel better.

10. Without warning, the car's brakes slipped just as he reached the

    bottom of the hill.

Nouns and verbs are the two most significant types of words in our language. As you have already observed, these two types form the core of all our sentences. While learning about nouns, keep in mind that they name something or someone. That's why they are classified as naming words. We will take up later exactly how these naming words function in a sentence (pp. 36–42). You have already seen the most important function of a noun: **subject** of the sentence.

You are not stuck with trying to memorize all nouns in order to identify them because English offers clues to a noun's identity. For instance, a noun will fit in the following slot:

> The _____ was bothering us.

Even if we made up a nonsense word, the new "word" would function as a noun although the meaning would be nonexistent. The wombon sneaked up behind us. You don't have to know what a *wombon* is to know that it acts like a noun:

1. It follows *The*.
2. It's the subject of *sneaked*.
3. If we put an *s* on the end, we would know that several "wombons" sneaked up behind us.

Methods for identifying a noun, then, include:

1. **Definition**: A noun names whatever can be named.

   Exercise 2 Fill in the blanks with nouns.

Persons	Things	Ideas	Emotions	Places	Activities
Bob Hope	footstool	honor	frustration	Mt. Baldy	eating

2. **Endings**: Nouns may have predictable endings, offering the careful reader or listener clues to identify nouns. We offer two examples, then ask you to fill in the blanks with two examples of yours. You will discover that you already know most, if not all, of this material.

   Exercise 3 Fill in the blanks with nouns.

   Predictable noun endings:

   -ist: dentist, therapist, _____ , _____

   -ance (also -ence): significance, reluctance, _____ , _____

   -tion: production, distribution, _____ , _____

   -sion: depression, regression, _____ , _____

   -ity: ability, deformity, _____ , _____

   -ness: wilderness, helplessness, _____ , _____

   -ism: Americanism, feminism, _____ , _____

   -or (also -er): driver, operator, _____ , _____

   -ment: government, judgment, _____ , _____

   -ship: friendship, kinship, _____ , _____

3. **Determiners**: We can observe certain words that determine a noun is coming. These signal words announce a noun, sometimes telling us whether the noun is singular or plural. The three most consistent determiners are, *a*, *an*, and *the*. We offer two examples; you fill in two other examples of nouns following the noun's determiner. Some determiners are adjectives; nevertheless, they announce that a noun is coming.

Exercise 4 Fill in the blanks with nouns.

a chair, flower, _____ , _____

an elephant, actress, _____ , _____

the horses, date, _____ , _____

some shells, views, _____ , _____

one woman, marriage, _____ , _____

all nations, trucks, _____ , _____

every fish, answer, _____ , _____

those rabbits, glasses, _____ , _____

that outfit, book, _____ , _____

All numbers:
one, fifty, coins, _____ , _____

Possessive words:
my, Aenea's, your, its, whose, her, glove, ski, _____ , _____

4. **Form**: Nouns take two forms, singular and plural. A good test is to fit the correct form in the slot following either *this* or *these*.

Exercise 5 Write two additional examples of nouns.

this	**these**
boat, shirt, _____ , _____ ,	boats, shirts, _____
woman, person, _____ , _____ ,	women, persons, _____
light, pen, _____ , _____ ,	lights, pens, _____

5. **Function**: Nouns function in any of six positions in sentences. Few professional writers stress learning these functions; rather, they place the emphasis on being able to use nouns properly, such as whether to use them in their singular or plural forms. By example, however, we

will demonstrate the use of six functions: **principal subject**, **direct object**, **indirect object**, **object complement**, **subject complement**, and **object of a preposition**.

Exercise 6 After each complete example, fill in the blank by choosing appropriate nouns.

1. **Principal subject of verb**. The subject is the person, place, thing, idea, emotion, or activity that the sentence is about.

> **The car started slowly**. What started slowly? *Car*.
>
> **Walking is my favorite pastime**. What is my favorite pastime? *Walking*.
>
> **That clock runs five minutes fast**. What runs fast? *Clock*.

   1. A _____ jumped straight up.

   2. The _____ broke down last week.

   3. My _____ is fifty years old today.

   4. Whenever Jennifer goes out, _____ talk with her.

   5. Some _____ never watch sports.

2. **Subject Complement**. A subject complement follows a linking verb (is, am, are, was, were, been) and renames the subject. (Another kind of subject complement, adjectives, will be discussed later.) The word *complement* means to complete or finish. Thus, a noun following a **linking verb** completes or finishes the subject by renaming or identifying it:

> **We were winners**. *Winners* renames *we*.
>
> **Our house is an old barn**. *Barn* identifies *house*.

   1. She was the best _____ .

   2. The music is a poor _____ .

   3. This is the _____ who robbed the bank.

   4. The letter was the _____ of his last request.

   5. When the night of the party finally arrived, Dalia was the _____ he took.

3. **Direct Object**. The direct object is the word that receives the action of an action verb. The direct object can be found by asking the action verb *who* or *what*.

> **We bought a new car**. We bought what? *Car*.
>
> **Sam, open the door over there**. Open what? *Door*.
>
> **The owner paid John**. Paid who(m)? *John*.

1. Our team broke _____ all afternoon.

2. After lunch, fix the _____ .

3. The store offered free _____ .

4. If you travel frequently, flying saves _____ .

5. Dr. Mundy, the attending physician, claims _____ of the incident.

4. **Object Complement**. An object complement renames the direct object.

> **They elected Joan mayor**. *Mayor* renames the direct object, *Joan*.
>
> **He practiced until he made his work an art**. *Art* renames the direct object, *work*.
>
> **After going to a great deal of trouble, Al called it a night**. *Night* renames the direct object, *it*.

1. The woman's incessant chatter made it a _____ to leave.

2. Having a dog makes walking a _____ .

3. We decided to elect Steve _____ .

4. Following their tedious deliberations, the committee appointed

   Kate their _____ .

5. An education can make life a _____ compared

   to life without one.

5. **Indirect Object**. If an indirect object is present in a sentence, it will always be between the verb and the direct object. An indirect object indirectly receives the action of the action verb. Further, you can place an imaginary *to* or *for* in front of the indirect object. Two verbs, in particular, tend to give us indirect objects: *give* and *send*.

> **Tom always gave girl friends great presents**. Notice than an imaginary *to* or *for* could be placed before the indirect object, *girl friends*.
>
> **Burl gave it a coat of paint**. Burl gave a coat of paint to what? To *it*.
>
> **I bought Marie a new car**. *I* bought a new car for who(m)? For *Marie*.

1. Doug gave _____ his telephone number.

2. James gave _____ a fine present.

3. Please send _____ the overdue notice.

4. She donated the _____ her art collection.

5. His innovative ideas earned _____ quite a reputation.

6. **Object of Preposition**. Prepositions are small words like *to, from, under, of, on, over*, and *between*. (They are discussed in detail in Chapter 3.) Prepositions indicate relationships to things, often telling *where* or *when*. Prepositions link a noun (or pronoun) to another word in the sentence. For instance, **We walked over the bridge**. *Over the bridge* is a prepositional phrase—*over* is the preposition and *bridge* is the object of the preposition. English tends to be filled with prepositional phrases. They are often three words long, but may be more or fewer.

> over the rainbow
> around the next corner
> until dawn
> to the lake
> from the new boss
> between the sheets

Typical sentences with prepositional phrases look like these:

>   prep   object   prep   object
> After the rain, the girls ran through the field.

>   prep   object   prep   object
> The men in the car have been sitting there for an hour.

1. The flowers sat on the _____ .

2. The train came very fast around the _____ .

3. The house on the _____ needed paint under the _____ .

4. Muriel took her friend for a _____ to the _____ .

5. A small stream weaved between the _____ as it ran from the

   _____ to the _____ .

Methods for identifying a noun include definition, endings, determiners, form, and function.

Nouns function in six sentence positions:

Principal subject, subject complement, direct object, object complement, indirect object, and object of a preposition.

Nouns are always the name of a person, place, thing, emotion, idea, or activity.

Exercise 7 Choose the correct letter for the noun in italics.

    a = Principal Subject
    b = Subject Complement
    c = Direct Object
    d = Object Complement
    e = Indirect Object
    f = Object of Preposition

_____ 1. Rock stars earn more *money* than doctors.

_____ 2. The lawyer sent *Jasper* a registered letter.

_____ 3. What we did taught me an important *lesson*.

_____ 4. They made the gardener *President*.

_____ 5. Over the *years*, our house grew smaller.

_____ 6. Never drink and then drive a *car*.

_____ 7. Brevity is the *soul* of wit.

_____ 8. The team was a *loser*.

_____ 9. The blue book lay on the *doghouse*.

_____ 10. The bedspread camouflaged the messy *bed*.

_____ 11. The colorful patterns of the *wallpaper* made the room comfortable.

_____ 12. She was an *actress* from the time she could walk.

_____ 13. *Edith* organized a stag party.

_____ 14. The pilot turned the *plane* gently.

_____ 15. The mattress was filled with chicken *feathers*.

_____ 16. Until yesterday, she kept her promise to *me*.

_____ 17. Although he is young, we unanimously elected him to be our new *president*.

_____ 18. Clark is a *person* who will not be rushed.

_____ 19. She told the district *attorney* that she never saw me before.

_____ 20. Tonight's *potpourri* has a definite Eastern flavor.

Exercise 8 Write clear, intelligent sentences using the following nouns in all six functions. Follow the order listed below. For example, here is *store* used in all six functions:

1. Subject: The *store* is only a mile from here.
2. Subject Complement: This building was a grocery *store*.
3. Direct Object: The owner bought the *store* at a good time.
4. Object Complement: Mr. Barbola made his dream a *store* with beautiful fixtures.
5. Indirect Object: Mr. Blake gave the *store* his time and energy.
6. Object of Preposition: Blake's Market was the name of the *store*.

1. radio

   a. _____

   b. _____

   c. _____

   d. _____

   e. _____

   f. _____

2. diligence

   a. _____

   b. _____

   c. _____

   d. _____

   e. _____

   f. _____

3. fireplace

   a. _____

   b. _____

   c. _____

   d. _____

   e. _____

   f. _____

4. dancers

    a. _____

    b. _____

    c. _____

    d. _____

    e. _____

    f. _____

5. wilderness

    a. _____

    b. _____

    c. _____

    d. _____

    e. _____

    f. _____

PRONOUNS

If someone asked you who did your homework, you would not use your own name, but would simply reply, "I did." The pronoun *I* is a convenient substitute word for one's name. Words that substitute, that stand in for nouns, are labeled **pronouns**. These words make our language much less cumbersome than it would be without them.

Tina went to Tina's house for Tina's clothes so Tina could spend the night with Tina's friend. That sentence is absurd. We use pronouns to calm it down: Tina went to her house for her clothes so she could spend the night with her friend.

Later on we will help you avoid the few problems that pronouns cause in written work. For now we will demonstrate the two essential characteristics of pronouns: (1) kinds of pronouns, and (2) case of pronouns.

Kinds of Pronouns

Few persons take the time to memorize the various kinds of pronouns. (Memorizing the parts of an electric mixer doesn't help make a cake.) Knowing the kinds of pronouns won't make you a better writer. However, in going through the kinds of pronouns and later the cases of pronouns, you might well discover an area that has troubled your writing before. Most beginning writers do make a considerable number of errors with pronouns. Your objective, therefore, is not memory work but discovery—discovery of how pronouns function and discovery of how to avoid common errors (these are dealt with in Chapter 8). Both discoveries can add substantially to your writing ability.

Personal Pronouns Some pronouns reveal whether a person is the speaker (called **first person**), someone spoken to (called **second person**), or someone spoken about (called **third person**). Number refers to one or more than one, singular or plural.

First Person (singular): *I* sent the letter today.
First Person (plural): *We* rode horses at the beach.
Second Person (singular or plural): *You* can begin now.
Third Person (singular): *She* went for the record.
　　　　　　　　　　　　　　He asked for a raise.
　　　　　　　　　　　　　　It just stands there on the mantle.
Third Person (plural): *They* offered to help work.

Additional examples:

I sent the letter yesterday. *I*, the speaker, is called first person singular because there is only one.

We were glad to be home. *We*, still the speaker, is called first person plural because *we* is clearly more than one.

You can walk home by yourself. *You*, the person spoken to, is called second person singular because only one person is addressed.

You must *all* bring your tests to the office after finishing the exam. *You*, the persons spoken to, is still called second person, but is now plural because more than one person is addressed.

She (or *He* or *It*) will need some time to settle down. *She*, *he*, or *it*, a person or thing spoken about, are called third person singular because they obviously refer to only one.

They are preparing a large picnic for next Saturday. *They* is called third person plural because *they* refers to more than one person being spoken about.

Therefore, the terms **first person**, **second person**, and **third person** refer to singular pronouns as well as to plural pronouns.

A personal pronoun is called *personal* because it designates

**The speaker (first person),
someone spoken to (second person), or
someone or something spoken about (third person).**

In addition, personal pronouns can be singular:

I, you, she, he, it

Or plural:

we, you, they

A brief interruption of the discussion is needed here. The concept of case will be fully discussed in the next section of this chapter, but here is the basic idea.

Some pronouns are used as the **principal subject of a verb** (**We drove slowly**.) while others are used as the **object of a verb** or the **object of a preposition** (**Howard and Ethel sent us flowers for them**.) while still others are used only as **possessive** words (**That house is ours**.).

> *I* bought a puppy.
> The puppy bit *me*.
> This puppy is *mine*.

Case, then, refers to how a pronoun is used in a sentence.

I, *me*, and *mine* are all words that refer to the speaker (therefore, all are first person singular), yet they cannot be interchanged. They are in different cases, meaning *I* can only be in a **subject** position (called **subjective case**); *me* can only be in an **object** position (called **objective case**), and *mine* can only be used in a **possessive** position (called, predictably, **possessive case**).

Exercise 9 Underline the correct pronoun.

1. John and (she, her) drove to his place to study philosophy.

2. When (we, us) were a young nation, government was small.

3. (You, Your) comments to her upset me.

4. (He, Him) told us not to listen to you.

5. (They, Them) said to meet them on the corner.

6. The last novel of Updike was (his, hims) best.

7. (I, Me) and Phil cannot agree on a candidate.

8. (You, Your) game is too easy for the children.

9. (She, Her) called to the man on the ledge.

10. (They, Them) wanted to move to another state.

Gender A few words tell the sex of the person or thing being spoken about. *She, her, hers*; *he, his, him*; *it, its* all reveal whether the person or thing is considered feminine, masculine, or neuter. Nouns do not change form (spelling) when we move them around in a sentence except when they are plural or possessive. Pronouns change form (spelling) a great deal when we move them around.

> Bob offered Mary a bargain on Bob's car.
>
> He offered her a bargain on his car.

Nouns are always in the third person. Pronouns can be either first, second, or third person.

Here is a matrix that visually demonstrates the qualities of personal pronouns showing **person**, **number**, **case**, and **gender**.

Number	Person	Subjective Case	Objective Case	Possessive Case
Singular	first	I	me	my, mine
	second	you	you	your, yours
	third	she	her	her, hers
		he	his	his
		it	it	its
Plural	first	we	us	our, ours
	second	you	you	your, yours
	third	they	them	their, theirs
Singular or Plural		who	whom	whose

The Problem with You and Numbers Beware of *you*. That's correct; be careful how the word *you* is used in a sentence. Remember that *you* is always someone spoken to, addressed, or spoken to directly. Careless writers often begin a sentence with one kind of pronoun and then shift to *you* (second person) elsewhere in the sentence.

When *I* boarded the bus, *you* could see that the seats were full.

If a writer shifts person in a sentence, the sentence is confusing.

We wanted to spend the night, but you knew no one would ask us.

We is the first person; *you* is the second person.

After we drove around, you could see we were lost.

We is first person, and *you* is second. The sentence should read, **After we drove around, we knew we were lost**.

Exercise 10 Find and correct the errors in the following sentences by crossing out the incorrect pronoun and writing the correct one in above it.

Example: I enjoyed the movie because it kept ~~you~~ me in hysterics.

1. They lived under a highway overpass, but you know they weren't poor.

2. I love his photography since you can always see something special in each picture.

3. Unless we water the plants, you know they will die.

4. We know that the government is in a mess, but you can't change it.

5. We lived there three years before you could feel at home.

Number Pronouns take the place of nouns.

> That dog has had its shots.

The noun to which a pronoun refers is called the **antecedent**. If the noun (antecedent) is plural, then the pronoun must also be plural. By the same token, if the noun (antecedent) is singular, then the pronoun must also be singular; for example:

> You ought to teach a *child* to respect authority before *they* get too old.

This sentence is incorrect since *child*, the antecedent noun, is singular, yet *they* is plural.

> *Computers* can be inexpensive, if you know where to buy *it*.

Again, this is incorrect. *Computers* is plural while *it* is singular in number.

Exercise 11 Correct the following sentences containing an error in pronoun number by crossing out the incorrect pronoun and writing the correct one in above it.

> them
> **Example**:   Groceries are not so expensive when you buy ~~it~~ at a discount store.

1. When a person studies, they should find a quiet place.

2. Check your calculations before you hand it in.

3. A woman can keep up with their competition.

4. Each member of the cast gave their best effort.

5. Anyone who loves killing should analyze their values.

Indefinite Pronouns Don't get discouraged because the information about personal pronouns took so long to discuss; the other kinds of pronouns are not so intricate. Some pronouns, unlike personal pronouns, do not refer to any particular person or thing. Following are **indefinite pronouns**.

one	each	neither	somebody
anyone	either	nobody	someone
anybody	every	no one	something
anything	everybody	nothing	everything

All these indefinite pronouns are singular. If they are used as the subject, then they require a singular verb. A few indefinite pronouns are almost always plural: *all*, *several*, *some*, *few*, *many*. These rarely offer any trouble. However, the singular indefinite pronouns offer considerable awkwardness at first.

> her
> Each of the girls went to ~~their~~ room.

The confusion with *their* stems from not distinguishing between the true subject (*each*) and the object of the preposition *of* (*girls*).

Everyone
Everybody
Each
Someone } gave her or his best effort.
Somebody
Each one
No one

Remember that a great many pronouns such as *everyone* and *everybody* are singular. They have a plural sound and feel to them, but they are not plural. If we separate them into *one* and *body*, both singular, we can see they mean only one.

A debate rages over whether *he*, *his*, and *him* should be used to include both males and females. Everybody wants (his) (his or her) (their) name in lights. The simplest answer traditionally is to choose *his* and let it represent both males and females. Others argue that *their* is clear, although grammatically incorrect, and should be accepted. Still others assert that *her or his* is the best modern solution. Here's a firm stand: you decide on the basis of your instructor's advice.

Informally, in speech, you can probably get by with this kind of sentence:

Everybody should do their own work.

But if your communication is written (and other than very personal correspondence), you should not choose *their* and expect your reader not to blink. *His or her* may be less than smooth, but this choice is acceptable to most editors and publishers. A few prefer that you avoid the problem altogether:

Everyone should do individual work.

Still others mix *her* and *his* randomly, allowing each one to suggest the entire population.

Exercise 12 Correct the following sentences either by crossing out the incorrect pronoun and writing the correct pronoun(s) above it or by rewriting the entire sentence.

1. Someone chose not to give their number.

   Rewritten: _____

2. Nobody will forfeit their place in line.

   Rewritten: _____

3. Any one of the children can offer their opinion.

   Rewritten: _____

4. Each parent was asked about their child.

   Rewritten: _____

5. Somebody left their gloves on the counter.

   Rewritten: _____

Interrogative Pronouns When certain pronouns are used at the front of a sentence, they ask questions. Thus, they are called **interrogative** which means question. Interrogative pronouns are *who*, *which*, *what*, *whose*, and *whom*.

These same words can also introduce a clause (discussed later), but when they introduce a clause, they are called **relative pronouns** (see below). Only when they ask a question are they called interrogative pronouns.

> *Who* is that standing over there?
> *Which* book is your favorite?
> *What* was your answer?
> *Whose* vote do you consider most important?
> *Whom* did you want elected?

Relative Pronouns Relative pronouns take the place of a noun that begins a clause (see pp. 33, 101) and link the clause it introduces with the noun it modifies or describes.

> John is the man.
> John is standing on the corner.

Notice that what happens when we substitute *who* for *John* in the second sentence and combine the two sentences.

> John is the man who is standing on the corner.

(1) *Who* takes the place of a noun (*John*) in the clause it introduces, and (2) *who* links the clause with the noun (*man*) it modifies.

Relative pronouns introduce **adjective clauses** (see p. 111). These adjective clauses begin with relative pronouns that are easy to remember: *who*, *whom*, *whose*, *which*, and *that*.

relative pronoun
> Our neighbor *who* pulled us out of the ditch last winter had his truck stolen.

relative pronoun
> We elected our friend, *whom* we liked best, to be our senator.

relative pronoun
> Our house, *which* we painted last summer, needs painting again.

relative pronoun
> Our dog *that* was lost stumbled home two days later.

Exercise 13 Underline the relative pronouns. Notice that they (1) take the place of a noun in the clause they introduce and (2) link the clause with the noun they follow and modify.

Example: The motocross race that we attended saw fourteen wrecks
in the first heat.

1. The old, oak table that we bought at a rummage sale turned out to be

    very difficult to refinish.

2. The relay satellite that everyone thought was lost started working again.

3. Microwave stations that are located about twenty-five miles apart

    provide the TV signal.

4. The actor who used to play on *I Dream of Jeannie* became J. R. on *Dallas*.

5. Cowboy boots that are made of solid leather tend to outlast the cowboy.

Demonstrative Pronouns Pronouns that point out something or someone are called **demonstrative pronouns**. English has only four demonstrative pronouns: *this*, *that*, *these*, and *those*. Notice that the word *them* is not among the four demonstrative pronouns. Do not confuse *them* with *those*.

> **Correct:**   We wanted to buy those shoes.
> **Incorrect:** We wanted to buy them shoes.

Sometimes a writer may incorrectly refer to an entire sentence with the words *this* or *that*. These two words are used to refer to specific persons or things, not to an entire sentence.

> After the movie, Sue and Darlene wanted to get an ice cream cone.
> **Incorrect:** This appealed to Marvin. (Incorrect use of *this*.)
> **Correct:**   This idea (plan) appealed to Marvin.

Exercise 14 Correct the use of demonstrative pronouns in the following sentences by crossing out the incorrect pronoun and writing the correct one in above it.

1. The army chose to divide the troops because of discipline problems.

    This disappointed the new recruit.

2. Our window box herbs grew enough to share with the neighbors. That

    appealed to everyone in the building.

3. Where did you get them buttons?

49

Reflexive and Intensive Pronouns Tom cut *himself* shaving. Notice the use of *himself*. The word *himself* tells us that the object of the verb *cut* is the same person as the subject *Tom*. A **reflexive pronoun** serves as an object and turns the action of the verb back toward the subject. Reflexive pronouns are always *self* words. and they are always written as one word, never as two words.

> Emil wrote himself a letter.

You can see how *himself* serves as the object of *wrote* and also how *himself* turns the action back to the subject.

Make sure you use the correct *self* word. Several words are **incorrect**: hisself, theirself.

Exercise 15 Underline the reflexive pronouns in the following sentences. Reflexive pronouns "reflect" the action back to the subject.

1. They informed themselves about the situation.

2. The director worked himself out of a job.

3. The little girl gave herself a haircut.

4. The dog barked itself into exhaustion.

Another use of the self words shows **emphasis** or **intensity**; thus they are called **intensive pronouns**. Notice the emphatic power in these sentences.

> My mother *herself* told us to be home early.
> The director *himself* complimented my work.

Intensive pronouns are used for emphasis.

> I *myself* accept all the credit.
> Our neighbors *themselves* wrote the letter.

One common error prevalent around the country is to use a self word after a preposition or a verb:

> me.
> The store gave a gift certificate to my roommate and ~~myself~~.

You can ask yourself, "Besides my roommate, the store gave a gift certificate to whom?" To *me*. The sentence should end with the proper pronoun, *me*.

Exercise 16 Correct the following sentences by crossing out the incorrect pronoun and writing the correct one above it.

1. Dr. Brooks hisself gave the order to operate.

2. Cory herself told Rodney and myself about the affair.

3. The team members theirselves are to blame.

4. George and myself told Hedda to come anytime.

5. Just between you and myself, I don't believe him.

Case of Pronouns

Jack rode to school.

He rode to school.

Dot bought Jack a gift.

Dot bought him a gift.

Notice that the noun *Jack* remains the same whether used as the subject of the sentence or as the object. But the pronoun taking the place of Jack does change.

This change is called **case**. When a word is used as the subject of a sentence, it is said to be in the **subjective case**. Likewise, it is called **objective case** when used as the object.

Nouns do not change whatsoever when moved from **subjective** to **objective** uses.

A noun does change to show possession: Where is Jack's chair? We add an apostrophe to show possession with a noun. But a pronoun changes form—*my* coat, *their* gloves, *her* pencil, *our* house. Almost no one has difficulty with possessive pronouns, except with *its*. *Its* (possessive of *it*) *never* uses an apostrophe.

But pronouns change to show subjective case or objective case.

We gave *her* a letter for *them*.

Bob and I gave Amanda a letter for Dirk and Con.

Notice how pronouns change and nouns do not.

Subjective Case When a pronoun is used before a verb, it is in the **subjective case**.

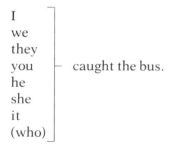

I
we
they
you
he
she
it
(who)

caught the bus.

The same words are used in formal constructions following linking verbs: *is, am, are, was, were, been*.

However, informally we use a more familiar pronoun.

Formal: It was *they* who came.
Informal: It was *them* who came.
Formal: This is *he*.
Informal: This is *him*.
Formal: It is *I*.
Informal: It's *me*.

There will be no question of correctness if you use the formal construction in your writing.

Objective Case When a pronoun is used as an object, then the pronoun is in the **objective case**.

The barbed wire fence caught

me
you
him
her
it
us
them
(whom)

This same list is used following prepositions.

When a pronoun is **doubled**, that is, used along with a noun or another pronoun, the pronoun must be in the correct **case** (subjective or objective). The way to tell which is correct is to use the pronoun as if it were alone.

I went shopping.
Dad went shopping.
Dad and I went shopping.

Look at this example:

Incorrect: Jon and me tried to catch the runaway car.

Notice that if you leave off *Jon and*, the sentence reads *me tried to catch the runaway car*. We know that's wrong; it should be *I*. **Jon and I tried to catch the runaway car**.

Sometimes writers and speakers are fooled by the fact that the pronoun is doubled with a noun or even another pronoun; however, you can choose the correct case of a pronoun by trying the pronoun by itself.

Exercise 17 Choose the correct case for the following pronouns by crossing out the incorrect pronoun and writing the correct one in above it.

1. The cat and myself liked the warmth of the fireplace.

2. Between you and I, this has got to stop.

3. He did a good job all by hisself.

4. My parents gave John and I new bookcases.

5. Save a ticket for we members.

6. They sent John and he an invitation.

7. George told them people to cooperate.

8. The mailman said the package was for she and I.

9. Juan and me hitchhike together in the summer.

10. The members theirselves voted on the raise.

11. Her and I both ran after the ball.

12. Each of we girls went to our rooms.

13. She does better in school than me.

14. Them kids are always getting into trouble.

15. Tom, Danny, and me are going to the movies this afternoon.

16. He told she and I about the mistake.

17. This book is either her or yours.

18. His brother, Tom, and him are going away to college next year.

19. I know them are the people whom just moved from New York.

20. Mine is the first new car on the block where him lives.

Case following <u>than</u> and <u>as</u>   Both *than* and *as* can be used to make a comparison.

> He owns a bigger car than I.
> Mother can't jump as high as she.

When we make comparisons using *than* or *as*, we often leave out some words.

> He owns a bigger car than I (do).
> Mother can't jump as high as she (can jump).

If you will supply the missing words when using *than* or *as*, you will have no trouble choosing the correct pronoun.

> Sam can read faster than I (can read).

The case of *who* and *whom*

***Who* is a subject word and is always in the subjective case. *Whom* is an object word and is always in the objective case. When in doubt, try the word *he* (or *she*) and if it fits, then choose *who*; or try *him* (or *her*), and if it fits, then choose *whom*.**

> If *she*, *he*—*who*.
> If *her*, *him*—*whom*.

> *Who* can fix the car?
> *He* can fix the car.

> *Whom* do you want to fix the car?
> You want *him* to fix the car.

> Our teacher was a woman to *whom* we went for help.
> We went to *her* for help.

The use of *who* or *whom* depends on how the word is used—as a subject or as an object.

Everyday use has diminished the use of *whom* considerably. In point of use, *who* has just about taken over for both words. But in writing, a careful writer still needs to choose the grammatically correct form. Further, it is better to know the standard written form and then relax the use of it than it is not to know and be handicapped by wrong usage.

Who and *whom* are pronouns that introduce **adjective clauses** (a group of words with a subject and a verb that modify a noun). See p. 111.

> The drummer (*who came* late) also forgot his drum.
> The drummer (whom *we knew*) could play for hours.

Look at the clause by itself: whom we knew.
Turned around we would properly say: We knew *him*.
Since *him* fits, we choose *whom*. Another way of saying it is that *whom* is the object of *knew* and, therefore, is in the objective case.
Here again is the list.

Subject Words	Object Words
I	me
we	us
they	them
you	you
he	him
she	her
it	it
who	whom

If the word in question—*who* or *whom*—is the subject of the verb, then always choose *who*.

> Who ran.
> Who were running.
> Who played the piano.

However, if *who* or *whom* is the object of the verb, then always choose *whom*.

> Whom we knew. (her, him)

Notice that the verb *knew* already has a subject *we*. Also notice that the object *whom* is before the actual subject.

> Whom the cat licked.   (him, her)
> Whom the teacher knew.   (him, her)

Exercise 18 Choose between *who* and *whom* by underlining the correct one.

Example: Mr. Lincoln was a man (who, <u>whom</u>) everybody respected.

Mr. Lincoln was a man (<u>who</u>, whom) respected everybody.

1. Mr. Arthur is a person (who, whom) sells cars.

2. Mrs. Arthur is a woman (who, whom) we know as a good neighbor.

3. People (who, whom) travel are usually tolerant.

4. Jon and Avi, (who, whom) are invited, are good musicians.

5. Buddy Rich, (who, whom) is known by many musicians, is a great drummer.

6. We want friends (who, whom) are honest.

7. We all want friends to (who, whom) we can turn.

Sometimes a short phrase like *I think* or *I suppose* will follow the relative pronoun. Pay no attention to such phrases when you choose *who* or *whom*.

> These are the girls <u>who</u> I think can win.
>
> Mr. Johnson is the man <u>whom</u> I suppose we want to run.

8. This picture was made by the man (who, whom) I think will be known for his photographs.

9. We just met Homer Reeves (who, whom) we guess you already know.

Sometimes *who* or *whom* is combined with *ever*—whoever, whomever. Adding *ever* changes nothing in the choosing process. Continue on the basis of subject or object.

> We gave the paper to (whomever, <u>whoever</u>) would take it.

10. Why don't you ask (whoever, whomever) wants to go?

11. Choose (whoever, whomever) you wish.

12. We gave the buckle to (whoever, whomever) they thought could ride the best.

13. We introduced Betty to (whoever, whomever) came first.

14. That's John (who, whom) I thought had already left.

15. (Whoever, Whomever) told you that bumblebees can't fly was mistaken.

16. My friend Larry, (who, whom) just transferred to State College, has been in a wheelchair since he was fourteen.

17. I told (whoever, whomever) it was to call back later.

18. They will hire (whoever, whomever) gets there first.

19. That woman is the one (who, whom) hires the bands and schedules the concerts.

20. (Whomever, whoever) it was, I'm sure he will be back.

VERBS

Nouns and verbs are the two most important words in English. (See Chapter 1.) Nouns name. A verb tells what is going on in the sentence. An action verb expresses physical or mental action. A linking verb links the subject with either an adjective or a noun.

The book *revealed* everything about the actor.

Revealed, a verb, tells what the subject does.

Mrs. Wheeler *is* a perfect neighbor.

Is, a verb, tells what the subject, Mrs. Wheeler, is—a neighbor.

Our favorite dessert *seems* too sweet sometimes.

Seems, a verb, tells what the subject, *dessert*, seems to be—too sweet.

With verbs we can make statements about people, places, things, ideas, actions, and emotions—in other words, about nouns. Verbs can be complex, but a few clues will help you identify them. In a future chapter, we will help you avoid common verb errors that plague writers. But for now concentrate on finding and identifying the verbs.

Exercise 19 In the following sentences identify the verb and its action by filling in the blanks.

Example: Robert Shaw starred as an ex-pirate.

The verb, <u>starred</u>, tells what <u>Shaw did</u>.

1. A married couple played a variety of roles in one show.

   The verb, _____ , tells what _____ _____ .

2. Every day the cars scramble for position during rush hour.

   The verb, _____ , tells what _____ _____ .

3. College demands time, energy, money, and goodwill.

   The verb, _____ , tells what _____ _____ .

4. The crippled airplane circled around the field several times before landing.

   The verb, _____ , tells what _____ _____ .

5. Bill Blass designed chocolates and dresses.

   The verb, _____ , tells what _____ _____ .

Two Kinds of Verbs

First a review.

Action: An action verb expresses either physical or mental action.

> The choir *sang* beautifully outside our dorm.

Sang, an action verb, tells what the choir did.

> My roommate *plays* an anti-establishment youth in the new TV show.

Plays, an action verb, tells what my roommate *does*.

Linking: A linking verb establishes a link between the subject and another word in the sentence.

> The antique car *is* thirty years old.

Is, a linking verb, tells what the antique car, the subject, *is*—thirty years old. Another way to say the same thing is to note that *is* links *car* and *old*.

> My brother *appears* sleepy most of the time.

Appears, a linking verb, tells what my brother *seems* to be—sleepy. And *appears* links *brother* to *sleepy*.

Typical linking verbs are *is*, *am*, *are*, *was*, *were*, *been*, *become*, *appear*, *seems*, *look*, *taste*, *feel*, *sounds*, and *grew*. These verbs are followed by a word that is linked with the subject. Note that the word linked is not an action verb. If it were, the linking verb would become a helper and the action verb would become the principal verb. Action verbs dominate linking verbs. In the following examples, note how clearly the linking verb links another word in the sentence with the subject.

> The candle *is* red.
>
> At Thanksgiving, Martha *appears* happy when her children come home.
>
> Buck *was* a truck driver in his youth.
>
> After each play, the disgruntled coach, along with his assistants, *became* increasingly embarrassed by the play of his young secondary.

Nearly always, you can reduce a sentence that contains a linking verb to three words: (1) the subject, (2) the linking verb, and (3) the completing word in the sentence called a **subject complement**. The word *complement* simply means completed or finished.

Exercise 20 List the three significant words in the following sentences.

Example: The busy marketplace is never a place to relax.

marketplace   is   place

subject   linking verb   subject complement

1. The children looked like ghosts in their costumes.

    _____   _____   _____
    subject   linking verb   subject complement

2. An embarrassment, that show became a loser.

    _____   _____   _____
    subject   linking verb   subject complement

3. Some TV programs are frank in their use of language.

    _____   _____   _____
    subject   linking verb   subject complement

4. That water looks too deep to wade in.

    _____   _____   _____
    subject   linking verb   subject complement

5. You are a beautiful person.

    _____   _____   _____
    subject   linking verb   subject complement

6. This horse is far too spirited for a child to ride.

    _____   _____   _____
    subject   linking verb   subject complement

7. Five miles seems like a long way to walk just for an ice cream cone.

    _____   _____   _____
    subject   linking verb   subject complement

8. That dress looks good on you.

    _____   _____   _____
    subject   linking verb   subject complement

9. Because my friend and teacher inspired me, giving me a direction in life,
    I became a world famous writer.

    _____   _____   _____
    subject   linking verb   subject complement

10. The cloudy, sullen sky appears ready to burst into a thunderstorm at
    any minute.

    _____   _____   _____
    subject   linking verb   subject complement

Some of the linking verbs—*is, am, are, was, were, been*—are indeed linking when used by themselves, but these same words, when used with action verbs, are no longer linking but helping or auxiliary verbs.

A good way to increase the effectiveness of your verb choice involves listing several alternatives.

Exercise 21 Take a few simple nouns and list at least five verbs that fit especially well.

Example: plants

grow
droop
decay
flourish
revive

1. water _____

2. wind _____

3. actors _____

4. ministers _____

5. politicians _____

More Than One Word

One verb may consist of one, two, three, or four words: *is walking, will be walking, might have been walking*.

Exercise 22 Form verbs by combining the words in columns 2 and 3, then add these verbs to a subject that you choose in column 1 so that you write a complete, simple sentence.

1	2	3
_____	have been	published
_____	has been	paid
_____	will be	restored
_____	should have been	preserved
_____	may be	collected
_____	are	obeyed

Remember, the verb may be more than one word. Often we need to use an additional word or two to help the principal verb. When more than one word makes up the verb, the principal verb is **always** the last one.

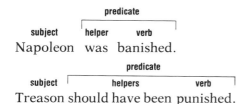

Often used helping words are: *be, is, am, are, was, were, been, could, shall, will, have, has, had,* and *may.*

Exercise 23 Identify the subject and the predicate, including the helpers and the main verb, by writing the words in as in the example above.

1. Sentences may be analyzed.

2. Columbus was imprisoned.

3. Grammarians will differ.

4. Sodom might have been spared.

5. The lovely crickets are chirping somewhere in the backyard.

6. I have never been so insulted in my life.

7. We had been gone about an hour before the earthquake hit Lake Arrowhead.

8. Never before has she looked so lovely.

9. Tomorrow it will be a week since I have had food or water.

10. Had it not been for you, we would be there by now.

11. In exactly one more month, she will have had ten years of driving experience.

12. I have one more semester to complete at community college before I transfer to a four-year university.

13. He once visited some universities in Texas and Pennsylvania.

14. By this time tomorrow we will have traveled over 3,000 miles.

15. Had she lived, she would have continued her career as a concert pianist.

16. I am never going to see him again.

17. They left a few minutes ago.

18. If you hurry, you can still catch up with the crew.

Exercise 24   Sentence Building Construct five intelligent sentences around these subjects.

1. Comets _____

2. Carpets _____

3. Summer _____

4. Fireplaces _____

5. Short stories _____

Additional Help for Recognizing Verbs

The form of verbs (actually nothing more than the spelling) depends on whether the verb is matched with a **singular** subject or a **plural** subject. With *he*, *she*, *it*, or a singular noun such as *the horse*, a verb will be spelled with an *s*; in other words it's singular.

> He, she, it, the horse *walks, runs, displays, rejects.*

However, with *I*, *we*, *they*, *you*, or a plural noun like *the horses*, a verb will be spelled *without* an *s*:

> I, we, they, you, the horses *walk, run, display, reject.*

The **tense** of a verb indicates the time—past, present, and future—that verb is expressing. Therefore, verbs can reveal changes in time.

> I *go* to class every day.
> I *went* yesterday.
> I *will go* tomorrow.

This change in the verb to indicate time is called **tense**, another word for time. Three other tenses of verbs—**present perfect**, **past perfect**, and **future perfect**—show that the action is already completed or perfected. The problems with tenses are discussed later.

> These are the tenses for one verb—to be.

Present	I am (going to work now.)
Past	I was (there yesterday.)
Future	I will be (there tomorrow.)
Present Perfect	I have been (working there for a year.)
Past Perfect	I had been (looking for that job.)
Future Perfect	I will have been (with the company two years in March.)

Exercise 25 Write the tense above the verb in each sentence.

1. The bird chatters incessantly.

2. The boots needed polishing.

3. I will paint the car next year.

4. Next month I will have driven 20,000 miles.

5. The police had raided the high school one time too many.

6. He has been in jail four days.

7. The aquarium needs more fish.

8. The blanket was woven by Navajos.

9. You should have been here earlier.

10. We stacked the wood on the porch.

Several problems with verbs are discussed thoroughly in Chapter 8. Here is a final exercise for you to practice choosing singular or plural verbs.

Exercise 26 Underline the correct verb.

1. Applause always (makes, make) me feel good.

2. Sharon and all her children (are, is) always late.

3. Someone in the bus (is, are) late.

4. Everyone in the stands (seem, seems) excited.

5. After he had been married one week, he (wants, wanted) to go fishing.

6. They were relieved that they (raise, raised) the corn.

7. When the child (cut, cuts) his teeth, he (cries, cried).

8. If I (was, were) rich, I would sleep more.

9. What (are, is) your telephone number?

10. Anybody who (believe, believes) in monsters (watches, watch) too much television.

11. Each of the men (is, are) interested in the project.

12. It (appear, appears) that your friend has left town.

13. Not one of those kids (want, wants) to leave camp.

14. She (describes, describe) the scene in perfect detail.

15. Everybody's rights to freedom (depend, depends) on personal responsibility.

16. As long as prejudice and greed (exists, exist), peace will be elusive.

17. All but one (remain, remains) to this day.

18. Neither of the boys ever (stay, stays) overnight.

19. Nothing on the planets we've observed (indicates, indicate) the presence of life as we know it.

20. Either of the women (are, is) fine for the job.

21. Persistence and hard work (accomplishes, accomplish) some amazing things.

22. Nobody (notice, notices) my new outfit.

23. We (was, were) standing in the middle of a vacant lot when the cloudburst caught us by surprise.

24. It (don't, doesn't) seem like your idea will work.

25. While walking last night, I (came, come) upon a family of raccoons.

26. (Did, Does) he intend to come with us before he broke his leg?

27. Something (tells, told) me I shouldn't have gone alone.

28. Those people (been, were) standing there for over an hour.

29. It would (appear, appears) that he is not coming to work today.

30. We have (gone, went) on several of these expeditions.

Exercise 27 Find the nouns, pronouns, and verbs, placing an *N*, *P*, or *V* above the appropriate words.

Although Coca-Cola® is the most popular and famous soft drink in the world, the exact ingredients in Coca-Cola remain a highly guarded secret.

In 1886 a pharmacist in Atlanta, Georgia, named John Pemberton, mixed the first syrup that was to become known the world over. Today, Coca-Cola is sold in 140 countries at the rate of 200 million drinks per day. But the syrup that Mr. Pemberton developed is still formulated only in the United States. The syrup is then shipped to various bottling plants, mixed with local water, then sold to the public.

You may have read that Coke® used to have cocaine in it. That statement is true, but the amount was actually very, very small. Yet when the news got out that Coke had a drug in it, the company dropped cocaine altogether. The lift one gets now arises from the sugar and caffeine.

In addition to water, sugar, and caffeine, Coke has caramel, phosphoric acid, "decocainized" coca leaves, cola nuts, cinnamon, nutmeg, vanilla, lime juice, and citrus oils. Plus, it has a totally secret ingredient referred to as *merchandise 7x*.

Just what 7x is only a few know. The story goes that the secret for Coca-Cola rests with only a couple of people who, when they travel, fly alone, taking separate planes—just in case.

REVIEW TEST

I. Nouns

Choose the letter of the noun.

_____ 1. The cowboys sang most of the stormy night.
                       a   b   c   d

_____ 2. The young woman rode the white mule around the terrace.
                       a   b   c   d   e

_____ 3. Most of the children loved the icy, cold drink.
                       a   b   c   d   e

_____ 4. Watt wanted to destroy most of their agreement.
                       a   b   c   d   e

_____ 5. Over the hill rode the masked man.
                       a   b   c   d

II. Uses of Nouns

Choose the correct letter for the italicized word.

a = Principal Subject
b = Direct Object or Object Complement
c = Indirect Object
d = Subject Complement
e = Object of Preposition

_____ 6. When the rains came, the birds lost their *songs*.

_____ 7. I've lived in this *house* for most of my life.

_____ 8. The book's black *cover* hinted of a drab subject.

_____ 9. We made Wanda *chairperson*.

_____ 10. We slipped down the sandy bank and over the broken *fence*.

_____ 11. They sent *Hilda* a brand new bulldozer.

_____ 12. In the dark closet, we stood watching the *party*.

_____ 13. She was a beautiful *dancer*.

_____ 14. Their neighbors became good *friends*.

_____ 15. My *dreams* center on happiness.

_____ 16. Demetri was a *sergeant* during the Vietnam War.

_____ 17. His friends call him a *success*.

_____ 18. The banker in the town gave the *children* a free token.

_____ 19. We had more than enough time on our *hands*.

_____ 20. The business group donated a circular *handsaw* to the class.

_____ 21. Guess what mother gave the *neighbors*.

_____ 22. The *mosquitoes* made life miserable in the summer.

_____ 23. The new pen wrote under *water* only.

_____ 24. The *subway* needed full-time guards.

_____ 25. Ken has told that same funny story to the *children*.

III. Pronouns

Choose the letter of the pronoun.

_____ 26. He can afford to pay her for the damage.
             a b c d   e

_____ 27. All of the boys gave their best efforts.
       a b   c   d   e

_____ 28. If we help each other, then everyone is helped.
       a b c   d   e

_____ 29. These problems need to be solved by us.
          a   b c d   e   f

_____ 30. I want that particular chair delivered to my house.
    a b   c   d   e

IV. Pronouns

Choose the correct pronoun, either *who* (a) or *whom* (b).

_____ 31. (Who/Whom) do you think I am?

_____ 32. We took the car to the mechanic (who/whom) we think can fix it.

_____ 33. Chris wanted to find out (who/whom) started the fire.

_____ 34. You can guess (who/whom) she said will be the winner.

_____ 35. Send the bill to (whoever/whomever) will pay for the damages.

V. Pronouns

Choose the correct pronoun.

_____ 36. She baked more bread than I, me.
                      a b

_____ 37. Please send this package to Mr. Greer and she, her.
                                 a b

_____ 38. My son and myself, I, me will backpack next summer.
              a   b c

_____ 39. Johnson started the rumor about Jim and they, them.
                                  a   b

_____ 40. Just between you and I, me, myself, we had better food at the picnic.
                         a b   c

VI. Verbs

Label the following verbs as either **action** (a) or **linking** (b).

_____ 41. Mrs. Kiper *is* a kind person.

_____ 42. The quarterback *passed* for over three hundred yards.

_____ 43. The rocker *was built* in the late 1860s.

_____ 44. Collecting old books *was* profitable for the wallet and the mind.

_____ 45. That rose *appears* to need food.

VII. Verbs

Choose the correct letter that describes the italicized word(s).

a = Action Verb
b = Linking Verb
c = Subject Complement
d = Direct Object

_____ 46. Your papers *should be* neat and interesting.

_____ 47. Sea gulls *love* flying near cliffs.

_____ 48. The old boatman gave a *nod* to the young sailors.

_____ 49. When you buy, buy the best *product*.

_____ 50. Small airplanes are great *fun* when the weather is clear.

CHAPTER 3

CLASSES OF WORDS: ADJECTIVES, ADVERBS, PREPOSITIONS, CONJUNCTIONS, AND INTERJECTIONS

MODIFIED SUBJECT

We interrupt our discussion of classes of words to show you how a modifier works; adjectives and adverbs will then have more meaning.

The subject and verb form the foundation of every sentence, as we have seen. No sentence can be built without them. While the principal subject and verb form the sentence foundation, they are made more precise by adding other parts.

The birds built a nest.
The song-filled mockingbirds built an intricate, soft nest.

The main word in the complete sentence is a noun or pronoun called the **simple** or **principal subject** and often shortened simply to the **subject**. The main word in the predicate is the **verb**. The subject with its modifiers is called the complete subject or **modified** subject.

The song-filled mockingbirds . . .

A modifier is a word or group of words joined to some part of the sentence to qualify, or limit meaning, or to describe: a modifier makes for a more precise meaning.

The genial summer days have gone.

Days is the one-word subject, a noun. Look at these simple sentences and notice that each one contains a modified subject.

The angry wind is blowing.
The dead leaves fell.
The turgid river roared.
Those elegant Etruscan vases are broken.

Exercise 1 **Sentence Building** Write at least two suitable modifiers for each subject.

Example: That enormous rock cliff stood silent.

1. _____ speaker appeared tired.

2. _____ difficulties proved troublesome.

3. _____ accident happened.

4. _____ books should be read.

5. _____ opinions prevailed.

6. _____ bedspread was worn.

7. _____ woman shuffled along.

8. _____ rocket will be launched.

9. _____ students have been there.

10. _____ sea pitched and swelled.

Exercise 2 **Sentence Building** Build these sentences by prefixing modified subjects.

Example: The swift, gray-coated fox escaped.

1. _____ frolic.

2. _____ chatter.

3. _____ flourished.

4. _____ whistles.

5. _____ are dashing.

6. _____ spread.

7. _____ are flickering.

8. _____ disappeared.

9. _____ has gone fishing.

10. _____ leaps.

ADJECTIVES

The words we added to the simple subject were modifiers called **adjectives**. English has two modifiers—adjectives and adverbs. Adjectives are limited to telling us about nouns and pronouns. Adverbs add information to a verb, an adjective, or another adverb.

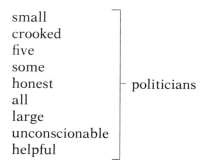

small
crooked
five
some
honest — politicians
all
large
unconscionable
helpful

An adjective is a word used to modify a noun (or pronoun, although very rarely is a pronoun modified).

Adjectives are words that tell about nouns.

      Several subsequent voyages proved disastrous.

Voyages is modified by *several* and *subsequent*. When the subject is a pronoun, the adjective commonly follows the pronoun.

      It was beautiful.

Pronouns are not often modified, however.

Exercise 3 Underline the adjectives in the following sentences.

Example: The whole earth smiles.

1. That dilapidated old wooden building has fallen.

2. An unyielding firmness was demonstrated.

3. The cold November rain is falling.

4. My valuable English watch runs smoothly.

5. The slender greyhound ran away.

6. Three of the playful dolphins rode the waves with the surfers.

7. The beautiful crystal lake glistened under the full moon.

8. This oppressive heat wave has lasted for at least a week.

9. Undisciplined children are a joy to a few.

10. Both boys were upset with their father.

11. Our new plan is working perfectly.

12. Steve's bionic system suffered extensive damage.

13. The revised edition is in the mail.

14. Migrating sparrows dotted the skies.

15. This vast desert wasteland has claimed many lives.

Exercise 4 Write in at least three adjectives to prefix the following nouns.

Example: programmed, workable, useful computer

1. _____ , _____ , _____ wilderness

2. _____ , _____ , _____ books

3. _____ , _____ , _____ government

4. _____ , _____ , _____ strength

5. _____ , _____ , _____ canyons

6. _____ , _____ , _____ mind

7. _____ , _____ , _____ streams

8. _____ , _____ , _____ mission

9. _____ , _____ , _____ wolves

10. _____ , _____ , _____ schedule

Adjectives help the reader know more about nouns by telling:

	Adjective	Noun
what kind	successful	trip
which kind	hunting	trip
which one	that	trip
how many	several	trips

Your own writing can improve at once if you substitute a precise adjective for a "lazy" one. For example, notice the difference in the clarity and interest when we change lazy adjectives to precise ones.

The enemy looked **funny**.
The enemy's beaded forehead puckered doubtfully.—*John Updike*

Notice the difference in the precise adjectives.

a nice person
{
a considerate
a thoughtful
a deliberate
a serious
a discreet
a sober
} person

Exercise 5 Fill in the blanks with precise adjectives, avoiding the temptation to choose the easy, lazy ones.

1. The _____ _____ horse galloped away.

2. Over the _____ _____ fire, the woman baked her

   _____ bread.

3. A _____ _____ man unknown to us telephoned.

4. After much _____ debating, the _____ warriors

   went home.

5. The _____ , _____ men played backgammon all day.

6. After using all their _____ bait, Gary and the _____ ,

   _____ man finally gave up and left the _____ dock.

7. Michelle's _____ , _____ parrot, Fruit Loops,

   answers to his name.

8. Shortly after arriving at the _____ lake, she and her

   _____ friend changed into their _____ swimsuits.

9. Tom's _____ , _____ boat began to take on water.

10. Her _____ , _____ hair flowing in the breeze behind

    her, the _____ , _____ girl dove into the

    _____ water.

Adjectives are easy to identify because they are associated with nouns. Single adjectives are found in two positions:

1. Immediately before a noun:

Adjective	Noun
azure	sky
stately	manner
stricken	animal
solemn	scene
bimonthly	meeting

2. Following a linking verb (*is, am, are, was, were, being, seem, look, grow, sound, feel*):

Subject	Linking Verb	Adjective
Janis	is	jubilant.
The book	sounds	interesting.
Richard	looks	vibrant.
We	are	depressed.

Look at the first set of examples and notice how each adjective could be moved from its position immediately before the noun to a position following a linking verb.

> The sky was azure.
> His manner is stately.
> The animal seems stricken.

Exercise 6 Fill in the blanks with the correct answers.

Adjectives are associated with _____ .

Adjectives come immediately _____ a noun.

Adjectives come after a _____ verb.

Exercise 7 **Sentence Building** Fill in the blanks with precise adjectives.

1. The _____ _____ girl was pleased to accept the

   _____ _____ package.

2. Betsy looks _____ in her _____ outfit.

3. The _____ waves caused Jim to hit his _____ head.

4. The best actor in the movie was _____ , _____ , and

   _____ .

5. Lawson feels _____ and _____ .

6. He went down the _____ trail to the _____ ,

_____ beach on the bay.

7. David has been _____ because his _____ ,

_____ wife just got a _____ job.

8. I don't know whether I am _____ or _____ .

9. I found her class to be _____ and _____ , yet

_____ .

10. This _____ _____ crowd is so _____

that they've been here protesting every day.

Exercise 8   Sentence Building Use each of the following adjectives in a clear,
interesting sentence.

1. highest _____

2. creative _____

3. crowded _____

4. brilliant _____

5. spicy _____

6. guarded _____

7. pensive _____

8. eager _____

9. fascinating _____

10. brightest _____

ADVERBS

Adverbs are like bouncers at a rock concert. They are present to help out but are often overused and generally found all over the place. Adverbs are close to the action but are never the center of a sentence; nouns and verbs are the center.

We just learned that adjectives modify nouns. English has another modifier—the **adverb**—that tells more about verbs by answering simple questions: When? where? how? how often? and why? And of these, *when*, *where*, and *how* will point to almost any adverb. The rather odd aspect of adverbs is that they can also modify yet another modifier, an adjective, for instance, or even another adverb.

Like bouncers, adverbs can be helpful if used correctly. Look at this sentence:

> Aenea skied.

The questions when? where? how? apply to the verb *skied*.

When?   Aenea skied *often*.
Where?   Aenea skied *everywhere*.
How?   Aenea skied *safely*.

Adverbs modify verbs, adjectives, and other adverbs.

Exercise 9 Fill in the blanks with words that answer *when? where?* or *how?*

1. G. W. worked _____ .

2. Jack drove _____ .

3. Raymond flew _____ .

4. Reece speaks _____ .

5. Emil paints _____ .

6. Dan climbed _____ .

7. She rides _____ .

8. The chimney smoked _____ .

9. Rob's car stalls _____ .

10. Jenny studied _____ .

Characteristics As you can see, adverbs modify verbs; remember that **modify** means to describe, limit, qualify—to make clear and precise. You recall that adjectives are themselves modifiers; they modify nouns and appear just before the noun they modify (**The** *beautiful* **coat was lost**), or they appear following a linking verb (**The coat was** *beautiful*). Adjectives occur in predictable, fixed positions in the sentence. Adverbs, on the other hand, move around freely in the sentence.

Notice the different places the word *only* could be placed in the following sentence. **You appear prepared for the test**.

_____ you _____ appear _____ prepared _____ for _____ the _____ test _____ .

Since adverbs move around freely in sentences, they may or may not be next to the verb they modify.

> Our women defeated the team from across town *easily*.
> *Annually*, the board offers almost nothing to the workers.

Exercise 10 Underline the adverbs that are separated from the verbs they modify.

1. Slowly, the rusted gears turned around the axle.

2. The instructor walked to school from his house occasionally.

3. The good players missed the basket rarely.

4. Fortunately, our house was insulated before winter.

5. Jonathan worked carefully on the cube.

6. Yesterday our neighbors bought a new car.

7. Perhaps you should avoid that road.

8. Mother could bake almost anything skillfully.

9. Regularly, the club conducted a membership drive.

10. One of the doors stuck open sometimes.

Adverbs can occur throughout a sentence and yet modify the verb, as you have seen. Another characteristic of adverbs is that many, though not all, end in -*ly*, especially when the adverb answers *how* and when the adverb has been made from an adjective.

Here is how the -*ly* gets added to an adjective to form an adverb:

quick	The *quick* paw caught the mouse. **Adjective**
quickly	The cat moved *quickly* to catch the mouse. **Adverb**
graceful	The *graceful* dancer captivated the audience. **Adjective**
gracefully	The dancer glided *gracefully* over the floor. **Adverb**
easy	We won an *easy* game. **Adjective**
easily	We won the game *easily*. **Adverb**

By no means do all adverbs end in -*ly*, but many do, especially those that are made from adjectives.

Exercise 11 Sentence Building Construct clear, interesting sentences using the following pairs of words.

honest	1. _____ .	adjective
honestly	2. _____ .	adverb
polite	3. _____ .	adjective
politely	4. _____ .	adverb
possible	5. _____ .	adjective
possibly	6. _____ .	adverb
graceful	7. _____ .	adjective
gracefully	8. _____ .	adverb
late	9. _____ .	adjective
lately	10. _____ .	adverb

In addition to modifying verbs, adverbs can also modify adjectives and other adverbs.

Adverbs are modifiers; they add information to a verb, as we have seen. Additionally they can add qualifying information to an adjective.

         adj   noun
The *cold winter* made life difficult for the animals.

        adv   adj   noun
The *very cold winter* made life difficult for the animals.

                     adj   noun
The _____ *trained athlete* captured three medals.

Note that an adverb such as *highly*, *extremely*, or *completely*, could fit in the slot before the adjective. Adverbs can qualify, limit, describe—modify—adjectives.

Exercise 12 Add an appropriate adverb in the blanks before the adjectives in the following sentences.

1. A _____ qualified driver won the race.

2. Margaret made a _____ blue housecoat.

3. The _____ exhausted deer made it over the fence.

4. Donna was _____ tired.

5. An _____ rising moon meant good fishing.

6. The _____ mown hay smelled sweet.

7. The boat ride was _____ smooth.

8. The bank teller appeared _____ dressed.

9. We bought an _____ old dresser.

10. The _____ hot sun made our eyes burn.

   Adverbs can also modify other adverbs. The adverbs *very*, *quite*, *rather*, *so*, *too*, and *somewhat* can intensify still another adverb. Notice that any of these words can be used before an adverb like *gracefully*.

          adv   adv   adj   noun
   A *very gracefully dressed queen* stood erect.

Rarely will the use of the double adverbs improve your writing. They can on occasion, however, add an element of intensity that makes the sentence more powerful.

                   adv   adv
   Brenda spoke a rare Russian dialect *very beautifully*.

Exercise 13 Add an appropriate adverb in the blank before the existing adverb in the following sentences.

1. The men worked _____ rapidly.

2. The pilots studied the gauges _____ carefully.

3. You are _____ possibly the best friend in the world.

4. Computers can be programmed _____ quickly.

5. The team won _____ easily.

ADVERB OR ADJECTIVE? A SPECIAL PROBLEM

A few verbs in our language that deal with our senses—*look, taste, smell, feel, sound,* and *hear*—can be used in two different ways. One use is **action** and requires an adverb to describe it.

Our dog quickly *smelled* the smoke.

In this sentence, *smelled* is **action** performed by the dog, and the adverb *quickly* appropriately modifies it. Any one of these sense verbs can mean a physical action.

What are the physical actions that are meant by these verbs?

look	physically moving the eyes
taste	_____
smell	_____
feel	_____
sound	_____
hear	_____

When these words mean physical action, then an adverb can be used to describe the action word. Although these sense verbs can be action, they are far more commonly used as **linking** verbs. Used as linking verbs, they link the subject **noun** with an adjective that follows the verb.

                 linking verb   **adj**
The flower *smells* sweet.

                action verb   **adv**
The dog *smells* the luggage *carefully*.

Look, taste, smell, feel, sound, hear,—

Most of the time these sense verbs are linking and must be followed by an adjective, not an adverb.

The shirt looked _____ . Would you properly use *nice* (an adjective) or *nicely* (an adverb) in the blank? It is clear that *looked* is **linking** and requires an adjective.

A good test to know whether the sense verb is action or linking is to substitute a form of *seem* in its place. If a form of *seem* fits properly, then the verb is linking and requires an adjective following it.

The blanket *feels* hot.

Is the verb *feels* used as an **action** verb or a **linking** verb? Since the word *seems* will properly fill in for *feels*, then we know the verb *feels* is linking.

Exercise 14 Identify the verbs as **action** (a) or **linking** (b). Don't neglect trying a form of *seem* to check your answer.

_____ 1. The old woman *tastes* her food carefully.

_____ 2. The wine *tastes* bitter.

_____ 3. The Snowcat driver *looked* cautiously at the snow bank.

_____ 4. The girls *looked* beautiful in their summer dresses.

_____ 5. This velvet *feels* smooth.

_____ 6. The blind man *feels* his way along with a cane.

_____ 7. The snake *smelled* the air with its tongue.

_____ 8. The smoke *smelled* acrid and harsh.

_____ 9. The radio *sounds* clear and crisp.

_____ 10. The fire station *sounds* the alarm for practice.

Never use an adverb to describe a noun that is following a sense verb. You must never use an adverb to describe the subject. Only an adjective can modify a noun.

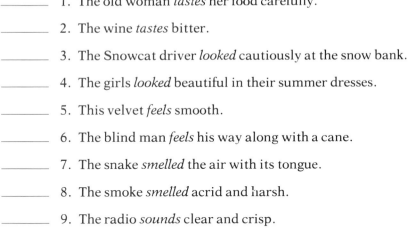

Incorrect: Our car   *looks   beautifully.*

Correct: Our car   *looks   beautiful.*

Exercise 15 Underline the correct word from the pairs of words in parentheses.

1. The musician sounded (happy, happily).

2. The dessert tasted (sweet, sweetly).

3. The driver looked (careful, carefully) before starting.

4. The wood looked (dry, dryly) on the ground.

5. Our desk feels (smooth, smoothly) to the touch.

6. Her voice sounds (clear, clearly) when she sings.

7. A fresh rose smells so (sweet, sweetly).

8. She feels (bad, badly) about the argument.

9. A thin suit feels (good, well) on a hot day.

10. Dr. James looked (angry, angrily) when he saw the bill.

11. My mother's voice sounds (happy, happily) on the phone.

12. The cup feels (rough, roughly) to the lips.

13. You can hear (good, well) under the water.

14. Our proposal sounds (honest, honestly) because of the subject matter.

15. She felt (cautious, cautiously) about his suggestion.

Exercise 16　Sentence Building　Fill in the blanks with precise adverbs.

1. Fred _____ enjoys walking _____ to work.

2. _____ , he ran to the cliff and dove _____

    into the water below.

3. _____ yet _____ , the boys

    _____ crept into the dark cave.

4. You should always drive _____ and _____ .

5. _____ gathering her wits, Mary peered

    _____ through the darkness.

6. Tamara is a (an) _____ competent attorney.

7. The crowd applauded her _____ executed

    performance _____ .

8. I believe it is _____ likely that he will

    _____ appear at our door.

9. He _____ strolls by my store _____ every

    day.

10. She is _____ either _____ agitated or

    _____ defensive.

PREPOSITIONS

In order to appreciate the function of prepositions, look at these sentences:

The car _____ the road was bright red.

The candle _____ the table burned for two hours.

Clearly, a word that shows **position** is needed: *near, in, on, by, across, under, beside,* and so on.

The car *near* the road was bright red.

The word *near* shows a clear relationship between *road* and *car.*

The candle *on* the table burned for two hours.

The word *on* shows a clear relationship between *table* and *candle.*

A preposition shows a clear relationship between a noun (or pronoun) and another word in the sentence.

A preposition and its noun (or pronoun) is called a **prepositional phrase**. The noun (or pronoun) that follows a preposition is called its **object**. (Other kinds of objects are the direct object, indirect object, and object complement, all discussed in Chapter 1.) A preposition is used to show position as we noted above: *under, over, across, on, behind, beneath,* and so on. Other prepositions show time: *during, after, until,* and *before.* Other prepositions show direction: *down, up, from, toward, to, off,* and so on.

In any case, remember that a preposition shows a relationship between its object and another word in the sentence.

A prepositional phrase is made of a preposition and its object.

Exercise 17 Label the prepositions and their objects, and underline the entire prepositional phrase.

                             prep   obj
Example: The man in the car was angry.

1. We sent her to the store.

2. Two of the boys went home.

3. They swam up the river when it was low.

4. The airplane flew through the clouds.

5. The aftermath of the horrible storm could be seen everywhere.

6. The colleges within the university followed different plans.

7. The boy with the bright blue eyes laughed heartily.

8. The cup on the small table looked empty.

9. A house on the riverbank seemed to be falling slowly.

10. We wanted a roof over our heads.

11. The child in the empty room played softly.

12. Every one of the boys is dripping wet.

13. Most of the groceries cost more this year.

14. Any one of the jury could have disagreed.

15. They actually drove through the lake.

16. The sailplane soared above the tiny little cloud.

17. In the summer, we go trout fishing.

18. Eating out on Sundays was a habit.

19. Throughout the play, the audience was quiet.

20. One of the women was always prepared.

A Troublesome Problem When we studied subjects and verbs, the sentences were generally constructed around a noun and a verb placed close together. However, a troubling problem arises when the subject noun (or pronoun) is separated from the verb by a prepositional phrase.

> subj   verb
> Everyone lost a friend.

> Everyone in the family lost a friend.

Notice that, although the prepositional phrase *in the family* is added to the second sentence, the subject remains *everyone*.

> subj   verb
> Some became angry.

> Some of the boys became angry.

The object of a preposition is never the subject of the sentence.

Exercise 18 Label the **subjects** and **verbs** and underline the **prepositional phrases** in the following sentences.

Example: subj
                A few of the cats eat with the dogs.
                              verb

1. Everybody on our team plays hard.

2. Someone in the choir is singing off key.

3. The parents of the twins couldn't afford new shoes.

4. Nearly all of the students liked the instructor.

5. Somebody on the bench thought we had gone too far.

6. Not one person near the scene of the accident came to help.

7. Neither he nor I, nor any of the boys, was willing to move from the cove.

8. The author of this book has agreed to meet with you under the condition that you come alone.

9. Some employees within this organization believe foul play was involved.

10. One of the tourists who is responsible for this situation has been found.

11. Most of the students went across campus for the concert.

12. Few of the missing bank notes will be found before morning.

13. Until now, no one on the board has been receptive to the idea.

14. None of the clues he gave you was legitimate.

15. Someone across the lake is in trouble.

16. One of these days in the near future will be sunny.

17. Everyone at the party danced until late into the night.

18. Somebody with incentive on this committee could solve this problem efficiently.

19. Either of the sites described in her report would be acceptable.

20. Somewhere over this embankment is a million dollars in gold ore.

Exercise 19   Sentence Building Fill in the blanks with appropriate prepositional phrases.

1. _____ and _____ we labored

   _____ _____ .

2. The small child shivered _____ , hiding as she was

   _____ _____ .

3. A rare and beautiful snow leopard crept _____ and surveyed

   the scene _____ _____ .

4. She has come _____ as I have.

5. Sneaking up _____ , the crouching cat waited

   _____ to strike.

6. _____ , it seems a lot easier to study.

7. _____ you hear from me, continue the project as planned.

8. Luke was _____ with grief _____ .

9. _____ I want you to memorize this formula.

10. When the brakes _____ slipped, it careened _____ .

CONJUNCTIONS

Conjunctions are words that join words or any sentence element: subjects, verbs, complements, phrases, and clauses.

Coordinating Conjunctions

Seven conjunctions are worth memorizing because knowing them will help you avoid one of the most troubling errors in writing—the run-on sentence. These seven **coordinating conjunctions** are *and, but, or, nor, for, so,* and *yet*. The last two are used the least, and the first two are used the most.

Coordinating conjunctions join elements of equal grammatical weight, equal rank, or equal value.

Coordinating conjunctions:

and, but, or, nor, for, so, and yet.

In good writing, two or more words are often used so that they show equal rank, value, or weight. Since they are equal, compound subjects, verbs, objects, complements, adjectives, adverbs, phrases, and clauses must be joined by the correct coordinating conjunctions.

Here are examples of each sentence element joined by the coordinating conjunction *and*, *but*, or *or*.

Compound subjects.

The horses *and* the cows were restless before the earthquake.

Compound verbs.

The cattle stomped *and* pawed the ground.

Compound complements (adj).

Amy is lonely *but* sad since the tragedy.

Compound adverbs.

Albert always drove very fast *or* very slowly.

Compound objects.

We bought cups *and* saucers at the swap meet.

Compound adjectives (complements).

The White House is beautiful *and* stately.

Compound prepositional phrases.

You can paint over the paper *or* over the plaster.

Compound clauses.

We wanted to know that you were safe *and* that you were well.

Clauses will be explained in detail later. Words, phrases, or clauses in a series are usually joined at the end of the series by *and* or *or*.

You may buy a new dress, coat, *or* hat.

For breakfast, we ate fresh grapefruit, fried potatoes, *and* crispy bacon.

We worked on the roof, under the sink, *and* between the walls during our stay at the cabin.

We knew who would join, who would pay, *and* who would work.

When you wish to combine two sentences with *and*, *but*, *or*, *nor*, *for*, *so*, or *yet*, you <u>**must**</u> **use a comma before the coordinating conjunction:**

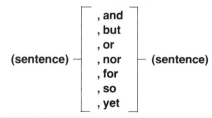

Coordinating Conjunctions and Punctuation Look at these sentences:

> The woman was very angry at the fox. She choked and beat it into unconsciousness.

If these two separate sentences are to be joined by a coordinating conjunction, then both a **comma** and a **coordinating conjunction** must be used. A comma alone is wrong; a coordinating conjunction alone is wrong. Read the following examples carefully, noting the correct use of the coordinating conjunction and the comma.

> The woman was very angry at the fox, *so* she choked and beat it into unconsciousness.
>
> I plant and grow tomatoes, *but* my friends eat them.
>
> We didn't want to ski, *nor* did we want to skate.
>
> The warranty was for one year, *but* we couldn't remember when we bought the tuner.
>
> The parachute was invented before airplanes, *and* no one knew how parachutes would later be used.
>
> The parachute was made to allow people to jump from burning buildings, *yet* parachutes became famous when airplanes were invented.

Again, when you connect two sentences with a **coordinating conjunction** (*and*, *but*, *or*, *nor*, *for*, *so*, or *yet*), you must also use a **comma**. Be aware, however, that the second part must be a complete sentence.

This sentence has a compound verb joined by *and*:

> The boxer's manager encouraged him with a smile *and* told him to be patient.

Notice that *and told him to be patient* is not a sentence; therefore, a comma is not placed in front of *and*. If you are in doubt about placing a comma in front of the coordinating conjunction, read the words after the conjunction to see whether or not they are a complete sentence.

Exercise 20 Place a comma where needed with the coordinating conjunction.

1. Henrik Ibsen wrote plays and he became bitter when a stroke prevented him from writing.

2. Ibsen's nurse encouraged him with tender words and hoped he would soon feel better.

3. He told her he was not feeling better so he turned to the window and died on the spot.

4. The year Ibsen died was 1906 and the place was Norway.

5. Money can't buy happiness but with money you can look for happiness in many places.

6. Some Japanese beef is especially tender but the way it is made tender is odd.

7. The steers eat in darkness and are fed beer.

8. Also the steers are massaged daily but we don't know if they like the massage or not.

9. You can imagine the steer's attitude and can imagine the masseur's attitude as well.

10. Someone said that reading makes an intelligent person and that writing makes an exact one.

Subordinating Conjunctions

A subordinate word group means that the word group is not a complete sentence. For instance, notice what happens when we take a simple sentence and place *although* in front of it.

> We could not pay our bills on time.
> Although we could not pay our bills on time . . .

The second word group is no longer a sentence but is a **subordinate clause**.

A subordinating conjunction makes an otherwise complete sentence into a lesser rank, a subordinate clause. Some typical subordinating conjunctions are:

> *when, before, after, until, since, while,*
> *because, if, unless, although, as, where.*

Some words—*before, after,* **and** *until***—are also used as prepositions (after the game . . .). When they are used as prepositions, they are still subordinate words because they introduce a word group that is not a sentence.**

Exercise 21 Change the first sentence into a subordinate clause by adding a subordinating conjunction. A comma will then follow the subordinate clause.

Example: I finally began to understand. The instructor changed the subject.

> When I finally began to understand, the instructor changed the subject.

1. The police conducted a three-year search. They found the man's body in his own house.

   _____

   _____

2. Mary Queen of Scots was beheaded in 1587. Her executioner discovered she was wearing a red wig.

   _____

   _____

3. The queen was forty-four years old. She was already gray-haired.

   _____

   _____

4. Her little dog had been hiding under her petticoat. It was not seen by the officials.

   _____

   _____

5. They could not get the little terrier to leave. They had to remove the queen's body.

   _____

   _____

6. We were glad to visit the mountains. We are happy to be home.

   _____

   _____

7. Somebody has warned her. There's no way she could have known about the trap.

   _____

   _____

8. I've never tried skydiving before. I'm willing to give it a try.

   _____

   _____

9. You're already here. We can settle this now.

_____

_____

10. She is waiting for an interview. She will have to wait a while.

_____

_____

When a subordinating conjunction begins a sentence, the subordinate clause will be followed by a comma.

After
Although
Before
Because   — **(subordinate clause), (sentence)**
Just as
Since
etc.

Subordinating Conjunctions and Punctuation When the subordinate clause is at the end of the sentence, no punctuation is required, with one exception. The *although* subordinate conjunction (*although*, *though*, *even though*, *as though*) will often be preceded by a comma.

He was a successful lawyer, although he never went to high school.

The other subordinate conjunctions do not require a comma when they are at the end of a sentence.

Exercise 22 Punctuate the following sentences properly or write *correct* in the blank.

_____ 1. The vests were warm although they left his arms exposed.

_____ 2. The driver's gloves are vented because the driver's hands need to breathe.

_____ 3. Since we went to Yellowstone no other park interests us.

_____ 4. Although the school's requirements were hard the rewards seemed worth the effort.

_____ 5. Because the fire went out the water pipes burst.

_____ 6. He suddenly joined the air force even though he never mentioned it to anyone before.

_____ 7. Beth hasn't seen her hometown since she was a child.

_____ 8. After Phil returned to school he decided that he liked it.

_____ 9. He stood there at my door as though nothing had ever happened.

_____ 10. Richard feels much better since he quit smoking.

Conjunctive Adverbs

In English we have trouble naming a few items. In theory, for instance, we should be able to say whether a word is an adverb or a conjunction. The trouble is that a few words act as adverbs because they modify clauses. They also connect parts of sentences; thus, they function as conjunctions. The easy way out is simply to call them both **conjunctive adverbs**. For a writer the issue is not what a word is called, but rather how the word is used.

When a conjunctive adverb is used <u>between</u> sentences, it is either preceded by a semicolon and followed by a comma, or it is preceded by a period, capitalized, and followed by a comma.

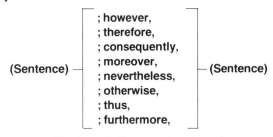

          (Sentence)   (Sentence)

or   **(Sentence). _However_, (sentence).**

When a conjunctive adverb is used <u>inside</u> a sentence, it is surrounded by commas.

                    We are, however, going to make it.

Exercise 23 Punctuate the following sentences properly.

1. The best way to read faster is to read more however most think there is some magic to faster reading.

2. Speed reading is not possible with some information therefore subjects like algebra must be read very slowly.

3. President Kennedy could read light material at an astonishing rate consequently he read several newspapers a day.

4. One key to good reading habits moreover is to read in phrases or word groups.

5. Some reading teachers flash short phrases on a screen however some
   students merely see the first word.

6. Speed reading can be very useful however most fine literature is
   meant to be savored slowly.

7. I'm in no mood for a party nevertheless I must go because I promised Sabbah.

8. Janet has neglected the maintenance of her car consequently the car
   will barely climb the speed bump.

9. I informed the family furthermore that a restraining order would be issued.

10. His immaturity far exceeds any good qualities he may possess
    therefore I've decided not to see him again.

11. Mark fell behind when he was sick and therefore has to study over the holidays.

12. One of the infected animals bit Rudy however we can still save him
    with the serum.

13. Despite Brady's attitude Marsha nevertheless agreed to the meeting.

14. There must be a way out of this forest moreover we'll freeze if we don't try.

15. She knew however that he was sure to call.

16. My trip will be delayed consequently I won't be returning as scheduled.

17. Orson has developed a steel alloy that is revolutionary furthermore
    no other country has considered his work.

18. Cheryl begged Rob to believe her nevertheless he refused.

19. I have consequently dropped all my subscriptions.

20. Brock was out of town on the afternoon of the robbery moreover he
    doesn't need the money.

Correlative Conjunctions

Correlative conjunctions are used similarly to coordinating conjunctions; that is, they join words, phrases, and clauses. No special problem of punctuation exists with these pairs. You use them to connect equally ranked items in a sentence.

> *Both* the lead guitar *and* the drums could be heard over the other instruments.
>
> She can choose a profession of *either* law *or* medicine.
>
> Some presidents are *neither* good speakers *nor* good writers.
>
> *Not only* gasoline *but also* plastic comes from oil.

A few conjunctions can be used in pairs:

   both . . . and,   either . . . or,   neither . . . nor,   not only . . . but also.

These pairs are called <u>correlative conjunctions</u>.

Exercise 24   Sentence Building Rewrite the following sentences using appropriate correlative conjunctions to produce concise, well-written sentences.

Example: Mike wants to major in music. Or Mike wants to major in art.
Mike wants to major in either music or art.

I don't have time to see him. I don't even want to see him.
I have neither the time nor the desire to see him.

1. Flora's not going to the lecture. James is not going either.

   (neither/nor) _____

   _____ .

2. Solar energy is an alternative to dwindling resources. Nuclear energy is gradually becoming more predictable.

   (not only/but also) _____

   _____ .

3. I'll call you this afternoon. You can reach me later tonight.

   (either/or) _____

   _____ .

4. She's been to stores in New York while trying to replace her lost coat.
   She has also searched stores in Los Angeles.

   (both/and) _____

   _____ .

5. I didn't understand the material. I didn't even understand the assignment.

   (neither/nor) _____

   _____ .

6. He denies any relationship with the senator. He claims they haven't even met.

   (not only/but also) _____

   _____ .

7. The major plans to arrive this evening. So do I.

   (both/and) _____

   _____ .

8. Chris might drop by the office with the papers. Tom might do it for
   her.

   (either/or) _____

   _____ .

9. I will not yield to their demands. I won't even listen.

   (neither/nor) _____

   _____ .

10. Several times she has been notified to send payment to us. She could
    also simply return the merchandise.

    (either/or) _____

    _____ .

INTERJECTIONS

Interjections are approximately as useful in writing (except fiction) as a heating lamp in the desert. They are expressions placed in front of a sentence, yet they have no grammatical relationship to the rest of the sentence.

> *Well*, it's time to go to dinner.
> *Darn*, that was a good movie.

As you can see, interjections are not very useful in the kind of writing required in college and on the job.

We do use interjections frequently in our speech. In fact, some persons seem to use mostly interjections. Someone once observed that the military would not function were it not for four-letter interjections.

In writing, if you have something strong to say, say it strongly inside the sentence rather than try for emphasis with an interjection. Many grammar textbooks no longer mention interjections.

SUMMARY

Label the adjectives, adverbs, prepositions, conjunctions, and interjections.

One of the most beautiful areas of the world for lovers of literature is the Lake District of northwestern England. The Lake District is designated as a national park, which means that its natural beauty is preserved for the enjoyment of all the people. The area is roughly nine hundred square miles of peaceful and tranquil scenery. One writer put it this way, "Austere but majestic craggy rock outcrops and bare mountainsides contrast with lush valley pastures; there are peat bogs and birch woods; bracken-clad fells and tree-covered islets; bubbling becks and dramatic cascades; deep-set lakes whose surfaces mirror their surroundings. . . ." In this historic area the traveler will also find prehistoric stone circles, ancient earthworks, some fifteen lakes, and gorgeous mountain passes.

Animals abound as well: deer, ravens, kestrels, curlews, nightingales, and lapwings. Daffodils, ferns, lobelia, and cotton grass are just some of the flowers nestled on the hills and in the valleys.

Because of the popularity of some of its residents, the area became known in the nineteenth century and even a bit earlier as the center for some great writers: Gray, Wordsworth, Coleridge, Southey, De Quincey, Ruskin, and Walpole. However, its magnetic appeal is hardly limited to writers. Backpackers, photographers, naturalists, and geologists as well as ordinary strollers find the place virtually irresistible. Indeed, the area calls visitors back again and again.

REVIEW TEST

I. Adjectives and Adverbs

For each numbered sentence choose the correct letter of the appropriate match.

_____ 1. The teacher looked strangely

_____ 2. My brother looked strange

_____ 3. Arturo feels bad

_____ 4. Mike feels badly

a. without his glasses.
b. at the board.
c. about the accident.
d. because he wears gloves.

II. Adjectives

Choose the letter of the adjective.

_____ 5. The dogs fought throughout the long night.
          a   b   c   d   e

_____ 6. She sits on the sideline where she used to play beautiful music.
       a   b   c   d   e

_____ 7. The sore and tired backpacker crawled back to camp.
              a   b   c   d   e

_____ 8. He tried to be a reasonable man.
        a   b   c   d   e

_____ 9. The artistic child could never find a playmate.
         a   b   c   d   e

_____ 10. Most famous people enjoy their privacy.
         a   b   c   d

III. Adverbs

Choose the letter of the adverb.

_____ 11. The pleased driver accepted the helpful aid gracefully.
            a   b   c   d

_____ 12. Frequently, the lights go out in Georgia.
        a   b   c d   e

_____ 13. Cese came quickly when the young girl called.
        a   b   c   d   e

_____ 14. We watched the steel workers walk carefully.
          a   b   c   d   e

_____ 15. They watched closely while the policeman approached.
        a   b   c   d

_____ 16. She clearly did not really understand the question.
        a   b   c   d   e

_____ 17. The road workers slowly poured the chemicals.
        a   b   c   d   e

_____ 18. He is a most conservative car dealer.
             a   b   c   d   e

_____ 19. The slowly approaching storm caused quick heartbeats.
                a   b   c   d

_____ 20. The dean responded very favorably to the suggestion.
             a   b   c   d

IV. Adjectives and Adverbs

Decide whether the words in italics are used correctly (a) or incorrectly (b).

_____ 21. The doctor seemed *surely* of his test procedure.

_____ 22. Tom felt *badly* about the harm he had caused her.

_____ 23. Always buy the stove that is priced most *reasonable*.

_____ 24. The team's trainer seemed to recover *quickly* from the accident.

_____ 25. Our kumquat tree has fruit that tastes *terribly*.

_____ 26. The smog moved in so *densely* that we couldn't drive.

_____ 27. James's friend ran *more faster* than anyone.

_____ 28. The roses in the spring always smell *sweetly*.

_____ 29. The children talked *confidently* about the sale.

_____ 30. An *early* rising sun caused the frost to melt.

V. Prepositions

Choose the letter of the prepositional phrase.

_____ 31. The car was stolen from the garage sometime last night.
                   a   b   c

_____ 32. We walked briskly down the dark, half-deserted street.
               a   b   c

_____ 33. That particular woman in the gray suit came over to our house for dinner.
                 a   b   c

_____ 34. The screwdriver rolled to the center of the car when I dropped it.
                 a   b   c

_____ 35. The monkey climbed to the top of its cage before throwing its food at us.
                a   b   c

_____ 36. The plumber fixed every drain in the house before he left.
                       b

_____ 37. He was hired because of his high grades on the tests.
                a   b   c

_____ 38. The astronaut flew in his small plane to the landing strip.
                a   b   c

_____ 39. When you leave, shut the door to the cabin and lock it.
               a   b   c

_____ 40. Apart from the raise, you have no reason to go to work early.
              a   b   c

VI. Conjunctions

Decide whether or not the conjunction separates two sentences: yes (a) or no (b).

_____ 41. She bought new tires, seat covers, *and* new windshield wipers.

_____ 42. She took care of the car, *and* he took care of the food.

_____ 43. The government cracked down on drugs; *however*, it did nothing about the cause of drug use.

_____ 44. Francis did not go to a big college *nor* to a poor one.

_____ 45. We got soaking wet; *therefore*, the fire felt good.

VII. Conjunctions

Choose the letter of the conjunction.

_____ 46. Any time the bird wanted, it flew in and out of its cage.
                                              a   b   c   d

_____ 47. Although the dog did no harm, he scared almost everyone.
                  a   b   c   d   e

_____ 48. They tried but failed to get the majority vote.
              a   b   c   d e

_____ 49. They went on a picnic since the rain had stopped.
                       a   b   c   d

_____ 50. Jane wanted the hot tub, but the boys couldn't carry it home.
                  a   b   c   d

CHAPTER 4
SUBORDINATE CLAUSES

To learn about clauses and to feel comfortable using them guarantees the writer a set of options that make for precision, clarity, and an interest in writing. Without the ability to use the subordinate clause, the writer struggles with simple sentences even when a more sophisticated structure would be easier to write and clearer to read. The beginning skier learns to snowplow—a fundamental step in learning to ski and a useful technique. To get beyond survival, however, and into skillful enjoyment, the skier must add the equivalent of clauses in writing, those extra elements, skills, and techniques that make skiing precise, secure, and fun.

Traditionally, teachers have identified two kinds of clauses: **main** (also called **independent**) and **subordinate** (also called **dependent**). The main clause can stand alone; therefore, a main clause and a simple sentence are the same thing.

$$\text{The movie ended.} = \left\{ \begin{array}{l} \text{an independent clause} \\ \text{a simple sentence} \\ \text{a main clause} \end{array} \right.$$

                 subj   verb

1. The *movie ended.*

                 subj   verb

2. After the *movie ended*

Both the first and the second examples contain a subject and a verb, but only the first can stand as a sentence. The word *after* prevents the second from being a sentence.

Traditionally, as we said, the first would have been labeled a **main** or **independent clause** and the second would have been called a **dependent** or **subordinate clause** because it **depends** on a main clause for meaning. We are not contradicting tradition, just simplifying some definitions.

---

1. **A group of words containing a subject and a verb that can stand alone is a <u>simple sentence</u> (also called an independent clause).**

2. **A group of words containing a subject and verb that cannot stand alone is called a <u>subordinate clause</u>.**

A subordinate clause is less than a sentence because the subordinate clause lacks completeness.

In Chapter 1 you studied the core elements of a sentence—a principal subject and a principal verb. And you went on to learn that to be a sentence these words must be able to function **independently**—to stand alone. Which group can stand alone?

The waiter fell.
When the waiter fell

Both word groups contain a subject and a verb, yet only one is a **sentence**. The other group, the one that cannot stand alone is called a **clause**, also known as a **subordinate clause**.

Exercise 1 Underline the subject once and the verb twice. Label the group of words as a sentence or a clause.

Example: A = clause   when we went home.
         B = sentence The rain finally stopped.

_____ 1. After the workers finished.

_____ 2. The cup on the table contained red paint.

_____ 3. When we plant tomatoes.

_____ 4. Because we love to eat fresh vegetables.

_____ 5. In the snow, the dogs felt at home.

_____ 6. Because they had their winter coats on.

_____ 7. Who teaches classes to the refugees.

_____ 8. That just came over on boats.

_____ 9. If possible, we will come over tonight.

_____ 10. The information proved more than helpful.

_____ 11. Whenever this project is finished.

_____ 12. Some drunken sailors sang and danced.

_____ 13. After the sunset, they left for home.

_____ 14. Every time the club met in the room.

_____ 15. Whenever you find the opportunity.

_____ 16. After she finishes her work.

_____ 17. When the price falls, he plans to buy the house.

_____ 18. Since he began playing the trumpet.

_____ 19. Because the trumpet sounded shrill.

_____ 20. We must hear more about the proposal.

_____ 21. Although the water was dripping.

_____ 22. Since the backpackers hiked into the canyon.

_____ 23. Nevertheless, they bought the old bridge's lumber.

_____ 24. As a result of miscalculations.

_____ 25. Tom never lost sight of the natural beauty.

A subordinate clause punctuated as a sentence is a **fragment**. A fragment is one of the worst possible mistakes for a writer because it announces to the reader that the writer is not in control and shifts the reader's attention away from the writer's ideas. Be absolutely certain that you avoid fragments. A subordinate clause affords the writer a great tool, but the clause must be connected to the main sentence in some logical way. Here is a subordinate clause:

1. Although the *subway was* noisy
   If we take away the word *although*, we have a simple sentence:

   The subway was noisy.

Here is another subordinate clause:

2. *That were* too tight
   This time we cannot merely take off a word in order to have a sentence; this time we must **add** something:

   I bought some new gloves *that were too tight*.

Look at this third subordinate clause:

3. Whatever *they said*
   Once again we need additional words to have a complete sentence:

   We believed *whatever they said*.

Number 1 is an **adverb** subordinate clause:

   Although the subway was noisy

Number 2 is an **adjective** subordinate clause:

   that were too tight

Number 3 is a **noun** subordinate clause:

   whatever they said

These subordinate clauses must be attached to a sentence in some logical way in order to be useful and to avoid being fragments.

Subordinate clauses function as if they were a single word—an adverb, an adjective, or a noun. Neither an adverb, an adjective, nor a noun alone can be a sentence. A subordinate clause cannot be a sentence.

ADVERB CLAUSES

Recognizing and Using Adverb Clauses

Adverb clauses answer simple questions about the action verb, questions like when? where? how? why? and under what condition? If you have trouble recognizing adverb clauses, look back at both adverbs and subordinating conjunctions. But you probably won't have trouble because once you practice identifying a few adverb clauses, they become easy to recognize.

First of all, adverb clauses will begin with a word that subordinates an otherwise complete sentence.

> We had good times around the dinner table.

Now notice what happens:

> Because we had good times around the dinner table,

The word *because* subordinates the sentence, making it a clause that can no longer stand alone. The clause is an adverb clause since it explains **under what condition** the rest of the sentence has meaning, why the family *felt* close.

> *Because we had good times around the dinner table,* our family always felt close.
>
> The manager started the meeting *early*.

Early answers the question *when?* and is an **adverb**.

> The manager started the meeting *when the room was available*.

The expression *when the room was available* also answers *when?* and functions exactly like the one-word adverb. We know that the expression is a clause since it has a subject and a verb: *room was*. Further, if we removed *when*, the expression would be a simple sentence: The room was available.

> The bread dough rose *quickly*.
> The bread dough rose *after we kneaded it*.
> The cat crept *silently*.
> The cat crept *as though it were walking on air*.

You can see that the adverb clauses function in these sentences just like the one-word adverbs function.

Exercise 2 Underline the one-word adverbs and the adverb clauses.

1. Our car started slowly.

2. Our car started when we jumped the battery.

3. Quickly, open the door.

4. When you hear the door bell, open the door.

5. The sand stretched everywhere.

6. The sand stretched as far as we could see.

7. The telephone will ring soon.

8. The telephone will ring after I sit down to read.

9. Patiently, the pilot landed the plane.

10. Because one engine had quit, the pilot landed the plane.

11. The train left early.

12. The train left before we arrived at the station.

13. He rides the bus often.

14. He rides the bus since his car broke down.

15. We boarded the ship quickly.

16. We boarded the ship when it docked.

17. They will leave immediately.

18. They will leave as soon as the meeting is over.

19. Carefully, they swam through the shark-infested waters.

20. Because the boat sank, they swam through the shark-infested waters.

   However, not all adverb clauses are extensions of one-word adverbs.
Most adverb clauses are used to express the exact relationship that the
author wants between two ideas, one being subordinate to the other. The
careful writer chooses subordinating words to express the kind of
information that is called for. Learn these indicator words.

Words that begin adverb clauses:

When?

after, before, when, while, whenever, even after, even when, as,
as soon as, until, since

Where?

where, wherever

How?

even if, as if, as though, just as

Why?
Under what condition?

because, since, so that, as, in case, if, unless, though, although, even if

While you will have more options available to you as a writer if you learn all these words, the most frequently used adverb clause indicators are: *when, before, after, until, since, while, because, if, unless, although, as,* and *where.*

A punctuation reminder: When an adverb clause begins a sentence, a comma follows the clause. If the clause is at the end of the sentence, no comma is used except with the *although* clause.

Exercise 3 Punctuate the following sentences or write *correct* in the blank.

_____ 1. Some people read astrology signs because they want to feel good.

_____ 2. When the dog wants strokes he sits at my feet.

_____ 3. Before you give up try more practice.

_____ 4. The best time to study begins after the noise dies down.

_____ 5. Too much emphasis is placed on sports although I do enjoy watching.

_____ 6. He'll continue to get in fights unless his attitude changes.

_____ 7. I've decided not to go even though Richard will be there.

_____ 8. He doesn't have an alibi even if his statements are true.

_____ 9. She sees his face wherever she goes.

_____ 10. If you don't hear from me see me in class.

_____ 11. He tried all the alternatives before he agreed to the operation.

_____ 12. Until mid-afternoon the doctor will be in her office.

_____ 13. Because of this delay we'll have to wait until tomorrow to leave.

_____ 14. The bartender threatened to throw them out if they didn't settle down.

_____ 15. Where there's smoke there's fire.

_____ 16. Since the accident he has been very depressed.

_____ 17. Although she does care for him she doesn't want to remarry.

_____ 18. Muriel studied all night because her grades were dropping.

_____ 19. When he left the party his car was gone.

_____ 20. While he's in town Mike wants to visit the botanical gardens.

The adverb clause indicators function as words that subordinate the words that follow, making them **subordinate adverb clauses**.

The fire went out.
Although the fire went out
Our blankets kept us warm, although the fire went out.

The word *although* subordinates and connects the adverb clause. Thus, we can say that adverb clause indicators are **subordinating conjunctions**—*subordinating* because the words that follow cannot stand alone, and *conjunctions* because the word connects parts of the sentence.

Remember that a few words are **coordinating conjunctions**: *and*, *but*, *or*, *nor*, *for*, *so*, and *yet*. These words do not subordinate the words that follow.

However, **subordinating conjunctions** do reduce the words that follow to a secondary position—a lesser position than a full sentence. Subordinating conjunctions, then, introduce adverb clauses.

Using Adverb Clauses to Improve Writing

A sentence constructed around one core subject and verb is called, as you might expect, a simple sentence. As you learned in Chapter 1, two simple sentences combined with *and*, *but*, *or*, *nor*, *for*, *so*, or *yet* (coordinating conjunctions) form a compound sentence. When we add a subordinate clause (as you have been doing with the adverb clauses) to a simple sentence, it becomes a **complex sentence**.

A complex sentence contains a simple sentence plus one or more subordinate clauses. Therefore, a sentence that contains an adverb clause is a complex sentence.

Subordinating one idea to another, more significant, idea allows the writer to show complex relationships that would not otherwise be possible.

Denise studied hard. Denise made good grades.

At first it might seem that the studying produced the grades, but what if you wanted to suggest that getting good grades encouraged her to study hard? Notice the subtle difference in meaning:

Denise studied hard *because* she made good grades.
When Denise studied hard, she made good grades.
Denise studied hard *after* she made good grades.

Constructing complex sentences provides you with a powerful option, increases reader interest, and energizes your writing.

The earthquake struck at six o'clock in the morning.
People were still at home. The damage was light.

You can anticipate how much better the ideas in these three short sentences would be if they were made into a good, complex sentence.

Because the earthquake struck at six o'clock in the morning while people were still at home, the damage was light.

Written this way, the emphasis is placed on the light damage. You could turn it around and place the emphasis either on the early morning part or on the fact that people were still at home. Notice the different meanings we get with different subordinating conjunctions: *until, although, if, when*.

We could not buy clothes _____ we wanted to.

Again, try each subordinating conjunction, noting the differences in meaning: *because, before, just as*.

The instructor saw the class _____ he wanted to.

Exercise 4 Combine the following sentences, making one of them a subordinate adverb clause. The completed sentence will be a **complex sentence**.

Example: Joey pulled off the crowded freeway.
The tire blew out.
The tire blew out *before* Joey pulled off the crowded freeway.
or
Joey pulled off the crowded freeway *when* the tire blew out.

1. Computer languages are similar to human languages.
   Children can learn either kind easily.

   _____

   _____

2. The parents looked at the children. Nothing had happened.

   _____

   _____

3. Mr. Danley always wanted a store of his own.
   He worked to get what he wished for.

   _____

   _____

4. We speak of possessions. No one admits to worshipping them.

   _____

   _____

5. Rock and roll music has been around for over 30 years.
   People of all ages enjoy the beat.

   _____

   _____

6. The Rolling Stones appeal to vast audiences.
   They can still draw audiences anywhere in the world.

   _____

   _____

7. Bruce Springsteen captures the audience's imagination.
   He has showmanship, charisma, and musical strength.

   _____

   _____

8. Several rock stars have been dead ten years or more.
   These heroes still inspire young followers.

   _____

   _____

9. Jimi Hendrix has inspired millions of followers.
   He has been dead since September 18, 1970.

   _____

   _____

10. Woodstock, held in 1969, remains *the* event of the Hippie Era.
    It brought together 500,000 music lovers.

   _____

   _____

11. The epidemic was of catastrophic proportions.
    People retained their sense of humor.

   _____

   _____

12. The doctor was buried. He was doing time in prison.

   _____

   _____

13. The rampaging sea continued its onslaught. The damage was extensive.

_____

_____

14. Her performance delighted the crowd. She played a few more songs.

_____

_____

15. Her car was towed away. The tow truck finally arrived.

_____

_____

16. We've learned how to treat phobias successfully.
    Nobody knows exactly what causes a phobia.

_____

_____

17. You have done your homework. You can go to the show.

_____

_____

18. They dug up the alleged vampire's grave.
    He was found to have fresh blood in his veins.

_____

_____

19. Skeptics say that reincarnation is wishful thinking.
    I think some people would rather not go through life on earth again.

_____

_____

20. He was American by upbringing.
    He went to Europe and was accepted into high society.

_____

_____

ADJECTIVE CLAUSES

Recognizing and Using Adjective Clauses

The **subordinate adjective clause** is used in a sentence just as if it were a simple adjective—to modify a noun. In the previous section, you learned that the adverb clause modifies verbs, adjectives, and other adverbs. Here we learn to deal with a more limited clause, limited because the adjective clause modifies a noun **only**. Further, in contrast to the adverb clause that can be found almost anywhere in a sentence, the adjective clause is found in only one position—right after the noun it modifies. The single adjective usually comes before the noun.

> adj
> She bought a *small* swimsuit.

> adj clause
> She bought a swimsuit *that was small*.

Notice how the single adjective comes before a noun or after a linking verb.

> adj   noun
> The minister spoke from a *black* notebook.

> noun   linking verb   adj
> The minister's book   was   *black*.

Now notice that an adjective clause comes right after the noun it modifies:

> noun   adj clause
> The minister spoke from a notebook *that was black*.

Exercise 5 Fill in the blanks with either *that* or *which* to make an adjective clause.

1. They rode an old bus. They rode a bus _____ was old.

2. The mechanic charged the dead battery.

   The mechanic charged the battery _____ was dead.

3. When they first appeared, only black phones could be bought.

   When they first appeared, only phones _____ were black could be bought.

4. The finest diamonds can cost millions.

   Diamonds _____ are the finest can cost millions.

5. Some thought the guillotine provided a humane means of execution.

   Some thought the guillotine provided a means of execution _____ was humane.

6. She chose the smallest puppy. She chose the puppy _____ was smallest.

7. The blond guy waved to you. The guy _____ is blond waved to you.

8. Burt took her to the new restaurant.

   Burt took her to the restaurant _____ is new.

9. He refused to listen to the offensive language.

   He refused to listen to the language _____ was offensive.

10. Larry brought the young woman to his house.

    Larry brought the woman _____ was young to his house.

11. The vicious tiger clawed his trainer.

    The tiger _____ was vicious clawed his trainer.

12. I decided to buy the most expensive dress.

    I decided to buy the dress _____ was most expensive.

13. The avocado tree grew fast. The tree _____ was an avocado grew fast.

14. They've gone to see their sick friend in the hospital.

    They've gone to see their friend _____ is sick in the hospital.

15. Denny's rare necklace has been stolen.

    Denny's necklace _____ is rare has been stolen.

16. The solemn procession marched past my store.

    The procession _____ was solemn marched past my store.

17. Her ignorant assumptions cost us the deal.

    Her assumptions _____ were ignorant cost us the deal.

18. His trip to the remote island gave him time to think.

    His trip to the island _____ was remote gave him time to think.

19. The glib boy talked for hours. The boy _____ was glib talked for hours.

20. David grew tired on the long trip.

    David grew tired on the trip _____ was long.

Five words introduce adjective clauses: *who*, *whom*, *whose*, *which*, and *that*. There is also a sixth word, *where*, which is rarely used.

We liked the house *where we lived*.

1. Some single adjectives are better expressed as a clause, while some are not. Emphasis is the difference.
2. The words *which* and *that* both introduce adjectives, and if the noun they modify is not a person, either word can properly refer to the noun. The word *which* should not be used to refer to a person. If the noun referred to is a person, then *that*, *who*, *whom*, or *whose* must be used.

These signal, indicator, or introductory words to an adjective clause are **relative pronouns**—*relative* because they can refer to any noun, and *pronouns* because they stand in for a noun.

Adjective clauses always follow the noun they modify.

Adjective clauses are introduced by relative pronouns:

who, whom, whose, which, and that.

When an adjective clause is removed from a sentence, a complete sentence remains.

Adjective clauses always follow the noun they modify because they are immobile; that is, when we try to move the adjective clause, the sentence falls apart and sounds awkward, if not meaningless. This lack of ability to move is in sharp contrast to the **adverb clause**, which can move to several places in a sentence.

Which clause can move?

adj
The man *who brought our dog home* refused any reward.

adv
After we lost our dog, we offered a reward.

A characteristic of both *adverb* and *adjective* clauses is that if we remove one of them, a complete sentence is left.

The flowers *that we loved* grew in the high country.
Our neighbor, *who broke his leg*, used to be a gardener.
The old man *whom we helped* finally left the neighborhood.
My friend *whose boyfriend owns a car* is coming to take us to the concert.
These are the burial grounds *which were mentioned in the story*.
He was lonely *before they met*.
While I'm here, I'd like to talk to you.
She became a great rock musician *because she was persistent*.

Exercise 6 Underline the adjective clauses. Remember (1) they will always follow the noun they modify, and (2) if you remove the adjective clause, a complete sentence remains.

1. The young woman who caught the largest fish piloted the boat.

2. I enjoy the television sets that have large screens.

3. New Year's Day has too many football games that few care about.

4. A diving instructor who could not swim would be less than easy to trust.

5. Muriel, who was always enthusiastic, drove a fast sports car.

6. He looks like the man who escaped from Alcatraz.

7. Our daughter, whom we sent to Europe, will return today.

8. The man whose wife was injured used to come by all the time.

9. This is the beach that allows nude sunbathing.

10. The lake where I spent the summer is frozen now.

11. Darcy, who is only ten years old, plays the piano quite well.

12. The maple tree, which was old, couldn't survive the blight.

13. Some of the kittens that were abandoned found homes.

14. A young girl who ran out of gas asked to use our phone.

15. She misses the bayou where she was raised.

16. The horse whose leg was broken has been shot.

17. His car, which was demolished in the race, can never be rebuilt again.

18. These are the people whom I introduced to you in my letter.

19. The bread that she baked was superb.

20. Her quiches, which she makes herself, are world famous.

21. The girl whose dog ran away is heartbroken.

Choosing correctly between who and whom Read, carefully, these examples using *who* and *whom*.

> John Jones was a farmer *whom other farmers trusted*.
> John Jones, *who was a farmer*, had the trust of other farmers.

If you recall, we studied *who* and *whom* as relative pronouns: *Who* is a **subject** word, to be used as the subject of the verb. *Whom* is an **object** word, to be used as the object of the verb.

   Here is how to know which is correct—the easy way. Remember we are studying the adjective clause, and a clause **always** has a subject and a verb. Read these isolated clauses.

subj verb	subj verb	subj verb
Who drove	Who sunned themselves	Who are late

Who is always a subject word or one used in the subjective case. Now look at *whom*.

subj verb	subj verb	subj verb
Whom we knew	Whom they trusted	Whom the car hit

You can see that a clause introduced by *whom* already has a subject. *Who* is always a subject word; *whom* is always an object word. *Whom* introduces a clause that already has a subject.

When *who* is used to introduce an adjective clause, then *who* is the subject of the clause:

> **The man who made breakfast went home early.**

When *whom* is used to introduce an adjective clause, then the clause will have a subject of its own:

> **The policeman whom we knew smiled at the children.**

Exercise 7 Fill in the blanks with *who* or *whom*.

 1. Jackie knows _____ has money.

 2. Travelers _____ are seasoned can take many hardships.

 3. Joe _____ he knew had been trekking in Nepal.

 4. Disk jockeys _____ talk too much should be fired.

 5. I trust Con, _____ I know to be honorable.

 6. Mary Ann, _____ lives on this street, has promised me her recipe.

 7. The man _____ the police took in for questioning is no longer a suspect.

 8. Ted, the good-looking man _____ I mentioned, has asked me for a reference.

 9. A woman _____ seemed to be ill was here collecting for the drive.

10. Their friend _____ flunked the test is going to study with them.

11. This is the woman _____ I'm going to marry.

12. The accountant _____ did my tax return is very competent.

13. The first person _____ is caught spying will be interrogated.

14. The man _____ I spoke to earlier has gone home for the day.

15. Her little boy, _____ she saved from drowning, stays away from pools now.

16. The cop _____ stopped me gave me a ticket.

17. Dr. Robbins, _____ I trust, will perform the surgery.

18. The individual _____ is persistent will succeed.

19. Marsha is the mechanic _____ fixed my car.

20. Don, _____ I've known for years, has joined the navy.

Sometimes prepositions are used before an adjective clause. The most frequently used prepositions in this instance are *to*, *for*, *from*, and *with*. Always use *whom* following a preposition.

> He is the man *in whom* we placed our faith.
> Our banker, *with whom* we had always dealt, went on a holiday.

Exercise 8 Choose *who* or *whom*.

1. The woman for _____ we had worked moved to Texas.

2. These are the tourists _____ came last year also.

3. Most Americans enjoy Canadians _____ are warm and friendly.

4. The ship was run by a man in _____ the crew had little trust.

5. My middle brother is a person _____ enjoys good conversation.

6. The man to _____ I spoke was helpful.

7. This is the boy _____ broke your window.

8. Mr. Edwards was the man with _____ I've exchanged services.

9. My friend, for _____ I'd do anything, is in serious trouble.

10. The man _____ I'm engaged to enjoys mountain climbing.

11. Wally is the one _____ won the tournament.

12. Here is the boy _____ I received flowers from.

13. The doctor, _____ I trusted, has betrayed me.

14. Mrs. Simms, the lady _____ designs clothes, lives next door.

15. He is the man for _____ I've worked.

16. My roommate, _____ I could discuss anything with, had gone.

17. His daughter, _____ wants to be a dentist, will graduate soon.

18. He's the man from _____ she's learned a great deal.

19. The children _____ I babysit for are wags.

20. He is the one _____ should have gone home early.

Using Adjective Clauses to Improve Writing

An adjective clause combined with a core sentence allows the writer to explain something about the sentence without writing two sentences. Further, the sentence with the clause in it will be smoother and easier to read. Once again, recall that in Chapter 1 we learned that two simple sentences with *and*, *but*, *or*, *nor*, *for*, *so*, or *yet* form a compound sentence.

Compound sentences work well some of the time, but writers need much more variety than they offer; in addition to compounding, writers need to subordinate to emphasize one element of the sentence over the other. When an adjective clause is added to a simple sentence, the new sentence becomes a complex sentence.

A complex sentence contains a simple sentence plus one or more subordinate clauses. Therefore, a sentence that contains an adjective clause is a complex sentence.

We'll practice subordinating some sentences, making adjective clauses out of some of them; the new clause will modify the noun it follows.

> My brother plays championship backgammon. He also writes poetry.
> My brother, *who writes poetry*, plays championship backgammon.

Two ideas are now expressed in one sentence: **brother writes poetry** and **plays championship backgammon**. The new sentence emphasizes *backgammon*.

An adjective clause works especially well when it is used to explain or to elaborate on the noun (or pronoun) it modifies:

> David scared the cat. It climbed up to the roof.
> David scared the cat, *which then climbed up to the roof*.

Exercise 9 Combine the following sentences making one of them an adjective clause.

1. The hens laid extra large eggs.
   They could always be found around six o'clock in the morning.

---

2. Some vessels carry blood from the heart. They are called arteries.
   (Be sure to place the adjective clause after the noun it modifies.)

---

3. One book outsells all others. It is called the Bible.

_____

4. The guns were fired at Lexington. They were heard around the world.

_____

5. Some rivers rise west of the Rocky Mountains.
   They empty into the Pacific Ocean.

_____

6. The doberman leaped four feet into the air for the Frisbee.
   He was the best dog in the competition.

_____

7. The Nazi troops invaded Denmark.
   They occupied that nation for five years.

_____

_____

8. The trip has been canceled. I told you about it.

_____

9. Woody Guthrie did several radio shows.
   His mother taught him the old songs.

_____

_____

10. She misses her home in the mountains. She grew up there.

_____

11. Larry has asked me out for another date. I like him.

_____

12. This is what's left of the building. It was leveled by the fire.

_____

_____

13. Ed found a lot of money. He found it in this vacant lot.

_____

14. Janet is a talented writer. I enjoy her company.

_____

15. His attorney defended him brilliantly.
    She has been practicing law for twenty years.

_____

_____

We can, if we choose, take an adjective and turn it into a short preposi-tional phrase or clause, giving us three options for modifying a noun:

1. an **adjective**   *energetic*
2. a **phrase**   *of energy*
3. a **clause**   *who has energy*
                       who is energetic

Look at this word—*wise*.

A *wise* woman will be honored.

Wise is used as a one-word adjective.

A woman *of wisdom* will be honored.

Of wisdom is a prepositional phrase modifying *woman*.

A woman *who is wise* will be honored.

Who is wise is an adjective clause modifying *woman*.

The first two are simple sentences. The third example is a complex sentence—a core sentence (*A woman will be honored*) and a clause (*who is wise*).

Exercise 10 Underline (1) the one-word adjective, (2) a prepositional phrase used as an adjective, or (3) the adjective clause.

1. An energetic student will succeed.

2. A student of energy will succeed.

3. A student who has energy will succeed.

4. The person who runs will catch the subway.

5. Henry Hudson discovered a large river.

6. Henry Hudson discovered a large river which bears his name.

7. Animals with backbones are called vertebrates.

8. Animals that have a backbone are called vertebrates.

9. Death is the black camel which kneels at every person's gate.

119

10. Our best friends are those who tell us our faults.

11. Rainy days are good for studying.

12. A day of rain once in a while helps us appreciate the sunshine.

13. There are always new adventures for kids these days.

14. We enjoyed a day of fun at the zoo.

15. One class in which I'm enrolled has been canceled.

16. They ignored the rules of the game.

17. After her exam, she was jubilant.

18. The man who called earlier is at the door.

19. This is the article that I told you about yesterday.

20. My best friend with whom I've spent so many summers has moved to the East Coast.

Exercise 11   Building Better Sentences Combine the following sentences, making one of them a subordinate clause. The completed sentence will be a complex sentence.

1. Ancient Greece was barely half the size of New York. It is the most noted country of antiquity.

   _____

2. Aesop was a slave. He wrote Aesop's fables.

   _____

3. The Mayflower was a strong ship for its time. It brought 101 men, women, and children to America.

   _____

4. Meridians are imaginary circles. They extend from pole to pole.

   _____

5. You can see Saturn with an inexpensive telescope. It has beautiful rings.

   _____

6. They were on their way to the moon. Man first set foot on the moon in 1969.

   _____

   _____

7. Algeria has over 16 million people. It's in North Africa.

_____

8. This is the woman. Her car was stolen.

_____

9. Albert Camus was a great author from Algeria. He was awarded the
   Nobel Prize.

_____

_____

10. The plane will be delayed for an hour. My son is on it.

_____

11. The three survivors were seriously injured. I tried to help them.

_____

_____

12. Latin was the first universal language. It was used during the Middle
    Ages and the Renaissance.

_____

_____

13. The old man has been retired for years. He used to own this shop.

_____

14. My daughter lost the tickets. I bought them last week.

_____

15. This is the day. I've been waiting for it.

_____

16. People live in the old mansion. They're very wealthy.

_____

17. Here is an article about cooking. I thought you would enjoy reading it.

_____

_____

18. Jill works long hours in her business. I believe she will succeed.

_____

19. Marian enjoys traveling in Europe. Her mother lives in Paris.

_____

_____

20. We watched our friend perform last night. She is a belly dancer.

_____

NOUN CLAUSES

Recognizing and Using Noun Clauses

Noun clauses form in our minds rather easily. When we want to question someone's ability to be clear, we say something like "What he said makes no sense."

> _What he said_ makes no sense.
> _He_ makes no sense.

The subject of the verb _makes_ is one word _he_ or a noun clause _what he said_.

A noun clause is used exactly as if it were only one word.

1. His _car_ was insane.   subject—_car_
   What he drove was insane.   subject—_What he drove_

2. She bought _clothes_.   direct object—_clothes_
   She bought _whatever she wanted_.   direct object—_whatever she wanted_

3. Mother gave _visitors_ fresh pecan pie.   indirect object—_visitors_
   Mother gave _whoever came by_ fresh pecan pie.   indirect object—_whoever came by_

4. This is our _principle_.   subject complement—_principle_
   Our principle is _that we should be free_.   subject complement—_that we should be free_

5. The community gave to _charities_.   object of preposition—_charities_
   The community gave to _whoever needed help_.   object of preposition—_whoever needed help_

Again noun clauses are used just as if they were one-word nouns.

   In almost every instance, an adverb clause or an adjective clause can be removed from a sentence without destroying the core sentence. A complete sentence will be left after an adverb or adjective clause is removed. Such is not the case with a noun clause. Except for the indirect object, a sentence will be ruined if you remove a noun clause from it. The reason is that a noun clause functions as an integral part of the basic sentence, such as a subject.

Exercise 12 Underline the noun clauses in the following sentences.

1. That nearly all children are intelligent is generally acknowledged.

2. That the moon is made of green cheese is believed by a few weird people.

3. I know which came first.

4. Plato taught that the soul is immortal.

5. Whether you come or not isn't important.

6. The instructor generally tells what you need to know.

7. How you bend your knees determines your weightlifting ability.

8. We never knew why they sold their house.

9. The radio was given to whoever bought the most gas.

10. The nurse found that everyone had a sore throat.

11. She reads whatever she can find.

12. What he did was inexcusable.

13. This is how I feel about it.

14. Old Mrs. Benchcroft will talk to whoever will listen.

15. We'll go to whatever store is open at this hour.

16. How she manages with twelve kids is a mystery to me.

17. Steve gives his attention to whatever appeals to him at the time.

18. He goes wherever his feet take him.

19. Generally, the rule is that no one discusses it.

20. He loiters on whichever street has the most shoe stores.

Using Noun Clauses to Improve Writing

A sentence built around a principal subject and a principal verb is called a **simple sentence**. As you learned in Chapter 1, two simple sentences combined with *and, but, or, nor, for, so,* or *yet* (coordinating conjunctions) form a **compound sentence**.

A complex sentence contains a simple sentence plus one or more subordinate clauses. Therefore, a sentence that contains a noun clause is a complex sentence.

Exercise 13   Building Better Sentences Fill in the blanks with noun clauses.
Remember the common words that begin noun clauses: *that, what, how,*
whatever, which, who, whom.

1. The army took _____ .

2. The dance instructor waited for _____ .

3. _____ must wait until later.

4. I wanted to know _____ .

5. _____ will not be forgotten.

6. James's girlfriend knew _____ .

7. _____ is no secret.

8. I know _____ .

9. The mother said _____ .

10. We gave the old car to _____ .

11. _____ is fine with me.

12. Richard likes to explore around _____ .

13. The results of an exam are _____ .

14. _____ greatly surprises me.

15. He spends most of his time _____ .

16. His philosophy is _____ .

17. The flyers were sent to _____ .

18. My dog loves to run in _____ .

19. I did _____ to pass the time.

20. She told _____ about her operation.

Exercise 14   Practice for Adverb, Adjective, and Noun Clauses Label the clauses in
italics as an **adverb** (a), **adjective** (b), or **noun** (c).

_____ 1. Crate makers contend *that their product is the best.*

_____ 2. A good shoe salesman is a person *who needs patience.*

_____ 3. *While we were camping last summer,* a snake crawled inside
the leader's sleeping bag.

_____ 4. *That we had sold the house* bothered my sister.

_____ 5. *As I talked to the policeman,* I found that we had been neighbors.

_____ 6. Where is the garden *that needs planting*?

_____ 7. Lynn, *who studied much of the time,* became a minister at age 41.

_____ 8. French is a language *that becomes more beautiful as time passes.*

_____ 9. The old cow came trotting home *because she knew a storm was approaching.*

_____ 10. The light blue plane *which was not paid for* was sold for taxes.

_____ 11. *Why she left the state* is something we'll never know.

_____ 12. People think that graffiti, *which is an ancient practice,* developed along with the modern bathroom.

_____ 13. He trusts no one *since she betrayed him.*

_____ 14. I finally have my car running again *after spending all my savings.*

_____ 15. The house *that suffered the most damage* has been leveled.

_____ 16. Bill doesn't understand *how you fixed it.*

_____ 17. The organization *for which Tamara works* is filing for bankruptcy.

_____ 18. Some people *who claim that they've seen UFOs* simply have good imaginations.

_____ 19. Carrie went to work *while Tony slept.*

_____ 20. I take time to see her *whenever I'm in town.*

Summary Exercise Underline the adverb, adjective, and noun clauses in the following sentences and label them **adv**, **adj**, or **noun**.

That we live in an increasingly crowded world and that we also live in an increasingly industrialized world places more pressure on all of us to develop less dependence on non-renewable fossil fuels. Because oil, gas, and coal cannot be renewed, a new emphasis is centering on wood, water, wind, and sunlight, all sources of enormous power that can help lessen the dependence on oil. Part of the new emphasis on "traditional" energy sources is that these sources will allow people to be in control of their own lives.

Since burning wood does add pollutants to the air, many feel that wood is no answer to the energy shortage. But the fact is that most of us are still in love with fireplaces, barbecues, and woodburning stoves. And wood is renewable. Certain kinds of wood that have been treated offer enormous sources of heat. Some residents in northern states are planting groves that will supply them with fuel for as long as they need it.

For those who live near small streams, water remains a cheap source of power. *Popular Science* published an article in 1947 showing the steps which one would take to develop a small electric generator. Some industrious persons are following this description and making a water-turned generator. Before the turn of the century, hundreds of towns had waterwheels that gave the town power. Now only a few remain. However, families throughout the northern part of the United States are finding that water-turned generators may once again be the best source of power.

Wind and solar energy are interrelated; they both involve outside devices to take advantage of natural elements. Windmills and solar collectors are making their progress felt around the world. The wind plants are not new, of course, since they were used throughout windy sections of the United States in the last century and the early part of this one. Solar collectors are already used extensively in Israel and other countries. No doubt these two forms of collecting natural energy will continue to intrigue persons interested in controlling their own lives.

D. S. Halacy, who wrote *The Coming Age of Solar Energy*, estimates that people the world over consumed 90 trillion horsepower-hours of energy in 1972; yet during the same year, the sun generated 1.5 million trillion horsepower-hours of sunlight. Add to those figures the consumable wood, usable water, and blowing wind, and one can see that alternative energy sources do exist.

REVIEW TEST

I. Subordinate Clauses

Choose the correct letter for a **sentence** (a) or a **subordinate clause** (fragment) (b).

_____ 1. We watched the train pull into the station.

_____ 2. Although it was three hours late.

_____ 3. Because the heat was extreme.

_____ 4. The fan ran all night long.

_____ 5. The tourists looked exhausted.

_____ 6. Who came late to our party.

_____ 7. That old car had never been there before.

_____ 8. I called the police soon afterward.

_____ 9. They came over in a flash.

_____ 10. The light on the car.

II. Adverb Clauses

Match the letter of the adverb clause with the proper sentence.

a. Although his motions are crazy,
b. After the rains came,
c. Whenever the sewing begins,
d. While Jimmy never plays hard,
e. Since we became friends,

_____ 11. ____, James always plays with verve.

_____ 12. ____, Rod sings with class.

_____ 13. ____, the mud slides began.

_____ 14. ____, I've seen her good qualities.

_____ 15. ____, I get out the thimble and needle.

III. Adverb Clauses

Decide if the sentence **does** (a) or **does not** (b) contain an adverb clause.

_____ 16. The rock concert consisted of several different groups that played for hours.

_____ 17. While the bands played, the two dogs slept quietly.

_____ 18. Although I married late, I always felt young.

_____ 19. The TV always broke when the best programs were coming.

_____ 20. I could never buy enough food because the goldfish ate too much.

IV. Adjective Clauses

Choose correctly between *who* (a) and *whom* (b).

_____ 21. The teacher ____ you gave your paper to is ill today.

_____ 22. Donald Sutherland, ____ had never played a similar role, gave a great performance.

_____ 23. The actress ____ Frank had interviewed left town suddenly.

_____ 24. My neighbor, ____ used to be a banker, now sells wooden fences.

_____ 25. We bought it from the boy ____ had worked so hard.

V. Adjective Clauses

Decide if the sentence **does** (a) or **does not** (b) contain an adjective clause.

_____ 26. The customs inspector was a man who worked very hard.

_____ 27. Jobs that pay well and are interesting are hard to prepare for.

_____ 28. While you were away, the flowers all died.

_____ 29. What goes up may not come down.

_____ 30. She paid eighty dollars for a special haircut.

VI. Noun Clauses

Match the noun clause with its proper sentence.

a. that we could not win
b. whoever has the best price
c. that she could bake
d. whoever made the ring
e. what we expected

_____ 31. ___ made it too big.

_____ 32. She said ___ .

_____ 33. Buy the bread from ___ .

_____ 34. This is not ___ .

_____ 35. ___ was made plain by the delicious cupcakes.

VII. Noun Clauses

Decide if the sentence **does** (a) or **does not** (b) contain a noun clause.

_____ 36. Albert likes his steak cooked for three minutes only.

_____ 37. Although the time is right, the place is wrong.

_____ 38. They said that we could rent the upstairs room.

_____ 39. The children who ride dirt bikes practice every day.

_____ 40. They fixed the fender which was not dented.

VIII. Adverb, Adjective, Noun Clauses

Choose the correct letter of the words in italics: **adverb clause** (a), **adjective clause** (b), or **noun clause** (c).

_____ 41. _When we phoned the fire department_, they had already left.

_____ 42. My mother, _who is 82_, still cans all summer long.

_____ 43. We rented _whatever we needed_ to make the film.

_____ 44. We bought the bike from the man _that talked too much_.

_____ 45. _When you get home_, I'll have dinner fixed.

_____ 46. The new sunglasses _that I bought_ had to be refitted.

_____ 47. The rain poured down _after the clouds became black_.

_____ 48. We bought new tires from _whoever could deliver them_.

_____ 49. Our calico cat, _which we bought as a kitten_, controlled even the big dogs.

_____ 50. We'll write the term paper _when we get time_.

CHAPTER 5
SUBORDINATION BY PHRASES

Both in the last chapter on clauses and in this one you are gaining experience with **subordination**, a device used by good writers to create mature, sophisticated sentences. When a writer subordinates an idea, she expresses that idea in a subordinate construction that is part of a sentence. A subordinate clause or phrase cannot be a sentence but will always be a part of the larger, more complete sentence.

We have already studied the **prepositional phrase** (p. 83) the **adverb clause** (p. 104), the **adjective clause** (p. 111), and the **noun clause** (p. 122). All subordinate word groups must be included in the larger, complete sentence.

VERBALS

A verbal is a word that retains some verb qualities—action for instance—but no longer functions as a verb. English has three verbals:

1. **participles**—The *growing* corn needed rain.
2. **gerunds**—*Growing* corn was hard work.
3. **infinitives**—*To grow* corn was difficult.

A verbal is a word that <u>cannot</u> function as a verb, although it may seem to possess verb characteristics. A verbal will function as a noun or a modifier.

Participles: Present

>the *green* corn—The word *green* is an adjective modifying the noun *corn*.

>the *growing* corn—Because *growing* also modifies the noun *corn*, *growing* is an adjective as well.

Both *green* and *growing* are adjectives because they modify a **noun**. Adjectives always modify nouns. Of the two words, *green* and *growing*, only one is formed from a verb. We get the adjective *growing* by adding *-ing* to the verb *grow*.

An *-ing* word used as an adjective is called a <u>present participle</u>. Any verb can become an adjective (present participle) by properly adding *-ing* to the simple verb form.

Exercise 1 Change the following verbs into present participles. Note that occasionally you may need to make spelling adjustments.

1. break _____
2. walk _____
3. lose _____
4. halt _____
5. plan _____
6. send _____
7. move _____
8. toss _____
9. drive _____
10. play _____
11. call _____
12. throw _____
13. give _____
14. study _____
15. sleep _____
16. turn _____
17. read _____
18. talk _____
19. graze _____
20. swim _____
21. be _____

Look at these three pairs:

> Our college has a *powerful* radio station.
> Our college has a *winning* radio station.

> The *white* geese waddled across the lawn.
> The *quacking* geese waddled across the lawn.

> The *sad* truth became apparent.
> The *crushing* truth became apparent.

Notice that the *-ing* word is an adjective and is made from a verb. These are examples of present participles.

Present participles are often used with accompanying words and with related words. Taken together—the participle and its related words—the group is called a **present participle phrase**. This phrase is used as an adjective just as if it were a single-word modifier.

> The *cold* rabbit hurried to the bushes.
> The *shaking* rabbit hurried to the bushes.
> The rabbit, *shaking with chills*, hurried to the bushes.

Shaking with chills is a present participle phrase modifying the noun *rabbit*.

Participle phrases can grace a person's writing. The phrases can often be moved around giving whatever emphasis is appropriate.

> *Crushing the grapes*, the couples jumped barefoot in the barrels.
>
> The couples, *crushing the grapes*, jumped barefoot in the barrels.
>
> The couples jumped barefoot in the barrels, *crushing the grapes*.

With simple punctuation, you can see that a participle phrase can be several words away from the word it modifies.

Exercise 2 Underline the present participle phrases.

1. Sally's smile is warm, giving a mild glow of friendliness.

2. The general, riding to the front, led the attack.

3. Rising quickly into the clouds, the balloon was lost from our sight.

4. The sun, rising slowly, dispelled the fog.

5. They boarded the ship lying in the harbor.

6. General Washington, having crossed the Delaware, attacked the enemy at Trenton.

7. Teaching the children about parenting, Miss Albaugh never lost her composure.

8. The guide, losing interest quickly, told us very little.

9. Glowing red, the candle lasted through four albums.

10. Smiling at everyone, the governor seemed plastic.

11. Moving the car just in time, Kathy avoided getting a ticket.

12. Pleading her client's case, the lawyer convinced the jury of the man's innocence.

13. The little dog, having been lost for a week, was overjoyed to be home.

14. His speech was excellent, stirring even the most cynical in the crowd.

15. The doctor, feeling guilty over the loss, tried to replace the money.

16. Having played cards all night with his friends, Ted then slept through his first class.

17. The young girl, seeing the approaching truck, waited to cross.

18. Profiting from his mistakes, Chad vowed never to procrastinate again.

19. The old man, shaking with the cold, slowly limped through the crowded streets.

20. The young gelding was nervous prancing before the crowd in the lighted ring.

Using Present Participle Phrases to Build Sentences

> She watched the children play. She looked sad behind the screened window.
>
> Watching the children play, she looked sad behind the screened window.

Notice how easily we can change two simple sentences into one much more powerful sentence, simply by turning one of the sentences into a participle phrase. Here is another example.

> Jo Ann stopped for a man. She thought she recognized him.
> Jo Ann stopped for a man, thinking she recognized him.

This practice, if used in your own writing, will help you build mature, sophisticated sentences with ease.

Punctuation of Participle Phrases

1. **Always place a comma after a present participle phrase if it is at the front of a sentence.**

   Shoveling his driveway, Granddaddy always kept ahead of the snow.

2. **If the present participle phrase ends a sentence, see whether the phrase modifies the subject at the front of the sentence. If the phrase modifies the subject, place a comma before the present participle phrase.**

   Granddaddy always kept ahead of the snow, shoveling his driveway.

3. **A present participle phrase that follows directly the noun it modifies should be set off with commas.**

   Granddaddy, shoveling his driveway, kept ahead of the snow.

Exercise 3 Subordinate the words in italics into a participle phrase.

1. *Jon needed to study.* He planned his day carefully.

   _____

2. *I bought several chances.* I had hoped to win.

   _____

3. *Bruce sauntered down the street.* He saw the accident.

_____

4. *Mr. Good emphasized good planning.* He wanted the students to succeed.

_____

_____

5. Mrs. Waldo screamed for the children. *She knew they were in danger.*

_____

_____

6. Our parents *knew the weather would be awful* and gathered plenty of wood for the fireplace.

_____

7. *We searched everywhere for a new car* and bought one from our next-door neighbor.

_____

8. Alita purchased the condo and *fixed it up with colorful furniture.*

_____

_____

9. *She ran for the train.* She fell.

_____

10. *He drank most of the time.* Tom finally lost many friends.

_____

11. Ted *walked into the office* and settled his account with Mr. Stevenson.

_____

_____

12. The detective *boarded the plane behind them* and continued to follow the couple.

_____

_____

13. *The kitten stretched sleepily* and padded toward the kitchen for his breakfast.

_____

_____

14. Alex ran every day. *He was planning to enter the Olympics.*

_____

15. Marilyn calmly left the store. *She took the pictures.*

_____

16. *He placed the binoculars to his eyes.* He saw the thieves enter the building.

_____

_____

17. *The dog was grossly overweight.* The dog was put on a strict diet.

_____

_____

18. Davis *heard about the heist from his stoolie* and arranged for his men to follow the crooks.

_____

_____

19. *She has seen him before.* I think she'll recognize him in the crowd.

_____

_____

20. Old Mrs. Mosley unlocked the cabinet. *She pulled out two crystal glasses and some sherry.*

_____

_____

Participles: Past

A present participle is always an **adjective** and always ends in *-ing*. Look at these pairs of adjectives.

the sprinkling water	the burning wood	the working horses
the sprinkled water	the burned wood	the worked horses

The *-ing* words are present participles. The *-ed* words are **past participles**. Past participles are used in the same fashion as present participles. The difference is that past participles indicate a condition already completed. Not all verbs spell the past participle with an *-ed*, however. Some other endings are *-en* (given), *-d* (told), or *-n* (blown).

The past participle form of a verb is the one that (when used as a verb) follows *have, had,* or *has*.

> have given
> had told
> has blown, etc.

Here are three pairs of sentences, one with a present participle phrase, the other with a past participle phrase.

present	*Parking our car in an alley*, we took the boxes in the back door.
past	Our car, *parked in an alley*, had a ticket on it.
present	The insensitive man, *smoking a cigar*, paid no attention to us.
past	*Smoked with cigar scent*, our clothes had to be cleaned.
present	*Exhausting as it was*, the hike was worth it.
past	*Exhausted by the hike*, we slept until noon.

Exercise 4 Underline the participle phrase and label the phrase as **present** or **past**.

_____ 1. Throwing snowballs, the entire team advanced on the coach.

_____ 2. The student, exhausted by study, fell asleep on the bench.

_____ 3. Finished by the last fight, the trout came to the boat.

_____ 4. The bird sat on the branch, scratching its head.

_____ 5. Carrying bright red backpacks, the three children stood out against the green meadow.

_____ 6. Looking throughout the house, Evelyn finally found the note.

_____ 7. The old horse, driven by the cold, plodded heavily toward shelter.

_____ 8. Maddened by the traffic, he parked his car and walked.

_____ 9. Lifting the heavy parcels, Charlie followed her into the house.

_____ 10. The prize bull was led off the ramp, sold to the highest bidder.

_____ 11. Merrilee became restless waiting in the car.

_____ 12. Disturbed by his tone, she wondered if he knew.

_____ 13. Debbie waited for hours, listening for his car.

_____ 14. Pressed for an answer, he told them a lie.

_____ 15. Encouraged by the new results, Glen felt as if a burden had been lifted

from his shoulders.

_____ 16. Dean's down jacket, worn by years of use, was covered with holes.

_____ 17. She barely slept because of the rain pouring down all night.

_____ 18. Dorian, tired from the long drive, went to bed early.

_____ 19. Cindy left for her vacation pleased with her progress.

_____ 20. Her fingers, flying over the piano keys, were only a blur.

All verbs have a past participle form, the one that follows have, has, or had. But when the past participle is used alone in a phrase, it is an adjective.

verb
We _had exhausted_ our water supply.

past participle phrase
Exhausted by study, she fell asleep.

Using Past Participle Phrases to Build Sentences Instead of writing two simple sentences like these:

The hiking trail was covered with moss. It was slippery.

Write:

Covered with moss, the hiking trail was slippery.

Punctuating a past participle phrase is done the same way as a present participle phrase (p. 134).

Also notice that a simple sentence with a compound verb can be made into a more mature sentence by making part of the sentence a past participle phrase.

The lovely valley was covered with wild flowers and grew trees in the rocky draws.

Covered with wild flowers, the lovely valley grew trees in the rocky draws.

Exercise 5 Change the following sentences into ones that contain a past participle phrase.

1. The small boys congregated by the pool of water.
   They were intrigued with the lazy fish.

   _____

   _____

2. A house was built for a clergyman and had seven gables.

   _____

3. The old man was given to yelling, and he struck the boy with a
   gold-headed cane.

   _____

4. He was delighted with the sweater, so he yelled with joy.

   _____

5. The men were transferred to a new camp and were troubled.

   _____

6. They argued for several hours. She was convinced that he was wrong.

   _____

7. The horses were exercised thoroughly this morning, and now they
   are hungry for their breakfast.

   _____

   _____

8. His shirt fit him perfectly and was sewn by hand.

   _____

9. Those two smugglers were finally arrested.
   They were caught at the border.

   _____

   _____

10. He and Cindy were made for each other, so they decided to get married.

    _____

    _____

11. Justin was tired from the party last night. He went to bed early.

_____

12. She left without him because she was disgusted with his drunken behavior.

_____

13. The tablets were translated from Greek into three other languages and displayed at the museum.

_____

_____

14. She was given directions and continued on her way.

_____

15. The little boy's efforts were thwarted, so he went home.

_____

16. The tree came down with a crash. It was felled with an axe.

_____

17. Pat was adopted as a small child and doesn't remember the orphanage.

_____

18. That extra parcel of land will be theirs as soon as the sale closes. It was included in the revised contract.

_____

_____

19. She was hired for the job and was experienced in her field.

_____

20. He was tormented by fleeting images of her face, but he tried to forget her.

_____

_____

Exercise 6 Underline the participle phrases and label the phrases as
present or **past**.

_____ 1. Debating the problem, the candidates finally became angry.

_____ 2. The dancers, entertained by the director, stood in awe when he danced.

_____ 3. Looking for a place to sleep, the old drunk scouted every alley.

_____ 4. The judge, frowning at the attorney, made his ruling.

_____ 5. Johnny Cash, having won dozens of awards before, seemed embarrassed.

_____ 6. She and Jody each left for their classes, agreeing to meet later.

_____ 7. Travis spent the holidays alone, alienated from his family.

_____ 8. Annotated throughout, the report had over two hundred pages.

_____ 9. Bill, freeing the trapped animal, smiled with satisfaction.

_____ 10. His car, insured only last month, exploded when the fire reached

the gas tank.

_____ 11. Disturbed over her test grade, Susan went to talk to her teacher.

_____ 12. That house, said to be haunted, is almost a hundred years old.

_____ 13. Caught in the act, he had no choice but to flee.

_____ 14. Seeing the futility of pursuing the matter, the young couple left

the credit department.

_____ 15. Andrea ran blindly through the rain, driven by fear.

_____ 16. Hoping to catch him before he left, Janet rushed to the train station.

_____ 17. The letter, discovered after the old man's death, explained everything yet

incriminated no one.

_____ 18. Fabian, regretting his harsh words, called to apologize.

_____ 19. Ed moved his family to the country, enchanted with the serenity.

_____ 20. Torn by indecision, Mary Ann was exasperated.

Gerunds

Jogging makes me sick.
The _jogging_ athletes were humorless.

In the first sentence, _jogging_ is the subject of the sentence. In the next
sentence, however, _jogging_ is an adjective. When a verb crosses over into
the adjective category, it's called a **participle**. An _-ing_ word functioning
as a noun is called a **gerund**.

An *-ing* word used as an **adjective** is called a _____ .

An *-ing* word used as a **noun** is called a _____ .

Noun *-ing* words are names of actions.

> *Basketball* is fun.
> *Walking* is fun.

Exercise 7 Underline the *-ing* words and label each as an **adjective** (participle) or a **noun** (gerund).

_____ 1. The chirping bird made my breakfast a delight.

_____ 2. Chirping must have been the bird's favorite pastime.

_____ 3. The working plumber soon became tired.

_____ 4. Spending is a great way to get in debt.

_____ 5. Running strengthens the heart.

_____ 6. The frowning girl soon got her way.

_____ 7. The chewing puppy ruined my boots.

_____ 8. Knitting is easier than I first thought.

_____ 9. The singing girls made it hard to study.

_____ 10. Flowing brushes created a sea of color.

_____ 11. Placing first in the race delighted her.

_____ 12. Dancing couples filled the ballroom.

_____ 13. Flying is all my roommate does on weekends.

_____ 14. Soaring seagulls swept over the shore looking for food.

_____ 15. The running stream makes me feel content.

_____ 16. Exercising benefits the mind as well as the body.

_____ 17. Jared's answering machine is broken.

_____ 18. Campaigning tires both politicians and voters.

_____ 19. He said nothing but gave her a knowing look.

_____ 20. Traveling is an education in itself.

Gerunds are not always just one word, just as participles are not always just one word. Rather, gerunds and their related words are called **gerund phrases**. You recall that participles and their related words are called participle phrases.

gerund phrase
Calling for help caused his sore throat.

gerund phrase
Her happiness was *taking good pictures.*

gerund   gerund phrase
He went from *eating* to *playing the piano.*

Exercise 8 Underline the single gerunds or the gerund phrases.

1. The children enjoyed playing in the snow.

2. Stomping their feet caused quite a commotion.

3. Swimming in the surf was a delight.

4. They took pride in building perfect birdhouses.

5. Being a teacher was her dream.

6. He spends all of his time either swimming or riding his surfboard.

7. Eating all the fudge made me sick to my stomach.

8. Waiting for her so often infuriates me.

9. Tipping the boat over was the least of his mistakes.

10. A knock on the door interrupted her grandmother's talking and reminiscing about

    the past.

11. Subscribing to that magazine for ten years has cost over three hundred dollars.

12. Waking up late ruined his morning plans.

13. Holding tightly to the pole was all the little boy could manage.

14. Reeling in that big fish was quite another matter.

15. All of those places are only interested in taking your money.

16. Encountering her friend at the restaurant surprised and embarrassed Betty.

17. His drinking may well destroy him.

18. Nothing could stop her from marrying John.

19. Following fire trucks and ambulances is dangerous.

20. It's frustrating but rewarding learning to play an instrument.

Since your goal in learning this material is to write better sentences, your best practice is to create sentences. In the following exercise, concentrate on making the end product a mature sentence. One method for making tired sentences (that have no energy in them) into more powerful expressions is to use a preposition in front of a gerund phrase. Here is the way it works.

Take two simple sentences:

> I studied several stereo sets.
> I chose to buy separate components.

To rewrite these into a better construction, begin with a preposition followed by a gerund phrase.

gerund phrase

> By *studying several stereo sets*, I chose to buy separate components.

Typical prepositions are *by, of, on, for, in, after,* and *before*. Here is another set:

> Harriet owns a set of clippers, and they cut thorny roses.
> Harriet owns a set of clippers *for cutting thorny roses*.

Exercise 9 Change the words in italics into a gerund phrase. Don't forget to use a preposition before a gerund phrase in some of the sentences.

1. *He was being obnoxious.* That is a fine way to lose his privilege.

   _____

2. *Tom stared down the opponent,* and he won the poker match. (use *by* or *after*)

   _____

   _____

3. *We took the examination early,* and we left for our vacation.

   _____

   _____

4. *The plumber worked all morning,* and he cleared the drain.

   _____

   _____

5. *We left for work,* but we did the dishes first. (use *before*)

   _____

6. *She pleaded with the judge.* It was her last resort.

   _____

7. *Wally worked on a fishing boat all summer.* It got him in great physical condition.

   _____

8. *He's an educated man,* but he has no trust in his own judgment.
   (use *for being*)

   _____

9. *That car horn was blaring.* It woke up the neighbors. (use *of the horn*)

   _____

10. *They drove fast.* They only saved three minutes. (use *by*)

    _____

11. We found them. *They were huddled on the bleachers.*

    _____

12. *I have been to the dentist before.* It wasn't very pleasant.

    _____

13. *Tom drove too fast.* It ruined the entire evening for her.

    _____

14. *She left the house* and called Ted again from a pay phone. (use *after*)

    _____

15. He caught the bus in plenty of time. *He left early.* (use *by*)

    _____

16. *My mother washed clothes every day.* It took all of her time.

    _____

17. I spent my summer break. *I vacationed in Paris.* (use *by*)

    _____

18. *Arnie saw Brad and Celia together constantly.* It reminded him of his own girl back home.

   _____

   _____

19. *That car was all he thought about.* It precluded his interest in school.

   _____

   _____

20. *He and I went to the concert.* We enjoyed the people as much as the music.

   _____

   _____

A gerund is an *-ing* word used as a noun.
A gerund and its related words are called a gerund phrase.

Exercise 10 Fill in the blanks with gerunds made from the verbs in parentheses.

1. _____ builds one's legs and lungs. (walk)

2. By _____ the bill, we avoided a scene. (pay)

3. After _____ her contract, Beth found a new job. (complete)

4. Without _____ a doctor, Sammy went on a fourteen-day fast. (consult)

5. _____ baseball forces a person to be patient. (play)

6. The student left the dean's office without _____ for a decision. (wait)

7. Bryant has a habit of _____ small children. (annoy)

8. By _____ the old carpet, we made the room inviting. (use)

9. _____ makes a person perfect, or so they say. (practice)

10. Cole tried to get out of trouble by _____ . (lie)

11. More than anything, Debbie enjoys _____ to music. (listen)

12. His _____ left a lot to be desired. (type)

13. _____ for his keys took almost an hour. (search)

14. The little boy's hands were shoved into the back pockets of his jeans, and he started

    _____ . (frown)

15. He howled with pain after _____ his thumb with the hammer. (hit)

16. The cheerleaders enjoyed _____ some new routines on the field. (try)

17. We met them while _____ in his car. (cruise)

18. Les shoveled the snow from the driveway before _____ the car. (start)

19. _____ the crying child was an impossible task. (comfort)

20. _____ the car up the hill had been the hard part. (push)

Exercise 11 Sentence Building Expand each of the following simple sentences
into sentences using the verb first as a participle phrase, second as a
single participle, and third as a noun.

Example: The stream flows.

1. The stream, *flowing gently,* crept through the meadow.
2. The *flowing* stream slipped away to the ocean.
3. The *flowing* of the stream caused a low murmur.

1. The sun rises.

    a. _____

    b. _____

    c. _____

2. Insects hum.

    a. _____

    b. _____

    c. _____

3. The wind whistles.

    a. _____

    b. _____

    c. _____

4. The tide changes.

    a. _____

    b. _____

    c. _____

5. The bells are ringing.

    a. _____

    b. _____

    c. _____

6. Couples stroll.

    a. _____

    b. _____

    c. _____

7. Their eyes pry.

    a. _____

    b. _____

    c. _____

8. The crowd murmurs.

    a. _____

    b. _____

    c. _____

9. Rain pours.

    a. _____

    b. _____

    c. _____

10. The boys laugh.

    a. _____

    b. _____

    c. _____

11. Baby ducks waddle.

    a. _____

    b. _____

    c. _____

12. The engine screams.

   a. _____

   b. _____

   c. _____

13. Snow falls.

   a. _____

   b. _____

   c. _____

14. The cheerleaders tumble.

   a. _____

   b. _____

   c. _____

15. Rockets explode.

   a. _____

   b. _____

   c. _____

16. The cats lounge.

   a. _____

   b. _____

   c. _____

17. Owls screech.

   a. _____

   b. _____

   c. _____

18. An old woman cries.

   a. _____

   b. _____

   c. _____

19. Some fish jump.

    a. _____

    b. _____

    c. _____

20. Birds migrate.

    a. _____

    b. _____

    c. _____

Infinitives

We have studied two uses of words that were verbs but are no longer acting as verbs—participles (adjectives) and gerunds (nouns). A third verbal is the **infinitive**, made of a simple verb plus *to*: *to see, to walk, to entertain*, and so on. Often you can turn a gerund into an infinitive:

> *Swimming* exercises all major muscles.
> *To swim* exercises all major muscles.

Exercise 12 Change the gerunds to infinitives.

1. Sightseeing gets on some people's nerves.

   _____

2. Playing the drums requires coordination.

   _____

3. Talking is Frank's strongest asset.

   _____

4. Working in a store teaches patience.

   _____

5. The neighbors' best quality is sharing.

   _____

6. She hated walking home alone.

   _____

7. Cooking is Ed's favorite pastime.

   _____

8. I don't like spending time in the kitchen.

_____

9. Marsha woke up late and quickly began dressing.

_____

10. Drinking and then driving isn't very smart.

_____

11. Coping with a teenage son is difficult for her.

_____

12. Julie loves dancing more than anything.

_____

13. Exchanging pesos for dollars is necessary after crossing the border.

_____

14. The entire herd of horses started stampeding.

_____

15. Nobody likes going to the dentist.

_____

16. Beginning any project is easy enough.

_____

17. The hardest part of any project is finishing it.

_____

18. Forgiving him may be impossible.

_____

19. Burl likes baking his own bread.

_____

20. Being a writer has been his dream as long as I can remember.

_____

An infinitive is made from a simple verb plus *to*:

to sing, to worship, to plan.

An infinitive, along with its associated words, is called an <u>infinitive phrase</u>.

***To play in the game* was his hope.**

Exercise 13 Underline the infinitive/infinitive phrase.

1. Donna always wanted to help with the house.

2. To swim is nothing short of exhilarating.

3. Dawn wants to sing and act for her school.

4. Tony and Sue hate to go out for breakfast.

5. She was beginning to dislike him for his rudeness.

6. He got his car fixed in time to go to the game.

7. To be in the hospital during Christmas was depressing.

8. To remember seems to be painful for her.

9. They went out to buy some beer.

10. We expect to meet our host shortly.

11. Her only concern was to keep her composure long enough to make the report.

12. Dean promised to call back last night, but he didn't.

13. The cars started to slip and slide on the icy roads.

14. Janet has chosen never to see him again.

15. Science is difficult for some people to understand.

16. To quit smoking takes a great deal of determination.

17. She fails to see the gravity of the situation.

18. To run before his leg is completely healed is asking for trouble.

19. It would appear that they were destined to meet.

20. To take him seriously, you need an open mind.

To create sentences with infinitives is easy enough, but they can be overworked. Be aware that a weapon in your arsenal against sameness and boredom is the infinitive. You can combine some sentences into one sentence with an infinitive phrase.

> Mike offered his car. He wanted to prove his fairness.
> Mike offered his car to prove his fairness.

Exercise 14   Sentence Building Build mature sentences by creating infinitive phrases with the italicized words.

1. Warren demanded a settlement. *This revealed his harsh attitude.*

_____

_____

2. *Up with People* gave a halftime performance. *They wanted their versatility shown.*

_____

_____

3. We own a house, *and we must paint it soon.*

_____

4. The priest demanded a decision, *and he wanted to go ahead with the building.*

_____

_____

5. To ban any discussion of emotions is *the same thing as banning communication.*

_____

_____

6. The coiled snake was waiting. *Striking was its intent.*

_____

7. She is the woman. *We should follow her.*

_____

8. He enjoyed the party, *but his purpose had been meeting the new girl.*

_____

9. The show started late. *That's because they wanted the basketball game finished.*

_____

_____

10. Ted left early. *He had several stops before he finished.*

_____

11. She lacks all the social graces, *so she couldn't meet the queen.*

_____

_____

12. *all day he plays his harmonica.* It's all he wants to do.

_____

13. Marie went jogging this morning. *She wanted a strong body.*

_____

14. *Having no friends made him sad,* but to have no fun was worse.

_____

15. The car didn't have enough gas. *It couldn't even make it up the steep incline.*

_____

_____

16. Marsha refused to call him first. *She wanted to avoid appearing too eager.*

_____

_____

17. Norm longed to own that sports car for years, *but it was another matter paying for it.*

_____

_____

18. *He knew he should compromise,* so he settled for half the payment.

_____

_____

19. The garage has the truck. *They're giving it a complete overhaul.*

_____

20. *All she wants to do is writing,* but she likes to play music for diversion.

_____

APPOSITIVES

The last phrase we study—the **appositive**—is not a verbal. The participle, gerund, and infinitive are all verbals. But two phrases—the prepositional phrase (p. 83) and the appositive—are not formed from verbs.

Look at this example:

> Frank controlled all the computer hardware. He was a programmer-analyst.

> Frank, *a programmer-analyst*, controlled all the computer hardware.

In this last sentence we took a sentence that explained who Frank is and changed the entire sentence into an appositive phrase that explained who Frank is.

> The artist painted with pastels on the sidewalk. His name was Tad, and he wore a suit and tie.

Look at how this last compound sentence can be reduced, can be placed just after *artist*, and can be made to identify or explain *artist*.

> Tad, the artist who wore a suit and tie, painted with pastels on the sidewalk.

One more example:

> Marie's apartment makes me feel warm and welcome. It occupies the entire third floor.

> Marie's apartment, the entire third floor, makes me feel warm and welcome.

An appositive is a noun (or pronoun) that follows, explains, and renames the noun it follows. An appositive along with its related words is called an appositive phrase. An appositive and an appositive phrase are set off with commas.

Daisie, my mother, lives by herself.

Exercise 15 Underline and punctuate the appositive phrases. Note that you can "hear" an appositive—the mind reacts to the commas with a slight hesitation.

1. Ruth Brown author of several books became a bartender.

2. Art awarded the gift a book of poems.

3. Sally a good plumber also drove a cab.

4. We decided to lease a new car a Corvette.

5. Julie our friend grew more anxious as winter approached.

6. *The Three Stooges* an old show is on television every day.

7. A mysterious stranger the woman waited in the shadows.

8. She left the hospital a depressing place to work.

9. Debbie Larry's girlfriend will finish law school this year.

10. Already a lawyer Larry has been able to help her occasionally.

11. My husband a musician travels throughout the country.

12. Cindy a poet who prints her own books has many talents.

13. They gave me the award a thousand dollar check.

14. Her friend the piano player from Philadelphia went home.

15. Jean lives in poverty an oppressive state of existence.

16. A chemist Bill works for the government.

17. Both of his sons gifted artists plan to go to medical school.

18. Phil and his wife Beth have been married a month.

19. Glen the man to whom I've been writing will be in town next week.

20. Harry saw his mother a remarkable woman last summer.

As you can see, appositives are easy to recognize and easy to punctuate. They are excellent devices for sharpening your sentences, for eliminating weak verbs like *is, are, was,* and *were* that are used in an explanatory sentence, and for adding variety to your sentence patterns.

Exercise 16 Rewrite the second sentence so that it becomes an appositive inside the first sentence. Don't forget the commas.

Example: Mr. Coogan played rugby. He was a large man.
Mr. Coogan, a large man, played rugby.

1. Cole and Lois managed an active college. They were both comptuer experts.

_____

_____

2. *Horticulture* and *Gardening* offer advice to people who raise gardens. They are organic-oriented magazines.

_____

_____

3. *Hamlet* makes me wonder about the nature of people. It is my
   favorite play.

   _____

   _____

4. Our visit included Mt. Vernon. That was George Washington's home.

   _____

   _____

5. Nancy and Bob loved to travel. They have been our longtime neighbors.

   _____

   _____

6. Steve spent the holidays with us. He is Fred's son.

   _____

7. Bob Barker will help host the Rose Parade. He's a TV game show host.

   _____

   _____

8. I read *Faust* three times. It's my favorite work by Goethe.

   _____

   _____

9. Harry is eager to get started. He's an ambitious man.

   _____

10. My mother has been depressed lately. She's usually a happy person.

    _____

    _____

11. Winning the football game is all my brother cares about. His name is Rob.

    _____

    _____

12. The benefit dinner was a success. It was a huge affair.

    _____

13. He finished in the marathon. It was a twenty-six mile race.

_____

14. Dorothy hired caterers for the party. She's such an organized person.

_____

_____

15. I wish I could play blues harp like Steve and Leroy. They're Larry's sons.

_____

_____

16. His daughter plays too. She's a beginner though, and her name is Rene.

_____

_____

17. Mrs. Keeney met Bill at the site. She is a strikingly beautiful woman.

_____

_____

18. Jordon was sick enough to go to the hospital for tests. He's my
    two-year-old nephew.

_____

_____

19. The boys won the game. It was a close victory.

_____

20. Layla and Carlos traveled to Spain together. They have been friends
    since childhood.

_____

_____

Now you need to heighten your sense of appositives by punctuating a few.

Exercise 17 Punctuate the appositives correctly with commas.

1. *Evita* a moving play brought tears to my eyes.

2. The houseplants some violets and ferns dried up before we could get home from Alaska.

3. The wall a gallery of oils made an imposing view.

4. The children Tammy and Josh walked to school.

5. Our favorite place is Morea a small French island.

6. Apel and Cynthia a happy couple celebrated their tenth anniversary.

7. We bought *Havana Moon* an albun by Carlos Santana.

8. A real estate salesman Mr. Frank works every weekend.

9. Bill's fiance Meg had to cancel the trip.

10. They urged the people to help fight that debilitating disease asthma.

11. The children missed seeing Farley their favorite uncle.

12. To learn word processing a practical skill is helpful in this computer age.

13. My veterinarian a devoted doctor offered to meet me at his office on Sunday.

14. An opera singer Pavarotti has a powerful voice.

15. The PTA meeting a regularly scheduled event has been postponed.

16. She does aerobic dancing to benefit the heart the most important muscle in the body.

17. His alibi an unlikely story checked out.

18. Her anguish stems from many strange occurrences a series of events too bizarre to be believed.

19. Volunteers at the hospital the women visited the bazaar with Mrs. Prescott.

20. Mr. Eliot the only man there felt out of place among the women.

Exercise 18 Find and underline the verbal and appositive phrases in the following paragraphs.

Making a Living

If you are having difficulty choosing your life's work, and if conventional fields just don't interest you, perhaps you should consider some of the more unorthodox occupations. Whatever time it takes for you to make such an important decision will be time well spent because what you decide can have a long-reaching effect on your life.

Chimney sweeps, who are respected professionals in Europe, are almost nonexistent in the United States. One chimney sweep, whose area covers much of Southern California, charges $25.00 for a job that takes one or two hours. This may be an up-and-coming profession.

If you like to make people laugh and you enjoy travel, you might apply to the clown training school of Ringling Brothers Barnum and Bailey Circus, which chooses about 30 students from approximately 300 applicants every years. Those who make it get a two-year contract with $200.00 per week starting pay.

In case solitude is your passion, there is a current demand for sheep-herders. Accompanied only by a horse, a dog, a rifle, and about 2000 sheep, you may find it to be lonely work, but that depends on the company you prefer. Sleeping under the stars after an eighteen-hour day could be your niche. Or you might contact the U.S. Forest Service in Washington, D.C., to apply for a job as a forest fire lookout. If you aren't afraid of heights and you enjoy your privacy, if you just need time to think about your career, or if you want to write the great American novel, this job may be for you. The pay starts around $10,000 per year, including generous health benefits, while you keep watch in a tower in a national park or forest preserve.

Street vendors can make amazing profits that come from working their own hours. You probably need a vendor's license, but the profits are your own. This is ideal for struggling artists and artisans whose profits can range from $10.00 a day to $250.00 per weekend depending on their products.

If you don't want to work a nine-to-five day and you enjoy playing cards, you could become a card dealer, a job that has flexible hours, exciting atmosphere, and excellent pay. Some places in Las Vegas and Reno offer trainee positions; however, manual dexterity is essential. Or, if you are a woman who enjoys good exercise and flexible hours, try belly dancing, which is a good way to work your way through school. Legitimate belly dancing is a well-paid art. Pay is commensurate with expertise, and it ranges from $5.00 to $15.00 an hour in clubs and restaurants. Interested men might well be pioneers in this potentially lucrative field.

The list stops only with your imagination. Think about what you like to do and how you want to do it, and then find a market for it. It can be a permanent occupation or a temporary position that might lead to something that is uniquely yours. The important thing to keep in mind is that you are unique, and whatever field you enter, even if it's a conventional one, will of necessity be uniquely you.

REVIEW TEST

I. Participles

Indicate whether the participles or participle phrases in the
following sentences are **present participles** (a) or **past participles** (b).

_____ 1. Ann, tired from running, walked to the gym to shower.

_____ 2. Thrown off balance by her tone, Ed was speechless for once.

_____ 3. Wanting to please me, my dog brought me her bone.

_____ 4. The grazing horses looked content in the meadow.

_____ 5. Having been duped so often, she is reluctant to trust anyone.

_____ 6. Disgusted, she left the room in a huff.

_____ 7. Beaten, the old woman slowly turned and left.

_____ 8. Halting, Doug listened in the silence for the sound of footsteps.

_____ 9. Her clothes, scorched by the fire, were ruined.

_____ 10. He moved quickly toward the child, seeing the danger.

II. Participles and Gerunds

Indicate whether the verbals in the following sentences are **past
participles** (a), **present participles** (b), or **gerunds** (c).

_____ 11. Their talking disturbed his studies.

_____ 12. Beginning classes just cover the fundamentals.

_____ 13. We found him hiding in the bushes.

_____ 14. Going to the beach on a holiday weekend was a mistake.

_____ 15. Cindy cried all night, feeling depressed due to the holidays.

_____ 16. My friend, Earl, hates wearing his new glasses.

_____ 17. It bored me being there last time.

_____ 18. The exhausted players left the field.

_____ 19. Our potted plants are thriving.

_____ 20. He planned to fail by failing to plan.

III. Gerunds

Match the following gerund phrases to the appropriate sentences.

———— 21. Being in the show

———— 22. By shopping early

———— 23. His bellowing

———— 24. Having been dropped from the organization

———— 25. Before giving himself up

a. saddened him.
b. was deafening.
c. he tried to make a break for it.
d. means everything to her.
e. we avoided the rush.

IV. Infinitives and Gerunds

In the following sentences, choose between using a **gerund** (a) or an **infinitive** (b), or mark *either* (c) of both could be used.

———— 26. She got up (console) the crying girl.

———— 27. His efforts at (comfort) her were useless.

———— 28. He always wanted (get) into the act.

———— 29. He likes (be) included.

———— 30. They were able to reach camp by nightfall by (rest) often.

V. Verbals—Participles, Gerunds, and Infinitives

Indicate whether the verbals in the following sentences are used as **participles** (a), **gerunds** (b), or **infinitives** (c).

———— 31. Her believing in him was a terrible mistake.

———— 32. The old man grew tired of sweeping the walk.

———— 33. I'm sick of dealing with her problems.

———— 34. He never had any intention of going.

———— 35. Dale rose, intending to leave, and then sat down again.

———— 36. Arthur Cassidy could never have anticipated what was to follow.

———— 37. He wants to leave his card.

———— 38. Owing back taxes, she left for Sweden.

———— 39. His goal has always been to be a dancer.

———— 40. Ben didn't know what to do with himself after he earned his degree.

VI. Appositives

Match the following appositives/appositive phrases to the sentences containing the nouns they modify.

_____ 41. The party ended early.

_____ 42. Clancy keeps everybody laughing.

_____ 43. My brother gives his first concert next month.

_____ 44. The club exists to help those in distress.

_____ 45. His wife called for help.

a. Beth
b. a musician
c. the office clown
d. a nonprofit organization
e. a total disaster

VII. Appositives

Indicate whether the following sentences are punctuated correctly (a) or incorrectly (b).

_____ 46. A sneak Grandpa Jonset snoops when we're gone.

_____ 47. My parents, an old-fashioned pair, never listen to anything I have to say.

_____ 48. The barking a raucous sound continued until late.

_____ 49. Her brother Bill is an angry young man.

_____ 50. Andy stood in the dark alley, a dangerous place.

CHAPTER 6
OVERCOMING SENTENCE PROBLEMS: FRAGMENTS

The sentence works as the fundamental unit of expression in writing; words make up the sentence, true, but the sentence performs the task of showing our words in such a way as to be understood. We can demonstrate, as we did earlier, that a jumble of words does not make sense, although we know what each word means: *dance, their, performed, storks, the, ritual, mating*. However, written in a complete sentence, these words express a complete thought: **The storks performed their ritual mating dance**. You can understand that a sentence is the writer's "face and personality" to the reader. The reader cannot see you physically while reading; therefore, you come across to the reader through your sentences. Studying sentence problems helps prevent any misunderstanding of your thoughts.

Look at these examples of sentence problems.

Example of problem	Name of problem
What they wanted to know.	Fragment
The rains finally came we planted the fruit trees.	Run-on Sentence (Chapter 7) (fused)
The soldiers were weary and tired, they needed food.	Run-on Sentence (Chapter 7) (comma splice)
To bake bread offers enjoyment, and canning fruit offers enjoyment as well.	Nonparallel (Chapter 7)
I found a tennis ball walking down the street.	Misplaced Modifier (Chapter 7)

A fragment announces to the reader that the writer does not know what is going on. Fragments get in the way of thoughts in communication. They take the reader's attention from the ideas and force attention on the flaws in the writing; they move the reader away from thought to poor writing, from the message to the writer's problems.

Look at these fragments that precede or follow the sentences. Notice the fragments fail to be complete sentences.

Listening to the waves roll in. We could have stayed there all day.

Most of us wanted to help. *Watching the puppy hurt.*

After a day of hard work. Then they wanted to play.

The groups of italicized words are fragments. They fail to be sentences because they fail to meet one or both of these requirements: (1) they must contain a subject and a verb; (2) they must be able to stand alone.

A fragment is a group of words punctuated as a sentence, although the words lack either a subject and a verb or completeness.

A sentence is a group of words that contains a subject and a verb; plus, the words can stand alone.

Causes of Fragments in Writing   In Chapters 4 and 5 you studied subordinate clauses and phrases. Both clauses and phrases are excellent methods of subordinating one idea to another while at the same time making a smoother, more mature sentence. But both phrases and clauses can encourage the writing of fragments if the phrase or clause is not properly attached to the main sentence. Often we write down one idea:

> John did not clean the apartment.

Then we think of something else to say after we have closed that first thought with a period.

> John did not clean the apartment. Thinking Lois would clean later.

You can see that a fragment results from this kind of writing.

PHRASES THAT CAUSE FRAGMENTS

Four kinds of phrases seem to cause the most fragments: (1) participle, (2) infinitive, (3) appositive, and (4) prepositional.

Participle Phrases

A present participle is a verb form ending with -*ing*:

Think*ing* we could win, we practiced every day.

A past participle is a verb form ending in -*ed* or -*en* (sometimes -*rn* or -*in*):

Disgrac*ed* by the incident, the judge resign*ed*.

Look at these typical examples of fragments caused by either present or past participles.

The surfer needed to practice every day. *Requiring a new work schedule.*

Corrected, the full sentence would not be broken by the period.

The surfer needed to practice every day, requiring a new work schedule.

The fragment can also be in the front.

Believing in my ability. I tried the thirty-foot diving board.

A comma instead of a period will eliminate the fragment.

Believing in my ability, I tried the thirty-foot diving board.

The past participle works the same way as the -*ing* forms.

Based on past experience. The neighbors planted potatoes early in the spring.

Corrected, the phrase is not separated from the sentence.

Based on past experience, the neighbors planted potatoes early in the spring.

Remember, a fragment is a serious error; do not punctuate participle phrases as if they were sentences.

Exercise 1 Underline the fragment and rewrite the fragment in order to have one correct sentence.

1. Waiting on the corner. The little dog saw his master coming.

   _____

   _____

2. We made some extra money. Writing children's stories.

   _____

3. Forced to work hard. The prisoner changed his mind.

   _____

4. The soccer ball bounced well. Pumped up with a needle.

_____

5. Taking his good, sweet time. James forced us to wait an extra day.

_____

_____

6. We learned a lot. Working with the animals.

_____

7. Smitten by the woman. He thought of nothing else.

_____

8. Tony left the room. Angered by the incident.

_____

9. Creating a need for his services. He made a great deal of money.

_____

_____

10. He fell into the ditch. Weakened by the heat.

_____

11. They went inside. Leaving him in the car.

_____

12. Hardened by prison life. They cared about very little.

_____

13. This manuscript has been well preserved. Written in the 15th century.

_____

_____

14. Impressed with his work. The manager gave him a raise.

_____

15. I'm not hungry. Having already eaten.

_____

16. She has very little time. Being a student.

_____

17. Ignored by his contemporaries. The young artist led a solitary life.

_____

_____

18. I'm glad to be working. Having experienced enough poverty.

_____

19. They bought the house the next day. Enchanted with its architecture.

_____

_____

20. Living in the country. He has learned to appreciate animals.

_____

Infinitive Phrases

An infinitive is a form of a verb used with a *to* in front: *to* walk, *to* procrastinate, *to* decide.

Infinitives can cause fragments the same way participles can; the writer fails to connect the phrase to the sentence, leaving it to be a fragment.

> *To read the whole book.* She needed both time and quiet.

Corrected, the fragment is connected to the sentence with a comma.

> To read the whole book, she needed both time and quiet.

> Denise rented another apartment. *To get her sanity back.*

You can see how to correct this type of fragment: connect it to the sentence.

> Denise rented another apartment to get her sanity back.

Exercise 2   Underline the fragment and rewrite in order to have one correct sentence.

1. To buy the car. She borrowed the money from the bank.

_____

2. Flora invited the other women over. To learn their new recipes.

_____

_____

3. The table needed work. To be sanded and to be painted.

_____

4. Everyone knew what he wanted. To become President.

_____

5. They knew he would come back. To get his bicycle.

_____

6. To reach the beach. They had to climb down the cliffs.

_____

7. She had already left. To go to the game.

_____

8. To get rid of the skunk's smell. She bathed the dog twice.

_____

9. To be ready for the final. Some started studying two weeks ago.

_____

10. I climbed the ladder. To wash the windows.

_____

11. They cleaned house all week. To be ready to receive their guests for
    the holidays.

_____

_____

12. To earn such a high salary. She must have worked for years.

_____

13. She got a second job. To be able to keep her house.

_____

14. To avoid any more problems. She had the locks changed.

_____

15. Everyone thought he was making a mistake. To be married so young.

_____

16. Ted will do anything. To play in the game.

_____

17. To discourage prospective buyers of the old mansion. The strange
man terrorized all who entered.

_____

_____

18. To teach his first class. He woke up early every day.

_____

19. To have enough money for Christmas. She saved all year.

_____

20. Dean let the horses out of the corral. To graze.

_____

Appositive Phrases

An appositive is a noun or noun phrase that repeats or renames the other
noun or pronoun that it identifies. Appositives start with *a*, *an*, or *the*.

> He plays baseball, *a game for the patient.*
> The old man, *a former astronaut*, told great stories.

You can understand that an appositive must be properly connected to
the main sentence or else it will be a fragment:

> The error was caused by Walter. *The first to miss the ball.*

Corrected, the appositive needs a connecting mark, a comma.

> The error was caused by Walter, the first to miss the ball.

The appositive can come at the front of a sentence as well:

> A man of the people, President Carter was not popular with the
> establishment.

As you can project, you can write a fragment as a sentence if you don't
think ahead to see how the appositive is connected to the sentence:

> A factor in our decision. The rain fell all day long.

To correct the error you need only connect the appositive to the sentence:

> A factor in our decision, the rain fell all day long.

Exercise 3 Underline the fragment and rewrite in order to have one correct
sentence.

1. The band enjoyed the melody. A tune that was popular forty years ago.

    _____

    _____

2. A comfortable seat. The chair was Dad's favorite.

    _____

3. We always got the munchies. A desire for any kind of food whatsoever.

    _____

    _____   _____

4. A lifelong occupation. Education is not just for the young.

    _____

    _____

5. A self-centered egomaniac. Harlan is impossible to get along with.

    _____

    _____

6. A voracious reader. He spent his evenings in the library.

    _____

7. Steve just got his driver's license. A sixteen year old.

    _____

8. A man with a conscience. He confessed his crime.

    _____

9. They had dinner at the new restaurant. The place where Janet works.

    _____

    _____

10. Larry finally did the dishes. A job he dreaded.

    _____

11. Only five years old. He surfs like a professional.

_____

12. She stayed up all night with her sick child. A devoted mother.

_____

13. We left for the cabin. A cozy place in the San Bernardino Mountains.

_____

_____

14. Jim is coming over in a few minutes. The painter.

_____

15. Anna had a great time at the party. An outgoing girl.

_____

16. A heavy drinker. Larry asked for some aspirin for his hangover.

_____

_____

17. A secluded meadow. It was her favorite picnic spot.

_____

18. An angry man. He always wore a sullen expression.

_____

19. She just finished reading the book. A story about knights in armor.

_____

20. Their house was furnished with antiques. A beautiful place.

_____

Prepositional Phrases

A preposition shows a relationship between the object of the preposition
(a noun or pronoun) and some other word in the sentence. Often the
relationship is one of position: _under, over, around, between, beside, above,
up, before, by, in, through, on, off, to, behind, within, across,_ etc. Other
typical prepositions are _about, after, as, because of, during, for, from, like,
until, with, without,_ and _in spite of._

Prepositional phrases seem to cause the most trouble when they are strung together in sets of two or three and punctuated as sentences.

> *During the period after the storm*. We couldn't get our minds clear.

As with the other fragments, you need to connect the fragment to the sentence.

> Before starting the car with the wet spark plugs, we raised the hood and let them dry out.

Exercise 4 Underline and rewrite the fragment in order to have one correct sentence.

1. By the smell of the grass and the blossoms on the vines. We knew her hay fever would return soon.

   _____

   _____

2. In a large square in London. They found a quaint bed-and-breakfast.

   _____

   _____

3. The Stevensons loved to travel. In this country and in England.

   _____

   _____

4. With inflation and with growing fear. The student considered a more practical major.

   _____

   _____

5. That was an odd time to have a performance. During the coldest season and before the smallest audience.

   _____

   _____

6. Between the two oak trees around the bend. The jewels are hidden.

   _____

   _____

7. They had to complete the exam. Within the hour.

_____

_____

8. Through the fence around the pasture. She watched the yearlings play.

_____

_____

9. Our kitten loves to sleep. Under the couch in the den.

_____

_____

10. We arrived before dark. In spite of the delay.

_____

_____

11. Like her mother and like her grandmother. She studied medicine.

_____

_____

12. Without any shoes, after the cloudburst. The kids went outside.

_____

_____

13. To the wet ground and climbed up the tree. The cat gracefully leapt
off the hood of the car.

_____

_____

14. My dog usually sleeps beside me. On the bed or on her pillow.

_____

_____

15. Over the peaceful grove and across the meadow. The falcon soared.

_____

_____

16. The party ended. About the time they arrived.

_____

_____

17. He's been released from jail. Until the trial.

_____

_____

18. Because of her illness. She has to stay home.

_____

_____

19. She decided to leave him. For her health and for her sanity.

_____

_____

20. Behind the music on the shelf above the piano. You left your glasses.

_____

_____

Exercise 5 Identify if the type of phrase that causes the fragment is a
participle (a), infinitive (b), appositive (c), or prepositional (d). Then
rewrite in order to have one correct sentence.

_____ 1. Requesting a rain check. Mary Ann traded in her ticket.

_____

_____

_____ 2. Over the counter and behind the cash register. We had looked.

_____

_____

_____ 3. They retired my brother. A man with enormous experience.

_____

_____

_____ 4. The refugee wanted to go home. To see his family.

_____

_____

_____ 5. To talk to the police. Henry decided.

_____

_____

_____ 6. Stunned by her silence. Ike went to the mountains alone.

_____

_____

_____ 7. Beyond the hills and through the meadows. The
meadowlark sang his lovely song.

_____

_____

_____ 8. We looked everywhere for the market. The one that sold
quality meat.

_____

_____

_____ 9. Kathy bought a bookcase. An old oak one with heavy shelves.

_____

_____

_____ 10. The picture looked nice. On the wall in front of the door.

_____

_____ 11. She decided to use garlic. To add some spice to the evening.

_____

_____

_____ 12. David went to traffic court. A tedious yet educational experience.

_____

_____

———— 13. Over the years at the same time each day. The fisherman
packed up his gear.

_____

_____

———— 14. Outraged by their attitude. The judge denied their release on bail.

_____

_____

———— 15. Running on the beach. Cindy found a ten-dollar bill.

_____

_____

———— 16. Burl went outside. To mow the lawn.

_____

_____

———— 17. Throughout the day and well into the night. They searched
for the survivors.

_____

_____

———— 18. A true pacifist. Chris actively protested the controversial war.

_____

_____

———— 19. Bitten by the dog. The child ran to his mother.

_____

_____

———— 20. To earn her degree. She has only another year of school.

_____

_____

Exercise 6 Indicate whether the words are a **sentence** (s) or a **fragment** (f).

Example: __f__   On the hill behind the barn.
                 __s__   We built a birdhouse.
                 __s__   They bought a house.
                 __f__   After the business was sold.

_____ 1. Required by law.

_____   The permit was bought from the state agency.

_____ 2. Sam always bought candy.

_____   The kind we all liked.

_____ 3. When Dawn came to dinner.

_____   After the movie.

_____ 4. I called the Thompsons.

_____   Our friendly neighbors.

_____ 5. Based on my experience.

_____   He doesn't know a good book from a poor one.

_____ 6. David's dream was to be a good teacher.

_____   And to be a playboy.

_____ 7. Talking for over an hour.

_____   They listened for only two minutes.

_____ 8. The average American woman is 5 feet 3.6 inches tall.

_____   The average American man is 5 feet 9 inches tall.

_____ 9. One half of the monkey's diet was fruit.

_____   The other was seeds.

_____ 10. We walked the two dogs.

_____   On a twisted beach.

_____ 11. To end the dispute.

_____   She quit her job.

_____ 12. A lonely man.

_____   He immersed himself in his work.

_____ 13. I found a water snake.

_____   In the stream running through the meadow.

_____ 14. He cut his first two classes.

_____ Needing more time to study for the test.

_____ 15. He went to the jazz festival.

_____ A yearly event.

_____ 16. Subdued by his outburst.

_____ She left the room.

_____ 17. Elaine lost track of the time.

_____ Doing her homework.

_____ 18. To see the movie.

_____ They stood in line all day.

_____ 19. Her ring fell.

_____ Down the drain of the kitchen sink.

_____ 20. An unsightly vehicle.

_____ The car was reliable transportation.

In this exercise, take a phrase and add a sentence of your own to the phrase. In other words, if left alone, the phrase would be a fragment, but attached to a sentence, it becomes part of a good, clear sentence.

Exercise 7 Building Mature Sentences Use the fragment as a part of a mature sentence.

1. With the wind blowing steadily

_____

2. To build an awareness of good health

_____

3. Threatened by the stares

_____

4. Because he was a student

_____

5. Waxing and polishing her car

_____

6. In the morning after breakfast

_____

7. To make the trip more enjoyable

_____

8. Written for a fast reader

_____

9. During my stay in New York

_____

10. With a little advice from friends

_____

11. The owner of a large estate

_____

12. A rope stronger than a cable

_____

13. Based on our wishes

_____

14. In front of the open fireplace

_____

15. By the smell of the flowers at our feet

_____

16. A performance to remember

_____

17. To get into shape

_____

18. Learning the language

_____

19. To be left alone

_____

20. A diver before the accident

_____

CLAUSES THAT CAUSE FRAGMENTS

Clauses do contain a subject and a verb, but they cannot be considered independent; they cannot stand alone as a sentence (see Chapter 3). If you have forgotten just what an adjective clause and an adverb clause are, then you might want to review them on pages 104 and 111.

Adjective Clauses

An adjective clause will typically begin with one of these words: *who, whom, whose, which,* or *that.* Further, the clause will follow the noun it modifies. Here are typical examples:

> The women played tennis on a concrete court *which made footing difficult.*

> The cow belonged to our neighbor *whose farm was next door.*

> We sanded and varnished an old table *that we had bought at a garage sale.*

You can see that if the clause is punctuated as if it were a sentence, you will have a fragment:

> Jim advises students. *Who enroll late in the semester.*

Make sure that an adjective clause follows the noun it modifies and that it is not punctuated as a separate sentence.

Exercise 8 Underline the fragment and rewrite in order to have one correct sentence.

1. The cake tasted like coffee. Which suited my taste.

   _____

2. We invited everyone, including Mr. Bill. Who just ruins a party.

   _____

   _____

3. The senator seemed afraid of the Soviets. Whose rockets impressed him.

   _____

   _____

4. Our cat liked cheese. That we had raised from a kitten.

   _____

5. The new barn served as a home to the robins. That still needed work.

   _____

   _____

6. We lost our red book. That had all our friends' phone numbers.

   _____

   _____

7. We always asked Dad. In whom we had complete trust.

   _____

8. All suffered through the test. Which was too long and too difficult.

   _____

   _____

9. John Belushi was a great comic. Whose sense of humor delighted everyone.

   _____

   _____

10. We sat and watched the breakers. That were blown back in the wind.

    _____

    _____

11. The man is being shipped overseas. Whom I love.

    _____

12. I mentioned the problem to the women. Who own the business.

    _____

    _____

13. She is the person. To whom I spoke.

    _____

14. Brad wants to go to law school. Whose father is an attorney.

    _____

    _____

15. The test has been postponed for a week. Which suits me just fine.

_____

_____

16. He finally bought the book. That he needs for his term paper.

_____

_____

17. She was the doctor. Whose work benefited so many people's lives.

_____

_____

18. Planes fly over my house. That sits on a hill overlooking the bay.

_____

_____

19. Noise pollution is a problem. Which isn't given enough attention.

_____

_____

20. I've been trying to find out. Who owns the cat.

_____

Adverb Clauses

Adverb clauses answer simple questions like when? where? why? under what conditions? and to what extent? An adverb clause, like the adjective clause, can often be shifted from the beginning to the end of a sentence or shifted the other way around.

> _When we were ready,_ the sun was not out.
> The sun was not out _when we were ready._

Check page 104 if you need a quick review of adverb clauses.

Adverb clauses begin with a subordinating word, a word that prevents the rest of the clause from being a sentence. Notice how the addition of the subordinating word _because_ prevents the other words from standing alone.

> The peanuts tasted good.
> Because the peanuts tasted good.

It is this characteristic that encourages fragments. If you left off the first word, then an adverb clause would be a sentence. (See p. 106 for punctuation rules and examples.)

Exercise 9 Underline the adverb clause and properly punctuate the
sentences.

1. Before we left mother made us clean the house

2. We left when we were ready

3. After the chair broke Helen lay there laughing

4. Whenever we go downtown we buy fresh bagels

5. Our condo would not sell although the price was low

6. As the grades got higher the student got more enthusiastic

7. The shoes would not stay on since they got wet

8. While the bees worked the birds sang

9. The towels were softer after we used rainwater

10. Since there is no end to this I shall be patient

11. If she doesn't arrive by tonight we'll have to meet her at the hotel

12. Willie never goes to concerts even though she loves music

13. I had to write my composition early this morning because I was too tired last night

14. Since I didn't see him last night let me know when he gets here

15. The boys may go out when they have finished cleaning the garage

16. Because she broke their engagement his grades began to fall

17. Before I'd go anywhere in my unreliable car I'd stay home

18. Since he missed the test he dropped the class after all that work

19. While we were walking we met the new neighbors

20. That's the site where they plan to build the new zoo

If **any** of the clauses you just underlined had been punctuated as a
sentence, it would have been incorrect—it would have been a fragment.
Therefore, when you write, be careful not to stop your thought short;
continue until you have a complete sentence.

Exercise 10 Connect the fragment to the main sentence. Do not rewrite the whole sentence.

Example: When we bought the horse _{, none} . ~~None~~ of us knew how to ride.

1. After the election was held. The candidates still would not speak.

   _____

2. You must work hard. Before the rent is due.

   _____

3. When the pipe is cold. It will break quite easily.

   _____

4. Because the picture was blurred. We thought it was a giraffe.

   _____

5. Until we meet again. Please take care.

   _____

6. The two men drove the old tank into the park. That was restored.

   _____

7. After they ran away from home. They didn't know where to go.

   _____

8. Her brothers will return tomorrow. Who are away at camp.

   _____

9. So that you'll know what to expect. You should make an appointment to talk to him.

   _____

10. She joined the honor society. Which greatly pleased her folks.

   _____

11. In case you have forgotten. You have a meeting in an hour.

   _____

12. Wherever I see her. She's reading a book.

   _____

13. They cleaned the entire house. While I was at the store.

_____

14. We watched that great movie about Hitler. That was
    on TV last night.

_____

15. Because he wanted to say good-bye before he left for New York.
    He came by.

_____

16. I've located the woman. Whose coat was found.

_____

17. There's nothing we can do. Until the doctor calls.

_____

18. The girl is getting married next week. With whom I used to jog.

_____

19. I like to play my harmonica. Whenever I'm under much stress.

_____

20. When I play my harmonica. My dog leaves the room.

_____

Exercise 11 Label the following as **correct** or as a **fragment**. If it is a
fragment, rewrite to make it a complete sentence.

a = Correct   b = Fragment

_____ 1. Going to the baseball game after dark.

_____

_____ 2. James Joyce was an Irishman who rarely lived in Ireland.

_____

_____ 3. The night the wind died down.

_____

_____ 4. Where the oil is deeper than sea level.

_____

_____ 5. She wore elegant, stylish dresses with appropriate accessories.

_____

_____ 6. While, at the same time, she never said hello.

_____

_____ 7. Which was no way to be.

_____

_____ 8. If you never met the manager.

_____

_____ 9. The king forced the officers to obey his orders.

_____

_____ 10. By devious means that worked every time.

_____

_____ 11. Whose job it was to correct it.

_____

_____ 12. To be able to afford the trip.

_____

_____ 13. To go is all I want.

_____

_____ 14. Leaving the cozy ski resort in the mountains.

_____

_____ 15. Worn from the evening's activities.

_____

_____ 16. Between the hedges around the side of the house.

_____

_____ 17. A tired old man from the hills.

_____

_____ 18. There he sat.

_____

_____ 19. Under no circumstances go across that wobbly bridge.

_____

_____ 20. During the trial for about five minutes.

_____

REVIEW TEST

I. Fragments—Phrases and Clauses

Indicate whether the following sentences are correct or fragments.

a = Correct   b = Fragment (Phrase)   c = Fragment (Clause)

_____ 1. Eddie went to pay his bills. After he got his paycheck.

_____ 2. He was frustrated. Owing so much money.

_____ 3. Jack has become a real danger. To himself as well as to others.

_____ 4. Pat has gone on a diet. Who just gained ten pounds.

_____ 5. Because there were so many safety hazards, they closed the plant.

_____ 6. Janet likes to jog. Whenever she gets the chance.

_____ 7. It had been a terrible mistake. To tell her so much.

_____ 8. A generous woman. She gave all her money to charities.

_____ 9. He started to go.

_____ 10. We tried the bread. Which he made himself.

_____ 11. Sally jumped. Startled by the crash.

_____ 12. There goes Meg. Whose mother I mentioned.

_____ 13. She wanted Dale to have a decent funeral.

_____ 14. Lou decided to call her. During the game or after the party.

_____ 15. She thought he'd never leave. An impossible bore.

_____ 16. There's the woman. In whom you were interested.

_____ 17. They tried to settle in. During the intermission of the play.

_____ 18. She was the first.

_____ 19. Before she sees him. She wants to gather her wits.

_____ 20. I got out of bed to look around. Disturbed by the strange noises.

II. Fragments—Phrases

Identify the type of phrase that causes the fragment.

a = Participle Phrase   b = Infinitive Phrase
c = Appositive Phrase   d = Prepositional Phrase

_____ 21. Hearing the phone and thinking it was her boyfriend calling.
Lee rushed to answer.

_____ 22. He signed up for dance lessons. Because of his date for the prom.

_____ 23. Jody swam. Across the lake during the storm.

_____ 24. A conscientious doctor. He always takes time to answer
his patients' questions.

_____ 25. Torn by the old washing machine. His favorite shirt was ruined.

_____ 26. He bought some plant food. To add to the bottles of water.

_____ 27. My favorite uncle. Uncle Charlie is going to live with us.

_____ 28. She and Dean sat and talked. On the bench in the park.

_____ 29. Jed fell asleep. Writing his term paper.

_____ 30. Excited, Jared and Dustin packed. To go to the mountains.

_____ 31. A sight to behold. The children had been playing in the mud.

_____ 32. She made plans with Cindy. To exercise at the spa.

_____ 33. Deceived by the woman. Jake vowed not to trust her again.

_____ 34. We have new neighbors. Down the road by the old well.

_____ 35. We've recovered the chair in the living room.
The one that had stuffing coming out of the arms.

III. Fragments—Clauses

Indicate whether the following groups of words are sentences or
fragments.

a = Sentence   b = Adverb Clause Fragment   c = Adjective Clause Fragment

_____ 36. I enjoy my fireplace the most whenever we have storms.

_____ 37. I met the new girl. Because she was the only reason I went to the party.

_____ 38. Before the show was over. She and Brad left for the parking lot.

_____ 39. Mr. Brady is the architect whom I referred to you.

_____ 40. Because she had the option to drop one test grade for the semester.
Melissa didn't take the test.

_____ 41. It must have been Bill. Who left the door unlocked.

_____ 42. She saw George. Before she saw his car in the driveway.

_____ 43. My sister didn't get to go on the trip. Which doesn't seem to
bother her much.

_____ 44. So that I'll know one way or the other, I wish you'd call.

_____ 45. Wherever I go. I see people with radio headphones.

IV. Fragments—Clauses

Properly connect the fragments to the sentences that they modify.

a. this probably doesn't surprise today's teachers.
b. there has been an explosion of new phobias.
c. you've had a common fear.
d. a fear that's as old as people.
e. that you can probably guess.

_____ 46. Since the development of the atomic bomb,

_____ 47. One general fear is fear of dying,

_____ 48. Nucleomitiphobia is a word with a meaning

_____ 49. While many people suffer from sophophobia, a fear of learning,

_____ 50. If you've ever had stage fright,

CHAPTER 7

OVERCOMING SENTENCE PROBLEMS: RUN-ONS, FAULTY PARALLELISM, AND MISPLACED AND DANGLING MODIFIERS

THE RUN-ON SENTENCE: COMMA SPLICE AND FUSED SENTENCE

The run-on sentence gets between the writer's message and the reader. The run-on sentence occurs whenever the writer runs one complete sentence into another complete sentence.

Recall that the fragment is less than a sentence, yet it is punctuated as though it were complete. The run-on is the other way around; the writer constructs two complete sentences, yet fails to punctuate the two correctly. It is as if the fragment is too little and the run-on too much.

The run-on sentence announces to the reader that the writer is not in control. Look at these examples of run-on sentences.

> The news came with a panicked voice but the aftershock stalked the house silently.

> Laughter had gone from her voice sadness had arrived to control her whole being.

> The instructor tried hard, he just couldn't teach.

If you can spot the errors—and fix them—then you will probably have little trouble with run-on sentences.

However, if you cannot spot or correct the run-on errors, take heart; these problems are surmountable.

Here is a graphic view of the run-on:

_____ _____

_____ , _____

_____ *and* (*but, or,* etc.) _____

A fused sentence is a type of run-on error and occurs under two conditions:

1. **When nothing (no punctuation, no coordinating conjunction) separates the two sentences:**

    The stars were bright they were twinkling everywhere.

2. **When a coordinating conjunction alone (no comma) links the two sentences.**

    That house needs a new roof and it needs a new coat of paint.

A comma splice is also a type of run-on error and occurs under one condition: when two sentences are connected by a comma only:

The pencil needed sharpening, the pen was out of ink.

Thus, two errors are known as run-on sentences: a fused sentence and a comma splice.

Exercise 1   Overcoming Run-on Errors Run-on errors are easy enough to fix, once you appreciate the problem. Remember, they occur when a writer runs two (or more) sentences together without proper separation; this is true whether the error is a fused sentence or comma splice (also known as a comma fault). You correct a run-on by separating the two sentences properly. But first you have to see that there are, in fact, two sentences.

Label the following as a correct sentence (a) or as a run-on sentence (b).

_____   1. The ear hears words like the palate tastes food.

_____   2. The Stones knew that buying a new car wouldn't be easy however they

felt they had no choice.

_____   3. Overwhelmed by his load, John decided to drop history.

_____   4. The review process, which I had dreaded, went very smoothly.

_____   5. She wanted to feel safer, therefore, she bought a German shepherd.

_____   6. The clocks worked beautifully but they were never together.

_____   7. When the moon begins to rise, the fireflies begin to light the evening sky.

_____   8. We knew not to drive fast in the fog however everyone else seemed to

speed up.

_____   9. Bob taught literature, Bernie taught logic.

_____ 10. Had the child asked, the teacher would have said yes.

_____ 11. We didn't want to go but he talked us into it.

_____ 12. The joke he told was quite good we laughed until we cried.

_____ 13. He wants to go to the beach although he can't swim.

_____ 14. Larissa is never home no matter what time I call her.

_____ 15. If your foal isn't better by tomorrow, we'll call the veterinarian.

_____ 16. Why he can't face reality is a mystery, she just can't figure him out.

_____ 17. Having been there before, I really don't care to see it again.

_____ 18. The show starts at 8:00 let's have dinner before.

_____ 19. Talk show hosts are a special breed, they all have lots of teeth.

_____ 20. I was overjoyed to see her after so long it's been three years.

How to Correct Run-on Errors

If the sentence is fused, then you have these choices:

1. **Place a comma and a coordinating conjunction between the sentences.**

    The rose was beautiful sitting on the table, but its beauty lasted only a few days.

2. **Place a semicolon between the two sentences.**

    We played all morning; we rested all afternoon.

3. **End the first sentence with a period.**

    The play was very boring. We decided to leave early.

If the two sentences have a comma splice, then you have these choices:

1. **Add a coordinating conjunction (*and, but, or, nor, for, yet, so*) to the already present comma.**

2. **Or you may opt for number 2 or 3 above. A final note of help: When two sentences are connected with a conjunctive adverb (*nevertheless, however, moreover, thus, consequently*, etc.), use a semicolon before the conjunctive adverb and a comma after it.**

    That florist is always helpful; moreover, he is quite knowledgeable.

Exercise 2 Go back to the previous exercise and correct any sentence that is run-on.

Exercise 3 Label and then correct the errors in the following sentences. If the sentences are correct, mark "c" in the blank.

a = Fused Sentence
b = Comma Splice
c = Correct

_____ 1. You make me laugh you should be on the Carson show.

_____ 2. The old clock never missed a tick, however, the newer one was more accurate.

_____ 3. Our couch is multicolored, our chairs are maroon.

_____ 4. The antique pistol on the wall reminded me of the Old West.

_____ 5. Framing pictures well adds to their beauty but adds nothing to their worth.

_____ 6. Cigarette smoking should be limited to the smoker's private quarters but this limitation will never come about.

_____ 7. I was born in the rugged hill country I still miss the grandeur of the mountains.

_____ 8. When the brakes failed, my heart followed the brakes' lead.

_____ 9. The wind blew shingles off the roof yet the house hardly moved.

_____ 10. A sense of humor makes life easier to take, however, a lack of humor adds a burden to living.

_____ 11. He's worked all these years to be an actor and he just got a role in a soap opera.

_____ 12. His picture was on the front page of today's paper, he wasn't as excited as I thought he would be.

_____ 13. There was nothing more for us to say, but, despite my misgivings, I agreed to the meeting.

_____ 14. They told me to call back later they said that it was too early to call on a Sunday morning.

_____ 15. It seems to be that everything is becoming so competitive somehow it doesn't seem right.

_____ 16. He ran all the way for a touchdown, that linebacker of yours is something else.

_____ 17. Eddie waited upstairs for Bill to get home but Bill didn't come home all night.

_____ 18. His school counselor was impatient probably he doesn't like his job.

_____ 19. Some springs were coming through the car seat, he tried to fix it himself.

_____ 20. He wasn't sick or anything that day, he just didn't think he had to be there.

Exercise 4   Fused Sentences (Run-on)   Label the following sentences as correct
(a) or **fused** (b). When you find a fused sentence, correct the error.

_____ 1. The baseball strike changed the game no sports group has
           ever struck before.

_____ 2. However, both sides lost.

_____ 3. The precedent had been set and nothing could prevent the strike.

_____ 4. The fans lost the most they lost their summer entertainment.

_____ 5. Some people just did not care; however, they did resent the
           media coverage.

_____ 6. He chose to go into the advertising field it promised a lucrative career.

_____ 7. She worked hard for an A on the test but she didn't quite make it.

_____ 8. Nonetheless, it has its effects.

_____ 9. She said she would try yet you have to meet her halfway.

_____ 10. They had only a few minutes to go in the game; as a result, the tension
            reached a fever pitch.

_____ 11. I waited too long to write the research paper now I'll be up all night.

_____ 12. She kept having the same dream but never understood its meaning.

_____ 13. He's always doing crazy things like that and no one is terribly surprised
            when he does.

_____ 14. I don't know if I can get a job it's been so long since I've had one.

_____ 15. Furthermore, I warned him.

_____ 16. The Naval Training Center begins drills very early in the morning, which
            I don't happen to like.

_____ 17. He may have gone to the store or he may be inside the house somewhere.

_____ 18. I may not make it in time so go ahead without me.

_____ 19. He doesn't like it nevertheless, I'll continue to do it.

_____ 20. Because of the money spent increasing our nuclear arsenal educational
            funds have been cut back.

Exercise 5   Comma Splices (Run-on) Label the following sentences as correct (a) or as **comma splices** (b). When you find a comma splice, correct the error.

_____ 1. Thoreau went to live in the woods, he wanted a simpler life.

_____ 2. One night he had a visitor, Emerson, a long-time friend, stayed several hours.

_____ 3. Although they sat in the same room for hours, neither of them exchanged more than a casual greeting.

_____ 4. They sat as if meditating, they appeared perfectly at ease.

_____ 5. Then Emerson rose to leave, he said to Thoreau that it had been a perfect evening.

_____ 6. Edgar Allan Poe was born in Boston, his parents were actors before they died.

_____ 7. He drank and gambled excessively, this alienated his adopted family.

_____ 8. He married his tubercular cousin, Virginia Clemm, who was only thirteen at the time.

_____ 9. Knowing Virginia was not going to live much longer, Poe went on drinking and opium sprees, he couldn't hold a job.

_____ 10. They had no money for firewood, Virginia died during the winter.

_____ 11. John Keats had a great influence on literature, he died at age twenty-five.

_____ 12. After he received his certificate to practice medicine, Keats decided to leave medicine and to write poetry.

_____ 13. He died of tuberculosis, so did his mother and brother.

_____ 14. Keats fell hopelessly in love with a beautiful young woman, Fanny Brawne, because he was dying, they couldn't get married.

_____ 15. His friend, Shelley, invited him to the warmer climate of Italy, there he produced some of his most beautiful writing in his letters to Fanny.

_____ 16. Molière was a playwright, his grandfather, who loved the theater, encouraged his career.

_____ 17. Molière had multiple talents, he produced farces, comedies, ballets, and masques for the court.

_____ 18. Louis XIV gave Molière's theater troupe permission to call themselves
the Troupe de Monsieur, before they were called L'Illustre Theatre.

_____ 19. Signifying a royal sponsorship, being called the Troupe de Monsieur was
important to them.

_____ 20. Molière is best known for his comedies of character, the device of
caricature was used to ridicule vices or affectations.

Next is a comprehensive exercise, which asks you to identify correct
sentences and run-on sentences.

Exercise 6 Label the following sentences as correct (a) or **run-on** (b). When
you find a run-on, correct the error.

_____ 1. English has used, up to now, the pronoun _he_ to mean both males and
females.

_____ 2. However, most well-read people are changing, they have been made more
sensitive to the overuse of male references.

_____ 3. Men have always called boats and ships by female references, these
references made some women angry.

_____ 4. A few people theorize that the sailors respected women only from a
distance up close they dominated the women around them.

_____ 5. Others felt that women were envious and deserved what they got.

_____ 6. A more reasonable view sees that all people possess both good and bad
qualities.

_____ 7. Aggressive behavior has long been associated with masculine qualities
but that's changing.

_____ 8. There has also been some confusion between aggressiveness and assertiveness even assertiveness is a quality that has been associated with
men.

_____ 9. Speculate on the semantic difference between _bachelor_ and _spinster_.

_____ 10. English has many "put-down" words about women but it has fewer about
men.

_____ 11. For example _old maid_ has no exact male equivalent.

_____ 12. *Broad* is another example and *chick* is still another.

_____ 13. Few men would want to be referred to as "the little man" however, these same men may well refer to their mates as "the little woman."

_____ 14. Women are often linguistically invisible, men are completely visible.

_____ 15. This leads to the final point then.

_____ 16. One way to avoid sexist English is not to specify gender unless it's relevant, this is difficult without a neuter third-person pronoun.

_____ 17. With conscious effort, sensitivity, and common sense, we can correct the problem even so it will take time.

_____ 18. Maybe that's all we need.

_____ 19. Time has a way of solving problems, this one is probably no exception.

_____ 20. It is, however, not solely the responsibility of women to change things but one that men share as well.

FAULTY PARALLELISM

Similar ideas need to be expressed in similar ways; if you express one idea in an adverb clause, then a parallel idea should also be expressed in an adverb clause. This concept of expressing equal ideas in equal constructions is appropriately called **parallelism**. Remember the end to Lincoln's Gettysburg Address: ". . . of the people, by the people, and for the people. . . . " That set of prepositional phrases remains a perfect model of parallelism.

Not to write in parallel fashion can cause a pothole in your otherwise smooth writing. Which sentence is parallel?

> We bought a video recorder to record late-night shows and that will be enjoyable to watch the next day.

or We bought a video recorder to record late-night shows and to enjoy them the next day.

In the last sentence, one idea was expressed in an infinitive phrase, and a similar idea was matched in an infinitive phrase.

Choose the parallel one of these sentences.

> Hugh enjoyed jogging each morning and to swim each afternoon.

> Hugh enjoyed jogging each morning and swimming each afternoon.

Parallelism is a kind of coordination; it's an arrangement of similar ideas in equal patterns: a noun with a noun, a prepositional phrase with a prepositional phrase, an adjective clause with an adjective clause, and so on.

Exercise 7   Recognizing Correct Parallel Elements Often beginning writers pay little if any attention to the structure of sentences. Thus, writing perfectly parallel elements is difficult at first.

In the following sets of sentences, one is written with correct parallel elements, one is not. Choose the correct one.

_____ 1. a. The tactful, friendly, and fair handling dispelled the old bitterness.
   b. The tactful, friendly handling and the fairness also dispelled the old bitterness.

_____ 2. a. The 1912 Stockholm Olympics used for the first time an electrical timing device, a public address system, and used wire cameras for photo finishes.
   b. The 1912 Stockholm Olympics used for the first time an electrical timing device, a public address system, and a photo-finish camera.

_____ 3. a. The hero of the 1912 games was Jim Thorpe, a half Sauk-Fox Indian, half Irish athlete.
   b. The hero of the 1912 games was Jim Thorpe, a half Sauk-Fox Indian, and he was an athlete who was half Irish.

_____ 4. a. Bright Path (his Indian name) trained hard for the Olympics; the question was, however, for which events he would compete.
   b. Bright Path (his Indian name) trained hard for the Olympics; the question was, which events would he go for, and for which competition in those events?

_____ 5. a. Thorpe won his chosen events, scoring twice as many points as his nearest pentathlon rival, and he breezed to win the decathlon title.
   b. Thorpe won his chosen events, scoring twice as many points as his nearest pentathlon rival and breezing to the decathlon title.

_____ 6. a. Running, walking, and to skate are my favorite forms of exercise.
   b. Running, walking, and skating are my favorite forms of exercise.

_____ 7. a. To be in his class and to study under his tutelage is invaluable to me.
   b. To be in his class studying under his tutelage is invaluable to me.

_____ 8. a. She is the smartest girl in the class, and she is also the most pretty.
   b. She is the smartest and prettiest girl in the class.

_____ 9. a. Both the television that he just bought and the radio that he just had repaired are broken now.
b. Both the television that he just bought and the radio, the one just back from the repair shop, are broken now.

_____ 10. a. What he needed was to study biology and a little brushing up on his chemistry.
b. What he needed was to study biology and to brush up a little on chemistry.

_____ 11. a. We called the exterminators to spray the fleas and to relieve our mother of the chore.
b. We called the exterminators to spray the fleas, and that will be a relief for our mother.

_____ 12. a. Herb decided to take a walk and some checking on her progress.
b. Herb decided to take a walk and to check on her progress.

_____ 13. a. We got home at one o'clock in the morning.
b. It was one o'clock in the morning when we got home.

_____ 14. a. Her calm, controlled response and the way she reacted so slowly surprised us.
b. Her calm, slow, controlled response surprised us.

_____ 15. a. Why Les did it and to do it so fast besides are both mysteries.
b. Why Les did it and how he did it so fast are both mysteries.

_____ 16. a. My oriental rug and my antique chair match perfectly.
b. My oriental rug and my chair that's antique match perfectly.

_____ 17. a. Knowing he was almost late and remembering the teacher's warning, he parked illegally to save time.
b. Knowing he was almost late and to remember his teacher's warning he parked illegally to save time.

_____ 18. a. Andy always wanted to work in a radio station hearing music all day.
b. Andy always wanted to work in a radio station and to hear music all day.

_____ 19. a. When he gets to the park, which is where he's going after the game is over, tell him calling me at home is necessary.
b. When he gets to the park after the game is over, tell him to call me at home.

_____ 20. a. Jennifer was sitting at her desk to file her nails during the break.
b. Jennifer was sitting at her desk and filing her nails during the break.

Exercise 8 Label the following as correct (a) or as containing **faulty parallelism** (b).

_____   1. His dream was to study hard, graduate early, and a good job
could be found.

_____

_____

_____   2. They looked at a menu of shrimp, Caesar, and fruit salads.

_____

_____   3. Running a vacuum weekly is easier than to run it once every month.

_____

_____

_____   4. Fire caused the house to sustain major damage: ruined the
carpets, smoked rooms, and the furniture had to be replaced.

_____

_____

_____   5. English is more than grammar, and writing needs good
handwriting too.

_____

_____

_____   6. Mountain climbing is dangerous but has excitement in it too.

_____

_____   7. Many English classes require that a paper have a
bibliography, outlining, and footnotes.

_____

_____

_____   8. The couple enjoyed going out to eat, drink, and take in a movie.

_____

_____   9. Many boat owners say it is better to rent than owning one.

_____

_____ 10. She likes having her cake and to eat it too.

_____

_____ 11. They played jazz and blues music at the concert, and they
also were playing some country music.

_____

_____

_____ 12. No matter who is calling or what they want, Mr. Bailey will
have to return their call.

_____

_____

_____ 13. Flying is all my brother thinks about because to fly his hang
glider is his favorite sport.

_____

_____

_____ 14. The list had cauliflower, lettuce, and to buy a roast written
on it.

_____

_____

_____ 15. Even though he enjoyed his cooking classes, to go to school
every day was difficult.

_____

_____

_____ 16. To be able to speak another language and learning to
pronounce it well can be very rewarding.

_____

_____

_____ 17. To live and to grow old with friends and family is to be very
rich indeed.

_____

_____

_____ 18. The remodeled kitchen has new cabinets, but we got a new refrigerator too.

_____

_____

_____ 19. That he passed the final was surprising, but his passing with such a good grade was amazing.

_____

_____

_____ 20. Freedom and to have liberty are the bases of our constitution.

_____

Exercise 9 Go back and rewrite each of the faulty elements; make them parallel. Try for smooth, mature sentences.

MISPLACED AND DANGLING MODIFIERS

Although the misplaced modifier and the dangling modifier differ to some extent, they are both errors that distract the reader; they move the reader's mind away from the true subject and toward the writer's mistakes.

A misplaced modifier is one that is out of proper sequence in the sentence; it does not refer clearly to the word or phrase it modifies.

Misplaced: Our neighbors watered the garden *in their blue jeans*.
Corrected: Wearing blue jeans (*or*, In their blue jeans), our neighbors watered the garden.

Modifiers may be one word, a phrase, or a clause.

One word: She looked at me as if I were the *only* man in the world.
            (See how many other places *only* will go in that sentence.)
A phrase: *Running the last leg*, Frank caught and passed the runner.
A clause: *When I graduated from high school*, the Army called me.

Exercise 10 **Recognizing Correctly Placed Modifiers** Write down the word, phrase, or clause that modifies the word in italics.

Example: We enjoy seeing roses *bloom* in the springtime. *in the springtime*

1. Reared in the mountains, *Leroy* could track anybody. _____

2. When she was twenty, *Alita* already had her pilot's license. _____

3. We ate at the *Fish House*, which serves brunch. _____

4. The *candle* on the nightstand burned for days. _____

5. That old *trunk* with the brass fittings must be a hundred _____
    years old.

6. Jumping over the fence, the *horse* ran into the field of tall grass. _____

7. Because he was a suspect, *he* decided to keep out of sight. _____

8. Exhausted, the little *dog* finally found its home. _____

9. I *tripped* when the phone rang. _____

10. The *fire* raged for hours, causing great damage. _____

11. That old woman *living* down the street takes in sewing. _____

12. We *found* out that the bones were three hundred years old. _____

13. My *friend* with the talking parrot lives nearby. _____

14. His favorite holiday is *Thanksgiving*, which is next month. _____

15. This is a picture of my *cat* that ran away. _____

16. The *car* with all the dents belongs to my brother. _____

17. I gave the little girl the *bracelets* on the table. _____

18. Troubled by the letter, *John* decided to call her that night. _____

19. That's the *girl* who dances so well. _____

20. A beautiful animal, the *cougar* disliked being caged. _____

Exercise 11   Recognizing Misplaced Modifiers These sentences contain a misplaced modifier. Underline the misplaced element.

1. They enjoyed the pigeons opening a six-pack.

2. The horse kicked him in the corral.

3. A young man was arrested with long hair.

4. I saw a man digging a trench with a long nose.

5. He died and went to his rest in New York.

6. An apartment was rented by two actresses thirty feet long and twenty feet wide.

7. A pearl was found by a sailor in a shell.

8. My boyfriend found a dollar running on the track.

9. She asked the waiter for more bread with a smile.

10. She loved the palm trees walking along the beach.

11. His dog bit him in the veterinarian's office.

12. After graduation, the company wants to hire him.

13. Planning strategy all night, the case was won by the lawyer.

14. It was so hot I cleaned the house without any clothes on.

15. The restaurant was redecorated by the owner with antique armchairs.

16. I left my dog at the kennel with the bad temper.

17. The woman tried on the clothes without any mirrors.

18. Joanie saw the armored car roller-skating past the bank.

19. Some popcorn was served by a waitress in a bowl.

20. The two men built the business over in the corner.

   We can illustrate the challenge of placing a modifying word correctly. Notice how we cannot be sure of the meaning in this sentence:

   Beverly turned to look at John typing his paper *for the tenth time*.

Did she look ten times? Or did John type his paper ten times? By moving the phrase to its correct position, the writer leaves no doubt about its meaning.

   Beverly turned *for the tenth time* to look at John typing his paper.

Exercise 12 The following have poorly placed word modifiers. Move them so that there is no ambiguity.

1. She told the children to eat their dinner *nicely*.

   _____

2. We buy our groceries from favorite stores *often*.

   _____

3. *Circling*, Sammy watched the birds.

   _____

4. His guitar instructor told him *strictly* to count the measure.

   _____

5. Five men climbed the mountain *only*.

   _____

Dangling modifiers have no words to modify; therefore, they indeed dangle.

When six years old, my grandmother died.

The question of *who* or *what* must be answered either inside the modifier (*when I was six . . .*) or at the very beginning of the sentence (*When six years old, I lost . . .*).

Exercise 13 Recognizing Dangling Modifiers In the following pairs of sentences, only one contains a dangling modifier. (1) Identify the correct sentence (write "a" or "b") and (2) underline the incorrect modifier in the other sentence. The first one is done for you.

____b____ 1. a. <u>Drinking their beer</u>, the party got louder.

   b. Drinking their beer, the partygoers got louder.

_____ 2. a. Going to school in the rain, the roads were slippery.

   b. While I was going to school in the rain, the roads were slippery.

_____ 3. a. By debating the issues, a compromise can be found.

   b. By debating the issues, we can find a compromise.

_____ 4. a. By studying radio signals, we can detect the enemy's position.

   b. By studying signals, the position of the enemy can be found.

_____ 5. a. Roughing the kicker, the linesman received a flag.

b. Roughing the kicker, a flag was thrown.

_____ 6. a. Working in the hot sun, the day never seemed to end.

b. Working in the hot sun, I thought the day would never end.

_____ 7. a. When I was only a child, my music teacher inspired me.

b. When only a child, my music teacher inspired me.

_____ 8. a. After teaching for so many years, students still didn't seem to care
about learning.

b. After Mr. Bonham had been teaching for so many years, students still
didn't seem to care about learning.

_____ 9. a. To learn a second language, some understanding of grammar
is important.

b. To learn a second language, one should realize the importance of
understanding grammar.

_____ 10. a. Leaving the airport, the car stalled.

b. As she was leaving the airport, the car stalled.

_____ 11. a. He asked for the list of library resources broken down into subjects.

b. He asked that the list of library resources be broken down into
subjects.

_____ 12. a. To write well, a person should read a lot.

b. To write well, reading a lot helps.

_____ 13. a. While I was getting out of the shower, my foot slipped.

b. While getting out of the shower, my foot slipped.

_____ 14. a. Because he was early, Mr. Dobson discussed the assignment with him.

b. Because Brad was early, Mr. Dobson discussed the assignment with him.

_____ 15. a. While going horseback riding, a rattlesnake crossed the path.

b. While Fred was going horseback riding, a rattlesnake crossed the
path.

_____ 16. a. Enjoying every minute, they stayed while the concert continued until late into the night.

b. Enjoying every minute, the concert continued until late into the night.

_____ 17. a. By following these instructions, the work isn't that hard.

b. By following these instructions, I've found that the work isn't that hard.

_____ 18. a. Upon my entering the class, the test began.

b. Upon entering the class, the test began.

_____ 19. a. Working at night, morning comes too soon.

b. Working at night, I think morning comes too soon.

_____ 20. a. When she was born, her daughter was very tiny.

b. When her daughter was born, she was very tiny.

_____ 21. a. While compiling the statistics, the pencil broke.

b. While I was compiling the statistics, the pencil broke.

Exercise 14   Revising Sentences with Dangling Modifiers Rewrite these sentences so that the dangling modifier no longer dangles.

1. They ate the steaks on the ground.

_____

2. You should put the car in the garage full of gas.

_____

3. Carrying the suitcases, a taxi could not be found.

_____

4. After complimenting the new couple, the phone became full of static.

_____

5. Consulting with his professor, the problem found a solution.

_____

6. Heidi eyed the birds with suspicion.

_____

7. He came home from the institution like a new person.

_____

8. Several people have tried I know and failed.

_____

9. They decided after the debate to go to lunch.

_____

10. Waiting for the bus, the hours seemed endless.

_____

11. If he comes early, the door will be unlocked.

_____

12. After eating lunch, the games began.

_____

13. Writing yesterday, the names have been compiled.

_____

14. To go to the show, a reliable car would be nice.

_____

15. Reviewing for the test, it looked easy to me.

_____

16. Getting up in the morning, the coffee pot begins to perk.

_____

17. Bert reliably wants to do the job.

_____

18. A painter all his life, the rewards were slow in coming.

_____

19. Sitting in the sun, the heat was intense.

_____

20. While talking on the phone, the other line rang.

_____

Exercise 15   Building Mature Sentences   Now we come to an exercise that asks you to practice what you have learned about misplaced and dangling modifiers.

Take the italicized words in one sentence and make them a modifier in the other sentence.

Example: The dancers completed the difficult finale.
They *raised their arms joyfully*.

Combined:
Raising their arms joyfully, the dancers completed the difficult finale.

1. I tried mountain climbing last summer. *I fell twice.*

2. Don wanted to see England every summer. *He worked extra hours.*

3. The pilot's heart raced. *His plane's engine had quit.*

4. *Harriet asked to see the manager.* Harriet was distressed with the service.

5. Dennis said he was resigning as chairperson. *He said that on Wednesday.*

6. Maggani revealed her plans to get married. *She revealed them last week.*

7. At his bar mitzvah, David received unusual gifts. *The little pickup had green wheels.*

8. The ruby has been known for its beauty. *This has been known for centuries.*

9. Con combines odd bits of food. *His assortment includes ketchup and ice cream.*

10. The officer advised Jack of his rights. *The booking was yesterday.*

11. Manhattan is a nice place to visit. *It's in New York.*

_____

12. The crew worked overtime. *They made twice as much money as usual.*

_____

13. I found a leak in the kitchen ceiling. *It had rained in my absence.*

_____

14. His platoon was ready to move out. *The enemy began to close in.*

_____

15. I want to take a shower. *My date arrives at seven-thirty.*

_____

16. *They all lined up to get his autograph.* They stood in line for hours.

_____

17. The equipment was loaded on the trucks. *Each truck could hold five thousand pounds.*

_____

18. The wind swept back her hair. *She was riding a horse.*

_____

19. *Leo called an hour ago.* Leo said he would call again.

_____

20. He was given a few weeks rest. *He had been having delusions.*

_____

REVIEW TEST

I. Run-on Sentences

Indicate whether the following are correct (a) or **run-on** sentences (b).

_____ 1. She didn't want to go to the museum, she wanted to go to the beach.

_____ 2. Annie was glad to see her they always have such fun together.

_____ 3. They finally reached the beach but then it rained.

_____ 4. Steven pleaded with her but to no avail.

_____ 5. We knew winter was coming soon it would snow.

_____ 6. I abandoned him in the treehouse; it had nothing to do with you.

_____ 7. She didn't like the way he treated her friends, so she stopped seeing him.

_____ 8. I hope this board fits, then we can nail it down.

_____ 9. The next flight to New York is at noon we think we can make that.

_____ 10. My dad was pleased to find out. My girlfriend is a doctor.

II. Run-on Sentences

Label the following sentences.

a = Fused
b = Comma-Spliced
c = Correct

_____ 11. He won't have any trouble finding a lab partner, he's an excellent student.

_____ 12. The officer didn't recognize the woman and couldn't understand why she would confess to a crime she didn't commit.

_____ 13. He found her roommate asleep on the living room floor and he decided to let her sleep.

_____ 14. Burl liked his new golf clubs, he had no time to play golf.

_____ 15. My father is getting ready to retire so he bought some land in Colorado.

_____ 16. Scotty got upset and left the party was too rowdy.

_____ 17. I found a silent partner, one who will finance the business while I do the work.

_____ 18. His secretary quit yesterday without any notice, now the office is chaotic.

_____ 19. Some people suffer from migraine headaches that must be miserable to get migraines.

_____ 20. Cindy knows all the new dances; I wish I could dance.

III. Parallelism

Indicate whether the following sentences are correct (a) or **faulty** (b).

_____ 21. People should take time to exercise as well as being able to function mentally.

_____ 22. He found honor without being victorious.

_____ 23. They are organizing the yearly event and planning a celebration.

_____ 24. Whenever he speaks and whatever topic he chooses, he always manages to find an audience.

_____ 25. Justin enjoys the yard and the gardening.

_____ 26. The troupe decided to give an extra performance and then that they would sign autographs afterwards.

_____ 27. Playing hockey is both dangerous and it has excitement.

_____ 28. I like hiking, swimming, and to go camping.

_____ 29. She couldn't decide whether to go to school or to get a job.

_____ 30. His mother told him to clean his room, to do his homework, and that he should be in bed by 9:00.

IV. Parallelism

Match these sentences to produce parallel elements.

_____ 31. I found him to be a knowledgeable man

_____ 32. Her work was mediocre

_____ 33. They ran through the rain talking

_____ 34. He talked too much

_____ 35. She loves to talk

a. but acceptable.
b. and to laugh.
c. and he bored me.
d. and laughing.
e. and an eloquent speaker.

V. Modifiers

Label the following sentences.

a = Misplaced Modifier
b = Dangling Modifier
c = Correct

_____ 36. Putting out the poison, the snails didn't have a chance.

_____ 37. Her horse balked when she tried to make him take the jump stubbornly.

_____ 38. Excitedly, the girls went out to build a snowman.

_____ 39. My mother brought us some homemade candy wrapped in plastic.

_____ 40. She spent all morning over the kitchen stove.

_____ 41. She served it lovingly to us.

_____ 42. When cooking, delicious smells come from the kitchen.

_____ 43. We hoped to work together desperately.

_____ 44. The doctor can thoroughly explain the problem to you.

_____ 45. The turkey was stuffed and served in an evening gown.

_____ 46. Rushing to the elevator, a trash can was overturned.

_____ 47. Crawling beneath the thick shag carpet, my dog followed the centipede.

_____ 48. Giving the recital, my hands shook nervously.

_____ 49. They take reservations before noon only.

_____ 50. The people applauded the band in the audience.

CHAPTER 8
OVERCOMING WORD PROBLEMS

ADJECTIVES AND ADVERBS: CHOOSING CORRECTLY

The difference between a skeleton sentence and a fully developed one
often rests with the appropriate use of adjectives and adverbs, which are
both modifying words.

Look at this bare-bones–fully developed pair.

She was lovely.

Alita, dressed in black silk, accepted politely the warm greetings.

Before you get the impression that we want all your sentences to be
flowery and flowing with modifiers, rest assured we do not. Often, good,
clear, short sentences are best.

Overdose:
The overly efficient secretary offered his boss the recent listings of
all her incoming telephone communications.

Simple and clear:
The secretary gave his boss her phone messages.

**A helpful guideline: offer the reader any information that will make the message
more readable, more clearly understood, and more enjoyable.**

Adjectives and Adverbs: Differences

All of us compare people and things.

The *new* couch is *larger* than the *old* one.
The jeep rode *more smoothly* after we bought *new* shocks.

Or we modify words to make the sentence accurate, interesting, and
clear for the reader.

Arturo talks *very loudly*.
The *paisley* dress accented her *natural* color.

Adjectives

As you learned in Chapter 3, adjectives describe nouns. More often than not, one-word adjectives come before the noun they modify.

> our white fence
> the delicate stitches
> an overwhelming experience
> a dirty floor

However, one-word adjectives may appear after a linking verb and modify the subject of the sentence.

> The flowers appeared fresh.   (*fresh* describes *flowers*)
> Douglas is boring.   (*boring* modifies *Douglas*)

Adverbs

Adverbs, more often than not, describe verbs. (See p. 76 for other uses.) An adverb that modifies a verb will usually answer the question *how?* when applied to the verb. Further, many one-word adverbs end in -*ly*.

> Karen drove slowly.   (*Slowly* answers *how* Karen drove. Or to say the same thing another way: *slowly* modifies the verb *drove*.)
>
> Marge sang beautifully.   (*Beautifully* modifies *sang*.)

Here are some adjectives and adverbs used correctly.

Adjective	Adverb
Janet was an exceptional driver. (*Exceptional* modifies *driver*.)	Janet drives exceptionally. (*Exceptionally* modifies *drives*.)
The baby is a quiet sleeper. (*Quiet* modifies *sleeper*.)	The baby sleeps quietly. (*Quietly* modifies *sleeps*.)
Melia was a steady worker. (*Steady* modifies *worker*.)	Melia works steadily. (*Steadily* modifies *works*.)

Adjectives modify nouns, often coming before the noun they modify.

> The *white* paper blew away.

The other position for an adjective is after a linking verb.

> The paper looked *white*.

Adverbs modify verbs, often coming after the verb they modify. One-word adverbs often end in -*ly*. When adverbs modify verbs, it usually answers the question *how*?

> The horse stood quietly.

When an adverb describes another adverb or an adjective, it often answers the question *how much*? OR *how often*?

> Tad talked *almost* incessantly.

Exercise 1 Change the italicized adjectives into adverbs.

Example: The dog's bark was *loud*.
          The dog barked *loudly*.

1. a. His moves were *smooth*.

   b. He moved _____ .

2. a. The family lived in *abject* poverty.

   b. In poverty, the family lived _____ .

3. a. That driver made *abrupt* lane changes.

   b. That driver changed lanes _____ .

4. a. Hugh had a *wistful* expression.

   b. Hugh stared _____ .

5. a. Greta's eyes were *languid*.

   b. Greta stared _____ .

6. a. He has a *certain* attitude.

   b. His attitude is _____ good.

7. a. He was a *meticulous* housekeeper.

   b. He kept house _____ .

8. a. The *testy* clerk threw down the change.

   b. The clerk threw down the change _____ .

9. a. The whole family was *amiable*.

   b. The entire family acted _____ .

10. a. The buttes were *prominent* against the sky.

    b. Against the sky, the buttes stood _____ .

Exercise 2 Underline the correct word (either an adjective or an adverb) in the following sentences.

1. The structure of the book remains (substantial/substantially) intact.

2. The actress stood (breathless/breathlessly) near the curtain.

3. The pilot sat (surprising/surprisingly) calmly.

4. The storm came over the hill (sudden/suddenly).

5. The (sudden/suddenly) announcement was shocking.

6. The (rapid/rapidly) rising stream looked angry.

7. They bought a (reasonable/reasonably) safe house.

8. Why does he eat so (exceptional/exceptionally) fast?

9. They talked so (serious/seriously).

10. Please don't talk (rapid/rapidly).

11. His presence made her feel (secure/securely).

12. Joe held his thumb (secure/securely).

13. Nadine paced the floor (nervous/nervously).

14. Her (nervous/nervously) pacing agitated Larry.

15. He eyed the money (greedy/greedily).

16. Sally walked with an (energetic/energetically) spring in her step.

17. She's always been a (vivacious/vivaciously) person.

18. Stu regarded him (suspicious/suspiciously).

19. Her dancing was incredibly (graceful/gracefully).

20. She walked (smooth/smoothly) and (confident/confidently) to the gate.

Nouns As Adjectives

Oddly enough, a noun can become an adjective when placed before another noun. For instance,

Baseball games can be boring.

Baseball, ordinarily a noun, modifies *games*; therefore, it functions as an adjective.

You will experience little trouble with such constructions unless you overdo the practice.

Overdone: The computer needs a *printout board interface cable* test.

Simple: The computer's printer cable needs testing.

Appropriate Forms: Positive, Comparative, and Superlative

A **positive** comment about the weather is stated directly:

The *warm* weather is invigorating.

But if we **compare** this month's weather with last month's we note:

The *warmer* weather this month . . .

Then if we compare this weather with all other warm weather, we say:

This is the *warmest* weather of the year.

Much of the time, short adjectives are formed like those above: *warm*, *warmer*, and *warmest*. That is, they add *-er* to form the **comparative** and *-est* to form the **superlative**. In fact, we can list short adjectives this way:

Simple form (positive)	Comparative	Superlative
warm	warmer	warmest
good, well	better	best
bright	brighter	brightest
big	bigger	biggest
pretty	prettier	prettiest

Longer adjectives and most adverbs form the comparative by adding a word—*more* (*less*); and they form the superlative by adding *most* (*least*).

Simple form (positive)	Comparative	Superlative
warmly	more warmly	most warmly
beautiful	more beautiful	most beautiful
graceful	more graceful	most graceful

A word of encouragement is in order: All of us (even teachers who write books) must look in the dictionary for an adjective or adverb when we aren't sure of its form. You should do so as well. In some instances, logic seems to have abandoned us. Many fine writers will use an illogical comparison when the adjective or adverb has an **absolute meaning**. For example, we can say "that was the *deadest* party," or "almostly completely filled." Logically when something is *dead*, the term means "without life." But emotional or psychologically, we know what "*deadest* party" means.

The best time to polish your adjectives and adverbs is when you rewrite, when you go back over what you've done and check for correct word usage.

Summary

Adjectives:

1. For the comparative form, add *-er* to one-syllable adjectives.
2. Add *more* to most of the rest. (When in doubt, look it up.)
3. Follow comparative adjectives with *than*.
4. For the superlative form, add *-est* to one-syllable adjectives.
5. Add *most* to almost all the rest. (When in doubt, look it up.)
6. Add *the* before a superlative if it sounds correct.

Adverbs:

1. For the comparative adverb that ends in *-ly*, add *more* in front of the adverb.
2. For the superlative adverb that ends in *-ly*, add (*the*) *most* in front of the adverb.

Exercise 3 Choose the correct comparative or superlative form of the adjective or adverb.

1. The mother was even (lively) _____ than her son.

2. Some movies are (easily) _____ followed than others.

3. The organist had a (unique) _____ approach to Bach.

4. James was the (tall) _____ of the three sons.

5. This tire is losing air (fast) _____ than that one.

6. This type of house appears (common) _____ than any other.

7. We gave (late) _____ scores to the operator.

8. His eyes were (red) _____ than I had ever seen them.

9. Maria writes (good) _____ than any other student.

10. Old men drive (slow) _____ than old women.

11. She noted with pride that her son's reactions were (quick)

     _____ than those of anyone else in the game.

12. He was one of the (good) _____ players on the team.

13. Of all the people I've ever known, he is the (mean) _____ .

14. Some foods are (readily) _____ digested than others.

15. Fran is the (spiteful) _____ woman I've ever known.

16. My brother, John, has always been (smart) _____ than I.

17. In fact, he's the (bright) _____ person I know.

18. He's the (fat) _____ man she has ever seen.

19. Emil's books are the (innovative) _____ of any I've read so far.

20. The vase she bought has (few) _____ flaws than any of the

     others.

Exercise 4   Adjectives after Linking Verbs, Adverbs after Action Verbs Linking verbs are followed by a noun or an adjective (see p. 14). Linking verbs are never followed by adverbs alone. The common linking verbs are *is, am, are, was, were, be, been, appear, seem, look, taste, feel, grew,* and *smell.*

> The cake tasted *delicious.*
> My children are *careful.*
> The flowers smelled *delightful.*
> The flowers smelled *delightfully fragrant.*

Action verbs are followed by an adverb if a descriptive word is needed.

> Ten minutes passed *quickly.*
> The corn popped *slowly.*

Underline the correct adjective or adverb.

1. The pancakes taste (different, differently) today.

2. Dad looked (angry, angrily) to Herman.

3. Dad looked (angry, angrily) at Herman.

4. Arthur felt (bad, badly) about losing the poem.

5. Dawn dances very (graceful, gracefully).

6. The delicate plant grew (slow, slowly).

7. That driver is (proficient, proficiently).

8. The dogs made a (hasty, hastily) exit.

9. The table appeared (odd, oddly).

10. Wherever we went, the countryside looked (inviting, invitingly).

11. The little boy yelled (gleeful, gleefully).

12. Terry check his answers (thorough, thoroughly) before handing in his test.

13. She reminded him to drive (defensive, defensively), but he has always been a (careful, carefully) driver.

14. When Brenda heard footsteps, she moved (furtive, furtively) to her closet and waited.

15. Her breathing was (rapid, rapidly) and (audible, audibly).

PRONOUN CASE AND ANTECEDENT

Pronouns are a bit like sand at the beach: valuable in its place, but grating and bothersome when found out of place, such as in bed. In this section, we will try to solve any grating problems you have with pronouns and to help you use them smoothly and efficiently. As you learned in Chapter 2, pronouns take the place of nouns.

> George told Sandra to buy the house.
> He told her to buy it.

Since pronouns are discussed in depth in Chapter 2, we will review here the problem areas and give you some extra help in avoiding the common pronoun errors.

In your family's life, your grandparents are your antecedents. That is, they came before you. In your grammar, you need to align all pronouns with the word they refer to, the word that came before.

Gender

As recently as ten years ago, using *he* to refer to both men and women was acceptable in published writing. This is no longer true.

Formerly acceptable:
Everyone in the class must bring his notebook.

Formerly acceptable:
A professor should always prepare before he comes to class.

Today, however, *he* or *his* cannot be used to refer to everyone, both men and women. To do so is unfair to women and therefore unacceptable. After all, *everyone* surely refers to both women and men.

Possible Solutions

1. One solution to the antecedent problem with *his* is to use both *his* and *her*:

   > Everyone should bring his or her own bedding.

   This option can become quite tedious, however, when used over and over again.

2. A few persons are now suggesting that we use *their*:

   > Everybody brought their own towel.

   The solution is as grating as the original problem: *their* is plural. Now the sentence has a basic error of grammar, although this option may become standard.

3. Make the antecedent plural to begin with, making the plural pronoun
   their appropriate:

   > All class members should bring their own bedding.
   > Bring your own towel.
   > Professors should prepare their lessons well before class.

4. Last, try to avoid all reference to gender, where appropriate.

   > Everyone bring bedding.
   > They brought towels.
   > Professors should prepare before class.

Exercise 5 Change the following to a more acceptable usage.

1. Anyone can see that he needs to write well.

   _____

2. Someone gave his last speech on the wrong day.

   _____

3. Whoever votes for that man loses his vote.

   _____

4. Every one of the girls gave their best effort.

   _____

5. Anyone caught plagiarizing will lose his priority.

   _____

6. The counselor gave somebody their bad news.

   _____

7. Each surfer gave their all for the team.

   _____

8. Nobody stood up to have his voted counted.

   _____

9. None of the team furnished their own equipment.

   _____

10. One of the kids brought his own TV.

    _____

11. Whoever comes in late won't be allowed to write their test with the others.

   _____

   _____

12. Someone left their coat in the classroom.

   _____

13. No one likes to do their homework when it's sunny.

   _____

14. Each of the workers put away his tools and left.

   _____

15. The soloist began singing his number as soon as the choir stopped singing.

   _____

   _____

Number

A singular pronoun refers to only one person or one thing; a plural pronoun refers to more than one.

Simple logic determines that if the antecedent is singular, then the pronoun must also be singular. A plural antecedent demands a plural pronoun.

> The *man* asked directions to *his* old high school.
> The *children* sang *their* very best.

Special Problems with Number Problems arise when various sentence elements are added to the pronoun and antecedent issue. Here are the main trouble spots with pronoun-antecedent number.

1. What happens if two nouns or pronouns are joined by *and*? Nearly every time that two nouns or pronouns are joined by *and*, they are considered plural.

> Adam and Eve are remembered for their garden.
> She and he bought their first car yesterday.

An exception: when two nouns or pronouns refer to the same person or thing, they are considered singular.

> The captain and quarterback was given his award.

2. If two nouns or pronouns are joined by *or* or *nor*, then the pronoun will agree with the second.

> Either the coach or the *players* will stay on the bus after *their* long trip.
>
> Either the little chickens or the *mother hen* will eat *her* corn first.
>
> Neither the child nor the *parents* wanted to give *their* facts away.

3. Collective nouns (*jury, chair, team*, and so on) are singular or plural depending on how they are meant.

> The jury gave *its* verdict.
> The jury gave *their* differing opinions.

4. Here is a valuable list of indefinite pronouns. Some are always singular; some are always plural; and a few are singular or plural depending on meaning.

Singular	Plural	Singular or Plural
another	both	all
anyone	few	any
anybody	others	some
anything	several	most
each		
each one		
either		
everyone		
everybody		
everything		
neither		
no one		
nobody		
none		
nothing		
one		
someone		
somebody		
something		

5. When a singular pronoun is followed by a prepositional phrase with a plural object, treat the pronoun as if the prepositional phrase were not present.

> **subj**   **prep phrase**   **sing verb**
> Each one   of the trees   is dying.
>
> Somebody on the bleachers is screaming loudly.

Exercise 6 Correct any errors in the following sentences.

1. The Yankees and baseball are known for its closeness.

2. Has anybody seen their script?

3. Few of the players seems ready to perform.

4. Neither the cows nor the calves wanted its feed.

5. The leader of the girl's team are too easygoing.

6. She and I was chosen for an award.

7. The truck, along with two cars, cost tens of thousands of dollars.

8. The team choose their own director.

9. Several of the chairs needs painting.

10. The department needs new furniture in their offices.

Case

Pronoun case is a phrase used to indicate how a few pronouns change their spelling to show whether they are used as a **subject** or an **object** or to show **possession**. (This material is also discussed on pp. 44–45.)

Subjective Case Any pronoun used as the subject of a verb is said to be in the **subjective case**. Here are the subject pronouns.

I	we
he	you
she	they
it	

IMPORTANT: *He, she,* and *it* require a verb with an *s*.

He *walks* tall.
She *is* at home.
It *wants* to be left alone.

The other subject pronouns—*I, we, you, they*—require a verb without an *s*.

I teach every day.
We sit together.
You bring the flowers.
They are on time.

Exercise 7 Underline the correct verb for the subject pronoun. You will find these easy to do.

1. We (drive, drives) the car on weekends.

2. After the class, I must (go, goes) to work.

3. During the winter months, she (make, makes) quilts.

4. We always (find, finds) great antique shops.

5. When did they (come, comes) to live here?

6. You (write, writes) very nicely.

7. It (sell, sells) well.

8. I (write, writes) every day.

9. She (buy, buys) groceries on Friday.

10. He (lose, loses) his gloves regularly.

11. They (want, wants) to see that new show.

12. It (look, looks) like it (is, are) going to be a nice day.

13. When he's not teaching, he (act, acts) in plays for relaxation.

14. I (close, closes) the restaurant when she's not there.

15. We (know, knows) he (was, were) lying, but we can't prove it.

Objective Case These are object pronouns.

me	her
us	them
him	whom

All object pronouns are used in one of three ways:

1. As the **direct object** or **indirect object**.

> The IRS sent *us* a refund.
> My father took my brother and *me* to the lake.
> Look at those apples; will you buy *them* for lunch?

Do not use expressions such as "my brother and *I*" as an object of a verb. The proper object pronoun is *me*.

---

2. As the **object of a preposition**.

> Just *between you and me,* I can't swim.
> *To whom* does this book belong?
> We always fought hard *against them.*

If you are in doubt about the correct form of a pronoun to choose when a double set is used (*you* and *me*, *her* and *him*, etc.), leave one of the two out and try the other one.

> **We bought a sweater for her and him.**

Try saying "for *he*," leaving out *her* for a moment, and you'll see that *he* would be wrong.

---

3. As the word before or after an **infinitive** (*to* go, *to* send, *to* contradict, *to* build, etc.)

> Our builder told *me to fasten* the windows.
> I wanted *to find her* and the cat.
> They asked Kelly and *him to go* home.

Using object pronouns with infinitives tends to be easy. Remember that when a double is used, choose the object one:

> **He wanted Bill and *me* to run the show.**

Exercise 8 Underline the correct pronoun.

1. The space shuttle looks intriguing to (me, I).

2. The rocket's noise makes (her and him, she and he) use earplugs.

3. Jon and (I, me) stayed to see the next blast.

4. The director showed Bill and (they, them) how to fire the retro-rocket.

5. My mother and (me, I) want to see the background film.

6. I knew the dog was going to bite the child and (he, him).

7. The inspector asked (me, I) to call the carpenter.

8. Their parrot sat next to (them, they).

9. The buyer offered John and (her, she) a bonus.

10. He was the man on (who, whom) we could count.

11. Stephen and (me, I) decided to go with (them, they).

12. (She, Her) and her boss tried to convince (him, he).

13. I've placed a great deal of trust in Mr. Bonhamm and (her, she).

14. Lucy sent (him, he) and his wife some cookies.

15. (We, Us) employees gave (her, she) a party because she was always a friend (who, whom) we could turn to.

Exercise 9   Additional Practice   Underline the correct pronoun.

1. The youngsters left (their, his) jackets at home.

2. When the parade was over, the crowd headed to (its, their) cars.

3. I became acquainted with Sue and (she, her).

4. (Who, Whom) is going to the movies?

5. Just between you and (I, me), I want out.

6. The actor (who, whom) I saw today stayed to chat.

7. Marilynn and (her, she) wrote very interesting papers.

8. To (whom, who) shall we send the fruit?

9. That old man asked John and (me, I) to sit by him.

10. That kind of pressure never affects (me, I).

11. Every one of (they, them) seems to have lost (their, his or her, his) perspective.

12. Please, let's keep this a secret between you and (I, me); no one will know but (we, us).

13. (Who, Whom) did you get this information from?

14. I've known (her, she) and Tad for years.

15. The committee voted her (its, their) new chairperson.

16. (Who, Whom) was that on the phone?

17. Peter drew on the pipe (him, he) got for his birthday.

18. My dog and (me, I) are going to the mountains to visit (they, them).

19. (She, Her) and Jessie gave (us, we) guys the brushoff.

20. The test didn't seem that hard to (me, I) but (who, whom) knows what the others thought of it.

VERB ENDINGS

All the verbs in our language are either action or linking (see p. 14). **Action verbs** show action:

The cars *slipped* and *skidded* on the sleet-covered streets.

Linking verbs link the subject of the sentence with another word in the sentence:

The weather *was* awful.

All verbs have three principal forms (**present**, **past**, and **past participle**) and two additional forms (**-s form** and the **present participle**).

Present Tense

The present form of a verb is the base or plain form and is the dictionary form of a verb. (Examples: *go*, *teach*, *walk*, etc.) The present form shows that the verb's action is occurring in the present and that the subject is a plural noun or the pronoun *I*, *we*, *you*, or *they*.

We *eat* pizza every Friday afternoon.
They *drive* an old Hupmobile.
Those trucks *haul* large jet engines.

-s Form

Except for *be* and *have*, the **-s form** of all verbs is made by adding *-s* or *-es* to the base verb: buy, buys; drink, drinks; eat, eats; congratulate, congratulates; draw, draws. The *-s* form of *be* becomes *is*, and of *have* becomes *has*. (Notice they still have an *s*.)

The -s form indicates present time. The -s form is used with a **singular** noun, a singular indefinite pronoun (*someone*, *anyone*), or the personal pronouns *he*, *she*, or *it*.

The chicken walks funny
That lecture invites disagreement.

Everyone asks the same question.
Everybody is hungry for spinach.

She strives to overcome.
It shines in the sunlight.

Subject and Verb Agreement **Agreement** refers to the relationship between a singular subject and a singular verb or between a plural subject and a plural verb. The spelling (form) of a verb must correspond to the subject. If the subject is plural, then the verb must have an appropriate plural spelling.

In most instances you will have little trouble.

Louise *wants* a ride home. (not *want*)
The school *offers* a good program. (not *offer*)
I *do* my own work. (not *does*)

Principles to follow:

Verbs must agree with their subjects in <u>number</u>.

sing   sing
The *line* of cars *was* endless.

pl   pl
The *lines* of cars *were* endless.

The subject and verb agreement problems center on the *-s, -es* ending on nouns (and a few pronouns) and the present and -s forms of verbs.

Some memory work is in order:

1. When the subject is a singular noun or pronoun (*she, he, it, this, each, everyone,* etc.), the present tense verb will end in an *s*.

> Barbara wants a new car.
> The light dims every morning.
> That plant in the bushes is pretty.

2. When the subject is a plural noun or certain pronouns (*I, we, they*), the present tense verb will **not** end in an *s*.

> The plants in the garden need water.
> The cars run smoothly.
> Our cats eat almost nothing.

Do not allow a prepositional phrase between the subject and the verb to fool you.

> That *boy* in the waves *struggles* against the odds.
> Those *boys* in the waves *struggle* against the odds.
> The *list* of names *is* small.
> The *lists* of names *are* small.

Exercise 10 Underline the correct verb.

1. Patricia (want, wants) to discuss philosophy.

2. The church (plan, plans) to hold a meeting.

3. The houses in the woods (cost, costs) more.

4. The reporters on most papers (send, sends) their news in early.

5. The TV set (sound, sounds) quite good.

6. The hero (don't, doesn't) care about the rules.

7. We (ask, asks) for our rights.

8. Seymour (drive, drives) like a maniac.

9. Our dog (play, plays) harder at night.

10. They (get, gets) books in the mail.

11. Leo (seem, seems) to be preoccupied today.

12. Her behavior (worry, worries) me.

13. I (think, thinks) the weekend will be fun.

14. No one (care, cares) about cleaning the apartment.

15. People in that profession (have, has) no life of their own.

Helping Verbs

Helping verbs (also called **auxiliary verbs**) are combined
with a verb's present form and past and present participle forms to show
time and other meanings. Typical helping verbs are these:

shall, will	have, has, had
do, does, did	is, am, are, was, were, been, being
can, could	became
may, might	should
would	ought

The *is, am, are, was, were, been* group all stem from the linking verb *be*
(see pp. 58–61). These words can be used alone as the main verb (**She** *is*
sad.) or as a helping verb (**She** *is going* **for a record**.).

Present Participles

The **present participle** is formed by adding *-ing* to the base verb, as in
constructing, drinking, writing. As a verb, the present participle **must**
combine with a helper (*is, am, are, was, were, has been, had been, have
been*). If the present participle is used alone, it is an adjective, not a verb:
evaporating water, **burning toast**.

> The children *were asking* for more homework.
> Those snakes *are striking* against the glass.
> We *had been drinking* for hours.

Past Tense

The **past tense** is the one that indicates that the verb's action occurred in
the past. The past tense works in a sentence without any helping verb.
Further, the past tense of regular verbs is formed by adding *-ed* or *-d* to the
present tense. Irregular verbs form the past tense by letters other than
-ed or *-d*.

> The owls *constructed* their nest in the barn.
> The little boy *nestled* into his mother's arms.
> We *brought* new recipes. (irregular verb)

Past Participle

The **past participle** form of a verb is always used with at least one helping verb (*have, has, had, be, is, was*). Regular verbs form the past participle by adding *-ed* or *-d*—just as the past tense does. (When the past participle is used without a helper, it is an adjective: **painted wall**. See p. 137.)

> The older birds *had constructed* their nest first.
> The candle *had burned* the table.
> We *had gone* to the lecture. (irregular verb)

Regular verbs form the past tense and past participle by adding *-d* or *-ed*.

present	past	past participle
look	looked	looked
mow	mowed	mowed

Irregular verbs form the past and past participle in ways different from *-d* or *-ed*.

see	saw	seen
hide	hid	hidden
take	took	taken

Irregular Verbs

Writers experience problems with the past and past participle forms when the sentence requires an **irregular verb**, one that forms the past tense and past participle by spellings other than *-d* or *-ed*. Irregular verbs form their past tenses and past participles in irregular ways.

Look at these examples:

Present	Past	Past Participle	Present Participle	-s Form
ask	asked	asked	asking	asks
plant	planted	planted	planting	plants
enjoy	enjoyed	enjoyed	enjoying	enjoys
go	went	gone	going	goes
see	saw	seen	seeing	sees
begin	began	begun	beginning	begins

Using the Correct Form of Irregular Verbs The following is a list of the most commomly used irregular verbs. Study them carefully and memorize those you do not know.

Present	Past	Past Participle	Present Participle	-s Form
arise	arose	arisen	arising	arises
beat	beat	beaten	beating	beats
begin	began	begun	beginning	begins
bend	bent	bent	bending	bends
bid	bid	bid, bidden	bidding	bids
bite	bit	bit, bitten	biting	bites
blow	blew	blown	blowing	blows
break	broke	broken	breaking	breaks
bring	brought	brought	bringing	brings
build	built	built	building	builds
burst	burst	burst	bursting	bursts
buy	bought	bought	buying	buys
catch	caught	caught	catching	catches
choose	chose	chosen	choosing	chooses
come	came	come	coming	comes
cut	cut	cut	cutting	cuts
dive	dived, dove	dived	diving	dives
do	did	done	doing	does
draw	drew	drawn	drawing	draws
dream	dreamed, dreamt	dreamed, dreamt	dreaming	dreams
drink	drank	drunk	drinking	drinks
drive	drove	driven	driving	drives
eat	ate	eaten	eating	eats
fall	fell	fallen	falling	falls
find	found	found	finding	finds
flee	fled	fled	fleeing	flees
fly	flew	flown	flying	flies
forget	forgot	forgotten	forgetting	forgets
freeze	froze	frozen	freezing	freezes
get	got	got, gotten	getting	gets
give	gave	given	giving	gives
go	went	gone	going	goes
grow	grew	grown	growing	grows
hang	hung, hanged	hung, hanged	hanging	hangs
have	had	had	having	has
hear	heard	heard	hearing	hears
hide	hid	hidden, hid	hiding	hides
hit	hit	hit	hitting	hits
hurt	hurt	hurt	hurting	hurts
know	knew	known	knowing	knows

lay	laid	laid	laying	lays
lead	led	led	leading	leads
leave	left	left	leaving	leaves
let	let	let	letting	lets
lie	lay	lain	lying	lies
lose	lost	lost	losing	loses
make	made	made	making	makes
pay	paid	paid	paying	pays
prove	proved	proved, proven	proving	proves
put	put	put	putting	puts
ride	rode	ridden	riding	rides
say	said	said	saying	says
see	saw	seen	seeing	sees
set	set	set	setting	sets
shake	shook	shaken	shaking	shakes
sing	sang	sung	singing	sings
sleep	slept	slept	sleeping	sleeps
sit	sat	sat	sitting	sits
slide	slid	slid	sliding	slides
speak	spoke	spoken	speaking	speaks
spring	sprang, sprung	sprung	springing	springs
stand	stood	stood	standing	stands
steal	stole	stolen	stealing	steals
swim	swam	swum	swimming	swims
swing	swung	swung	swinging	swings
take	took	taken	taking	takes
tear	tore	torn	tearing	tears
throw	threw	thrown	throwing	throws
wear	wore	worn	wearing	wears
weep	wept	wept	weeping	weeps
wind	wound	wound	winding	winds
write	wrote	written	writing	writes

Exercise 11 Write the correct form of the verb in parentheses in the blank.

1. The cost of cosmetics has (rise) since last year. _____

2. I had (do) my work before breakfast. _____

3. We are (wear) our thermal underwear. _____

4. His canteen (spring) a leak during the hike. _____

5. The note was (write) and therefore binding. _____

6. Our cat has been (sleep) more since she had kittens. _____

7. Bret has always (arise) at dawn and (go) to bed shortly after sunset. _____

8. That boy has (give) them trouble for years. _____

9. We (bring) the firewood down from the shed. _____

10. This must be the craziest thing he's ever (do). _____

11. Pat (cut) the lawn every Saturday. _____

12. Someday he's going to be (make) a lot of money. _____

13. You shouldn't have (eat) so much. _____

14. We must have (drink) four pitchers of beer last night. _____

15. Her fidgeting (make) me nervous. _____

16. She (choose) the puppy with the black and white face. _____

17. They just (stand) there watching, unable to move. _____

18. I'm (wear) my new clothes to the party. _____

19. When my sister heard the news, she (weep) for hours. _____

20. The tree in our front yard (bend) in two during the storm. _____

21. My brother has had his nose (break) three times. _____

22. After what seemed like hours, the storm (begin) to break. _____

23. I (dream) about them the other night. _____

24. The girl was (speak) so quietly that we barely heard her. _____

25. The troop had (sing) the final song of their tour. _____

Exercise 12 Fill in the blanks with the correct form of the verbs in parentheses.

1. Although they were _____ the car, they had _____ no laws.

   (drive, break)

2. Our dog _____ the steaks that we had _____ to cook for the party.

   (eat, plan)

3. The cat has been _____ for hours _____ the bird. (sit, watch)

4. He has _____ around so long that he's _____ to get

   on my nerves. (is, begin)

5. When I _____ up on him, he _____ to get the picture. (hang, begin)

6. They had _____ that they had _____ to her house before. (forget, is)

7. We are _____ town until this entire affair is _____ . (leave, forget)

8. That plant had been _____ well, but now it's _____ limp.

   (grow, lay/lie)

9. Every time he _____ he _____ money. (go, lose)

10. She _____ her own clothes before she _____ her job. (make, get)

11. He was _____ that the incident left him _____ . (say, shake)

12. Darlene had never _____ so much in her life as on the day she _____

    with Eddie. (swim, dive)

13. I haven't _____ a horse in years, but I have a friend who _____ them.

    (ride, break)

14. We were _____ up on the news when the wind _____ out the candle.

    (catch, blow)

15. Nell has always _____ into tears and has begun _____ things when

    she hasn't _____ her way. (burst, throw, get)

Troublesome Pairs: Sit, Set, Lie, Lay

Especially in speech, these two sets of verbs can be confusing. A key to remembering them is to realize that *sit* and its forms do not have a direct object following them.

Sit, sat, sat, sitting, and *sits* take no direct object.

>I sit in the same chair every day.
>They are sitting by the window.
>The dog sits quietly.

Set and its forms usually require an object when the verb means "to put" or "to place," but when the verb *set* means to become hard, then it has no object: The cement will set very hard.

Set, set, set, setting, and *sets* require a direct object.

>The hairstylist is setting her hair in large curlers.
>Please set the table.
>We set the plane down on a dirt road.

The two verbs *lie* and *lay* follow the same pattern.

Lie, lay, lain, lying, and *lies* do not require a direct object.

>The records lay where I had left them.
>She lies down every afternoon.
>The papers had lain in the floor for days.

Lay, laid, laying, and *lays* require a direct object.

>We laid the boards end to end.
>The hen is laying two eggs per day.
>He lays down the ruler before each race.

Exercise 13 Choose the correct verb, then choose the correct form of the verb.

1. The records _____ where we had _____ them. (lie *or* lay; sit *or* set)

2. Those birds _____ in their nests before _____ eggs. (sit *or* set; lie *or* lay)

3. Mother _____ the baby in the crib and _____ waiting for the phone to ring. (lie *or* lay; sit *or* set)

4. I _____ them down somewhere when I was _____ on the sun deck. (lie *or* lay; sit *or* set)

5. She spends all day _____ in the sun and all night _____ under the stars. (sit *or* set; lie *or* lay)

6. She has always _____ them on the table; she couldn't have _____ them anywhere else. (lie *or* lay; sit *or* set)

7. He _____ right in that chair and _____ next to me. (sit *or* set; lie *or* lay)

8. The cement had already _____ and all he could do now was _____ and wait to be rescued. (sit *or* set; lie *or* lay).

9. Take the eggs that were _____ this morning and _____ them in the bowl. (lie *or* lay; sit *or* set)

10. With her hands _____ on her lap, she just _____ there looking at me angrily. (lie *or* lay; sit *or* set)

Exercise 14 Building Sentences Provide the missing forms of the following verbs. Then write a good sentence for those forms.

Example:

present	past	past participle
lie	lay	lain

Conrad lay down in his office.
He has lain there for hours.

Present	Past	Past Participle
1. break	_____	_____
2. _____	froze	_____
3. _____	_____	chosen
4. see	_____	_____
5. _____	arose	_____
6. _____	_____	taken
7. speak	_____	_____

8. _____ slid _____

_____

9. _____ stood _____

_____

10. wind _____ _____

_____

Exercise 15 Add the correct form of the verb in parentheses. Do not forget to include the -s and -ed endings where needed.

We _____ (use) to _____ (ask) for favors from our neighbors. They

would _____ (give) us anything we _____ (want). But that

_____ (be) before the accident. After the train wreck, they were

_____ (wear) out from all the hassle of lawyers and courts. We

_____ (keep) in touch by _____ (write) them every week. They were

_____ (keep) in Europe for six weeks. And they _____ (get) out only

after _____ (choose) to allow the railroad to pay their way home.

Exercise 16 Correct the following gross errors by writing the correct verb in the blank.

1. Those things have not came today. _____

2. I done all my work before breakfast. _____

3. I come in a little late yesterday. _____

4. He has went to my house without permission. _____

5. That stupid fellow just set down on my new hat. _____

6. He sat the chair in the corner. _____

7. He brung the letter with him. _____

8. Sit that plate on the table. _____

9. I have set in this position a long time. _____

10. That child will not lay still or set still a minute. _____

11. I laid down under the tree and enjoyed the scenery. _____

12. Lie that comb on the table, and let it lay. _____

13. Those girls were drive out of the parking lot.   _____

14. I have rode every ride at Disney World.   _____

15. I done what I could to save the trees.   _____

16. The President has not spoke all week.   _____

17. The leaves have fell from all the trees.   _____

18. This sentence is wrote badly.   _____

19. He teached me grammar.   _____

20. I seen him when he done it.   _____

21. Julie was chose to be the leader.   _____

22. Bill has took my favorite film.   _____

23. I begun to sing after the fireworks.   _____

24. We drunk from pure Rocky Mountain water.   _____

25. I should have laid down before dinner.   _____

REVIEW TEST

I. Adjectives and Adverbs: Choosing Correctly

Indicate whether the words in italics in the following sentences are
used correctly (a) or incorrectly (b).

_____ 1. Grady is an *eloquent* speaker.

_____ 2. He has always acted *responsible* before.

_____ 3. She's beginning to act *weirdly* around me.

_____ 4. I've never seen him react so *strong* to anything.

_____ 5. The whole incident was *vaguely* disturbing.

_____ 6. He looked *shyly* to her.

_____ 7. She offered him the food *enticingly*.

_____ 8. The little boy glared *angrily* at her.

_____ 9. His headache made him feel *badly*.

_____ 10. It is *well* and good that things turned out this way.

II. Adjectives and Adverbs—Nouns As Adjectives

In the following sentences, indicate whether the words in italics are
used as **nouns** (a) or as **adjectives** (b).

_____ 11. *Construction* workers break the monotony by heckling passing women.

_____ 12. Not *all* construction workers are hecklers.

_____ 13. Most women view this behavior as *chauvinistic*.

_____ 14. *Some*, however, are flattered by the attention.

_____ 15. Construction of a *building* is hard work.

III. Adjectives and Adverbs—Appropriate Forms

Place the letter of the correct sentence in the blank.

_____ 16. a. She is the most prettiest girl I've ever seen.
   b. She is the prettiest girl I've ever seen.

_____ 17. a. Dancers carry themselves more gracefully than most people.
   b. Dancers carry themselves more graceful than most people.

_____ 18. a. He's more smarter than I am.
   b. He's smarter than I am.

_____ 19. a. The cold weather is invigorating.
   b. The most coldest weather is invigorating.

_____ 20. a. She is the better of the two cooks.
   b. She is the better than the two cooks.

IV. Place the letter of the correct verb or the correct possessive pronoun in the blank.

_____ 21. The oppression and poverty of Coketown (was, were) not the worst of
   a   b
   the workers' problems.

_____ 22. Everyone arrived promptly to take (his, their, the) test.
   a   b   c

_____ 23. The group presented (their, its) individual demands for change.
   a   b

_____ 24. All I want (is, are) a chance.
   a   b

_____ 25. Nobody seems to trust (their, the, his or her) doctor
   a   b   c
   anymore these days.

_____ 26. Neither the church nor its affiliates could justify (its, their)
   a   b
   expenditures.

_____ 27. The team gave (its, their) best effort.
   a   b

_____ 28. The wife and mother of his children (is, are) leaving.
   a   b

_____ 29. None of the houses (is, are) still standing.
   a   b

_____ 30. Either my friends or I (are, am) going to clean up after the party.
   a   b

V. Pronoun Cases—Subjective and Objective

Choose the letter of the correct pronoun.

a = Subjective   b = Objective

_____ 31. My uncle sent my brother, my sister, and (I, me) a ten-dollar bill each.
                                                          a b

_____ 32. (Who, Whom) was the phone call for?
                 a   b

_____ 33. I sent (him and his friend, he and his friend) to the store.
                      a   b

_____ 34. (We, Us) kids don't get enough allowance.
                 a   b

_____ 35. He has more money than (me, I).
                                       a   b

VI. Subject and Verb Agreement—Verb Endings

In the following sentences, choose the letter of the correct verb.

_____ 36. They should have (arose, arisen, arised) earlier.
                                  a   b   c

_____ 37. We had (began, begun, beginned) to understand when the class ended.
                       a   b   c

_____ 38. Those dishes have (laid, lain, lied) in the sink for three days.
                                  a   b   c

_____ 39. Our whole team was upset over having been (beat, beaten, beats).
                                                          a   b   c

_____ 40. Harold (come, coming, comes) by every single day.
                       a   b   c

_____ 41. We (done, does, did) the work you wanted.
                   a   b   c

_____ 42. I had a headache, so I (lay, laid, lied) down for a while.
                                       a   b   c

_____ 43. By tomorrow, I will have (drawed, drew, drawn) a hundred sketches.
                                         a   b   c

_____ 44. She said she (seen, see, saw) them leave through the back door.
                            a   b   c

_____ 45. Whenever I take my dog for a walk, she (lead, leds, leads) me on the
                                                      a   b   c
              leash.

_____ 46. He saw the pies (sitting, setting, lying) on the windowsill.
                               a   b   c

_____ 47. My dad always used to (loses, lost, lose) his keys.
                                     a   b   c

_____ 48. The kids (swings, swang, swung) on that old tire all day.
                        a   b   c

_____ 49. Abby has (wrote, write, written) over thirty books.
                        a   b   c

_____ 50. They (choosed, chosed, chose) my little brother for their team.
                    a   b   c

CHAPTER 9
REFRESHING SENTENCES

When the traffic ruins a sunny morning, when assignments, overtime, or a roommate invades our tranquility, or when the sight of cigarette butts, an overdue bill, plastic milk cartons, and unwashed dishes add more strife to our lives, we yearn to find calm, quiet, and invigorating surroundings. Each of us experiences the need for freshness, for unruffled times and places.

Persons who read a great deal as a function of their jobs—managers, editors, teachers—experience a similar desire for fresh, clear writing. That wish is similar to the desire for pleasant mental and physical surroundings. A refreshing sentence, a refreshing paragraph, and, finally, a refreshing essay add to the reader's understanding and appreciation just as a walk in the park makes a day go better. Good sentences that are clear, refreshing, and mature are truly worth striving for.

No one method or set of exercises will teach you how to write good, clear sentences. But you can begin. If you genuinely desire to write well, then you can succeed. Acknowledge that a clear sentence is better than a muddled one and that an interesting phrase is better to read than a worn-out one. Several principles can be illustrated and practiced: combining choppy sentences, controlling word choice, achieving sentence variety, and changing from passive to active voice.

COMBINING VARIOUS KINDS OF SENTENCES

You can profit from exercises in combining simple statements into complex and compound sentences and in resolving complex and compound sentences into simple sentences. In combining sentences, it is an excellent practice to contrast, expand, transpose, and substitute different words, and thus learn to express the same thought in a variety of ways.

Exercise 1 Combine each of the following groups of sentences in at least three different ways.

Example: This man is to be pitied. He has no friends.

      a. This man has no friends, and he is to be pitied.
      b. This man is to be pitied because he has no friends.
      c. This man, who has no friends, is to be pitied.
      d. This man, without friends, is to be pitied.
      e. This friendless man deserves our pity.

1. The ostrich is unable to fly. Its wings are not in proportion to its body.

    a. _____

    b. _____

    c. _____

2. Egypt is a fertile country. It is annually inundated by the Nile.

    a. _____

    b. _____

    c. _____

3. The nerves are small threads, or fibers. They extend from the brain. They spread over the whole body.

    a. _____

    b. _____

    c. _____

4. Johann Gutenberg published a book. The book was the first one known to have been printed on a printing press. He published it in 1455.

    a. _____

    b. _____

    c. _____

5. The human body is a machine. A watch is delicately constructed. This machine is more delicately constructed.

    a. _____

    b. _____

    c. _____

6. Water is needed for all building functions in the body. It dissolves and transports other nutrients. It also helps regulate body temperature.

    a. _____

    b. _____

    c. _____

7. The circulating bloodstream is very complex. It is composed of twenty-five billion cells. They are microscopic. These cells travel through the entire body every fifteen to twenty seconds.

    a. _____

    b. _____

    c. _____

8. Hunza is one of the leading human longevity sites on earth. It is located in a remote valley about 200 miles long. It is only one mile wide. Hunza sits at an elevation of 8,500 feet.

    a. _____

    b. _____

    c. _____

   You can see that short statements closely related in meaning may be improved by combining them. But beginning writers frequently use too many *ands* as well as other connectors, making their sentences too long.

Short, choppy sentences should be combined to make clear, longer ones. Long sentences should be broken up into short ones when the relations of the parts are not clear.

Exercise 2 **Sentence Building** Use the following phrases as **subjects** of sentences.

Example: Watching the burning candle allowed me to meditate.

1. Walking in the garden _____ .

2. Her writing that letter _____ .

3. Breaking a promise _____ .

4. Creeping up to the house _____ .

5. Looking at the accident _____ .

6. Riding a motorcycle _____ .

7. Finishing my homework _____ .

8. Observing the old couple _____ .

9. Getting out of bed on an icy morning _____ .

10. Going to a concert _____ .

Combining long, awkward sentences into clear, simple sentences is also excellent practice.

Exercise 3 Combine the following awkward sentences into a good, simple sentence.

Example: Hannibal passed through Gaul, and then he crossed the Alps, and then he came down into Italy, and then he defeated several Roman generals.

Hannibal passed through Gaul, crossed the Alps, came down into Italy, and defeated several Roman generals.

1. The light stood on the shelf, but it could never offer enough light. It was too high.

_____

_____

2. The day started as usual. It followed the usual patterns. Then it began to get hectic. Finally, it edged over into chaos.

_____

_____

3. He got a big break. He secured a new invention. He figured out a way
   to sell it nationally. He then became rich.

   _____

   _____

4. Harold finally finished his term paper, but before he did he went
   through a lot of hassles. He lost his book. He ran out of paper.

   _____

5. Their dad was just being stubborn. He refused to see the doctor. His
   arthritis was bothering him. He complained constantly.

   _____

   _____

6. Some of the girls took pictures. The pictures were taken on a
   camping trip. They took the trip that summer. It was an
   unforgettable trip.

   _____

   _____

7. The strange woman started to meditate. She started to levitate. Her
   body was suspended. It must have been two feet from the floor.

   _____

   _____

8. The Bradfords showed home movies. They invited their friends over
   to watch. The movies were of their trip to Europe.

   _____

   _____

CONTROLLING WORD CHOICE

When you become more secure and practiced with word choice, you may wish to check with your instructor about books with more information on diction or word choice. Here you will learn the basics. One basic is unavoidable: choosing the best word depends on a large vocabulary. To develop a large vocabulary requires dedicated reading and studying over a number of years. You can always begin.

Abstract and Concrete

Abstract words refer to qualities and ideas; these words apply to intangibles. Examples of abstract words include *happiness, curiosity, democracy, judgment, common sense,* and *fun.* **Concrete words** refer to specific objects, to details, to particulars. Examples of concrete words include *birthday party, boiling, bread,* and *cola.*

General and Specific

General words refer to large classes, to broad areas, to many things, whereas specific words refer to a particular thing, a particular case. A general word like *vegetation* is made specific by narrowing to *bermuda grass.* Clearly some overlapping exists between **abstract**, **concrete**, **general**, and **specific**. In another course, you may profit from a more detailed study of these concepts. Here, you can learn an important principle—be as concrete and as specific as you can when discussing abstract and general ideas.

•

Offer concrete details, examples, and illustrations when discussing abstract concepts.

        abstract   concrete
Democracy—Voting in a New England town meeting.

Follow general words with specific words that focus the reader's mental picture.

        abstract   concrete
Music—Placido Domingo sings Spanish folk songs.

Always use examples, illustrations, and details to make clear for your reader any abstract or general words.

Exercise 4 Label the following words as either **abstract** (a) or **general** (b).

_____ 1. disaster   _____ 11. growth

_____ 2. fear   _____ 12. luxury

_____ 3. plants   _____ 13. elegance

_____ 4. buildings   _____ 14. right and wrong

_____ 5. beauty   _____ 15. food

_____ 6. weather   _____ 16. reasoning

_____ 7. fun   _____ 17. animal

_____ 8. facial expression   _____ 18. safeguards

_____ 9. tools   _____ 19. rich

_____ 10. hues   _____ 20. education

Exercise 5 Choose the letter of the most **concrete** word in the following groups.

	a	b	c
_____ 1.	idea	conception	truth
_____ 2.	respect	honor	discipline
_____ 3.	probability	tendency	characteristic
_____ 4.	anger	emotion	feeling
_____ 5.	respect	awe	worship
_____ 6.	dependability	trustworthiness	truthfulness
_____ 7.	luxury	grandeur	prosperity
_____ 8.	quality	nature	nobility

Exercise 6 Underline the most **specific** word in the following groups.

1. animal   mammal   dog

2. trip   transportation cruise

3. meeting house   worship   white church

4. aircraft   airplane   engine

5. dust   clean   tidy

6. operator   driver   coachman

253

7. vines ivy plants

8. paintings representations Rembrandts

As you read, you will notice that good writers follow abstract and general words with concrete and specific examples, illustrations, or instances. Notice that in the following paragraph the writer begins with general words, *traditional* and *better ideas*. Then a short sentence follows that leads the reader into a paragraph made of specific words.

> We were considering making a traditional Christmas wreath this year until someone came up with an even better idea. Her suggestion was simple. Take the abundant wildflowers and native grasses of the area and incorporate them into a wreath that would be festive enough for the holidays. And we used heather, bachelor buttons, prairie clove, wild lupine, wildfire top grass, and moss to form the wreath. It lasted for weeks, hanging on the front door, and added a festive touch to our house.

You can readily see that naming the wild plants adds details, making the paragraph better.

Exercise 7 Sentence Building Rewrite (and add a sentence if you need to) the following sentences, adding concrete words for the abstract ones and specific words for the general ones.

Example: Every year about this time, nature tells us of her power.

Rewritten: Around Thanksgiving every year, nature reminds us of her miracles. Frost turns the lawn brown, winds blast bare branches, and the gathering chill humbles even the hardiest rose.

1. Stop what you are doing, and get ready.

   _____

   _____

2. The meal was delicious.

   _____

   _____

3. We attended a performance.

   _____

   _____

4. I can relate to having a lot of fun.

    _____

    _____

5. Trusting her can be dangerous.

    _____

    _____

6. He turned and faced her, and the color left her face.

    _____

    _____

7. It's good to know I can talk to you.

    _____

    _____

8. The truck traveled on the highway.

    _____

    _____

Choosing the Appropriate Word

What's the difference between "cry," "weep," and "sob"? Many writers, when careless, use words that are not appropriate for the sentence. The failure results from not paying attention to the emotional impact of the words. What is the difference in emotional impact between the following sentences?

> My dad grabbed my head.
>
> My father tousled my hair.
>
> Run-down house with need of work for sale. Two small bedrooms with old-fashioned bath.
>
> For sale: Rustic, cozy hideaway. Use your imagination with two intimate bedrooms. Shower in private bath.

A good method for finding just the right word, the one that offers the correct emotional impact, is to look up the word and find a synonym. Then try several words until you find the exact one.

> The old man *walked* home.

After looking up *walked,* you might try several synonyms until you find the one that suits you: strode, strolled, sauntered, ambled, or paced.

Exercise 8 Rewrite the following sentences, changing one or more words to create a more pleasing emotional impact.

Example: The officials talked about the consequences.

The two vice-presidents hotly debated the financial report.

1. After the chemistry lab, John *stood* for another hour. (Consider the difference between *remained, tarried, lingered, endured,* and *lasted.*)

   _____

2. The weather *changed* quickly.

   _____

3. Arnie's girlfriend left him, and he was *unhappy.*

   _____

4. They went to walk on the beach to try to come to an *agreement* on their relationship.

   _____

5. We've been *looking* for Cindy, but we can't find her, so she must have gone.

   _____

6. The *person* started the car and drove it around.

   _____

7. The animals and plants were interesting and *pleasant.*

   _____

8. I felt *emotional* when I heard the poem.

   _____

Exercise 9 Choose the word that appropriately completes the sentence.

_____ 1. _____ in children the love of learning.
_____ 2. New ideas _____ a department until they became

permanent.
_____ 3. _____ fuel into the engine.

a. instill
b. inject
c. infuse

_____ 4. Acrobats learn how to fall so they won't _____ themselves.
_____ 5. Nadine meant him no _____ .
_____ 6. The _____ was almost more than he could bear.

a. harm
b. hurt
c. injure

_____ 7. Only his hope _____ him.
_____ 8. Lucy tried to _____ him in any way she could.
_____ 9. The police claim that they can _____ the charge.

a. support
b. sustain
c. assist

_____ 10. The artist _____ his masterpiece out of nothing but scrap

metal.
_____ 11. My brother and his wife plan to _____ their own house.
_____ 12. Gathering her wits, she began to _____ a plan.

a. construct
b. build
c. create

_____ 13. His little sister _____ his style.
_____ 14. Her first impulse was to _____ from his sight.
_____ 15. My mother used to _____ her own orange juice.

a. shrink
b. cramp
c. squeeze

ACHIEVING SENTENCE VARIETY

The need for sentence variety arises wherever paragraphs are burdened with sentence sameness. This sameness may be choppy, short sentences and may result from a sentence pattern being repeated again and again. Sentences rarely stand alone; they are connected to those before and after. As clauses may be joined to form sentences, so sentences may be united to make a paragraph. Good writers know that sentence variety—variety in length and in pattern—aids the reader's understanding and appreciation of the message and medium.

When, Where, Why, How

No pattern, no length, no order for sentences works all the time; variety serves the writer best. The simple sentence should never be thought of as "simplistic." For making direct statements, the simple sentence performs well.

> The earth slows down one second every thousand years.
> Prices continued to rise.

Further, simple sentences can be made longer by adding modifiers.

> Television sets, large and small, have come down in price.
> Yesterday, after a week of rain, was a bright, warm spring day.

And simple sentences can be strengthened by answering *when, where, why,* and *how.*

> Our closest friends dropped by.
> (Add *when*)
> Our closest friends dropped by our house on Christmas Eve.

Exercise 10 Write new sentences adding *when, where, why,* or *how* words.

1. The vegetable garden failed.   (why)

_____

2. Her tights fit.   (how)

_____

3. Children need tender care.   (when)

_____

4. The crippled plane landed.   (where)

_____

5. Chris looked at her.   (how)

_____

6. Larry dialed the wrong number.   (when)

_____

7. The storm settled in.   (where)

_____

8. The test has been canceled.   (why)

_____

9. Animals make good friends.   (why)

_____

10. People boarded the plane.   (how)

_____

Embedding

Recall that a simple sentence can have modifiers.

My grandfather lived in Oklahoma.
He was a working cowboy.
My grandfather, a working cowboy, lived in Oklahoma.

This embedding of one idea inside a sentence will give your sentence greater maturity and greater variety.

Exercise 11 Rewrite the short sentences, embedding the information from one sentence into the other.

The director depends on Julie.
She is his research assistant.
The director depends on Julie, his research assistant.

1. a. The film was made in Athens, Georgia.
   b. It is a friendly, old-fashioned town.

_____

2. a. The director spoke about the difficulties.
   b. He talked about creative problems.
   c. He talked about bureaucratic difficulties.

_____

3. a. The boys are both in the band.
   b. They go to school together.

_____

4. a. Deaf people aren't any different from people who can hear.
   b. They are sometimes called "invisible citizens."

___

5. a. The shop has gone bankrupt.
   b. It sold antiques.
   c. It was in a bad location.

___

6. a. The committee discussed their plans.
   b. They reviewed the blueprints for the site.

___

7. a. Rick wants to marry Joan.
   b. He wants to take her to his country home.
   c. He wants her to meet his family.

___

8. a. Paul's grandfather lives in the hills of Kentucky.
   b. He lives in a serene valley surrounded by the hills.

___

Length

Sentence length must be considered with paragraph length writing. All long or all short sentences make a paragraph seem like a song with only one note.

Exercise 12 Rewrite the following paragraphs, varying the sentence length.

Example A: A police officer has many duties. Some are dangerous. I have had many duties in my day. I have been scratched. I have been kicked. I have been pushed. I have been knocked to the ground. I have been spit on, screamed at, and even bitten.

Example B: The duties of a police officer can be extremely dangerous. In the course of my duties, I have been scratched, kicked, pinched, knocked to the ground, spit on, screamed at, and even bitten.

A. Police work has rewards. It is like most other occupations. It is not like nine-to-five jobs. The rewards greatly outweigh the negative aspects. One reward is the greatest. Police officers are able to experience things. These things are the whole spectrum of human emotions. Police work is almost never dull. It is not mundane. It is not repetitious. This is because of surprises. This is because of humorous situations. But the greatest reward is the sense of accomplishment that comes. It comes from knowing I've helped someone.

B. _____

_____

_____

_____

_____

_____

A. Grocery shopping is frustrating. It's hard to walk around. This is true when there are too many people. There aren't enough checkers. It's frustrating to have to wait. Most people are in a hurry. This is too bad. But it could be more pleasant if people talked to each other. But they don't, except for meaningless exchanges.

B. _____

_____

_____

_____

_____

_____

A. Ralph sent Carl a letter. Carl is his brother. The letter told him off. It told him that Ralph didn't like things. He didn't like things that Carl was doing. Carl took him for granted. Carl forgot his birthday. Carl wouldn't take him seriously. Carl treated him like a kid. He was not a kid. He hoped the letter would help. But it didn't because Carl laughed.

B. _____

_____

_____

_____

_____

_____

A. Jack went for an interview. The interview was for a job as manager of an apartment building. The building in question is big. It has fifty apartments. It has a swimming pool. It has a tennis court. It has a game room. Jack would have to do maintenance. He would fix plumbing. He would fix locks. He would fix the elevator. He would answer complaints. These complaints would come from the people who lived there. He would hear complaints a lot. But he would get a free apartment. And he would get a salary.

B. _____

_____

_____

_____

_____

_____

Openers

English sentences tend to flow from the subject to the predicate, going from the noun to the verb to the complement when a complement is present. However, changing the beginning can add new emphasis and interest. Used sparingly, varied sentence openers work in the writer's behalf. Here, for instance, is a sentence with three different openers. The best choice depends on the writer's purpose.

> The captain was determined.
> His ship was a submarine.
> He followed the cargo ship.
> He pursued the cargo ship for thirty-two hours.

Notice the different emphasis when varied openers are used.

> The determined submarine captain relentlessly pursued the cargo ship for thirty-two hours.
> For thirty-two hours, the relentless and determined submarine captain stalked the cargo ship.
> Relentless and determined, the submarine captain . . .

To improve your own writing, practice and experiment with various sentence openers.

Exercise 13 Rewrite these sentences at least twice, varying the opening. Find one suggestion in parentheses.

> She asked numerous questions.
> She demanded to know his background.
> (Begin one sentence with "Asking.")
>
> Asking numerous questions, she demanded to know his background.
> She asked numerous questions, leading to his background.

1. Golf keeps growing in popularity. Racquetball also keeps growing. (Begin one sentence with "growing.")

   _____

   _____

2. Denise worked on her paper for eight hours. Then she went to class. (Begin one sentence with "for.")

   _____

   _____

3. Jack claims he can explain. It could help clear up this mess if you listen to him. (Begin one sentence with "listening.")

   _____

   _____

4. We went to an Indian burial site. We found some old spearheads. We walked around. We found part of an old bow too. We were lucky. (Begin one sentence with "finding.")

   _____

   _____

5. They discussed the problems with the manager. It was a hopeless situation. (Begin one sentence with "discussing.")

   _____

   _____

6. Jason is a hard worker. He's determined. He has built his own empire. He quit school in the ninth grade. (Begin one sentence with "determined.")

   _____

   _____

263

7. Alan bought a new sports car. This made his wife mad. This delighted his son. (Begin one sentence with "angering.")

_____

_____

8. My mother cooks all day. It makes her tired. She goes to bed early. (Begin one sentence with "tired.")

_____

_____

Transitions

The connection between two sentences, between two ideas, can be thought of as a transition, a bridge between one part and another. Frequently used by good writers, these words significantly add to the writer's bank account of sentence variety.

Suppose you wish to link one idea to another; use words such as _and, but, moreover, further, plus, likewise, first, for instance, however, therefore, in addition, since, although, if, after, in spite of,_ and the like.

Exercise 14 Use the word in parentheses as a suggestion for connecting the two thoughts. Then write another version using your own choice.

People buy computers. Many machines never get used. (Although)

Although people are buying computers, many are not using the machines.

_or_   Many computers are not used although people are buying them.

1. The cost of college is going up. Many students will not attend. (therefore)

_____

_____

2. Long-distance running requires dedication. It also requires a great deal of time.   (in addition)

_____

_____

3. Sully is furious. He's making no secret of the cause.   (moreover)

_____

4. We have to read the first fifty pages in the biology book this week. We have six books to read before the semester ends.   (in addition)

_____

_____

5. The police caught the robber. There were no witnesses. (in spite of)

_____

_____

6. Tom may call before I return. Ask him to call back tonight.   (if)

_____

_____

7. The car sped by Maureen, nearly hitting her. When it passed, she was shaking with fear.   (after)

_____

8. Willie Nelson has begun another tour through the country. So has Dolly Parton.   (likewise)

_____

_____

9. My little sister hasn't seen her husband for a year. Now the navy has delayed their reunion for another six months.   (further)

_____

_____

10. My dog had an encounter with a skunk. She'll spend the day outside.   (therefore)

_____

_____

Active and Passive Verbs

When the subject of the sentence acts, its **voice** is **active**:

>The mail carrier drove the car.

If, on the other hand, the subject receives the action, the verb is said to be in the **passive** voice:

>The car was driven by the mail carrier.

Generally the active voice makes a stronger sentence. To rid a sentence of passive construction, rearrange or change the subject and object.

>The government was dissolved by parliament.
>Parliament dissolved the government.

Exercise 15 Reconstruct the following sentences, changing passive verbs to active ones.

>During the snowstorm, frightened rabbits were seen by us.
>During the snowstorm, we saw several frightened rabbits.

1. Look carefully at the directions. Every step that is emphasized should be followed.

   _____

2. The purse was found by Skip.

   _____

3. He was driven into outer space by the invaders.

   _____

4. Nat Adderly was heard in concert last night.

   _____

5. The puppy was bought for the little girl.

   _____

6. The flag was raised on the Fourth of July.

   _____

7. A six-foot jump was cleared by the horse.

   _____

8. That book was written by Mark Sassoon.

   _____

9. The government was criticized by us for interfering.

_____

10. Our test was given this morning.

_____

11. They were told by her that the book was lost.

_____

12. Four harmonicas were bought for his collection.

_____

13. Jazz styles are being studied in our class.

_____

14. My writing workshop is fun for me.

_____

15. His reaction to Mavis was one of fear and dread.

_____

16. He knew there were powers she had, and he was afraid of her.

_____

17. Thomas was seen running from the building by the witness.

_____

18. The notes were found in his closet by the agents.

_____

19. The shop was closed down by the government after the incident.

_____

20. Elaine was caught by Joey just as she was about to leave the house.

_____

REVIEW TEST

I. Combining Various Kinds of Sentences

In the following sentences, choose the combination that best exemplifies what you've learned about combining sentences.

_____ 1. a. Nolan and Elise grew up in the same neighborhood right next door to each other. Then they lived together for two years. They were always talking about getting married. Now they've split up.

b. After growing up next door to each other, after living together for two years, and after endless discussions about marriage, Nolan and Elise have separated.

_____ 2. a. Needing money desperately and wanting to avoid returning to her old job, Marsha started her own interior decorating business.

b. Marsha was broke and needed money desperately. She didn't want to go back to her old job. She started her own business. She's an interior decorator.

_____ 3. a. My dad and my brother went fishing. They left early in the morning. They caught their quota of fish. They got home by the time the sun was going down. Then they cooked them, and we had a great fish dinner.

b. My dad and my brother went fishing at dawn, caught their quota, returned by dusk, and prepared a fine meal.

_____ 4. a. When she was small, my sister liked to rided horses more than anything. She likes it just as much now. As a result, she now trains horses. She does it for a living.

b. Enjoying horseback riding since childhood, my sister now trains horses for a living.

_____ 5. a. Before I can accept his date for the dance, I have to finish my book report, study for my French test, and clean the house.

b. I can't give him an answer about the dance because I have work to do, and I can't go out until it's done. I have to finish my book report, and I have to study for my French test. And I have to clean the house. If I get done with everything in time, then I can go.

II. Controlling Word Choice

Label the words in italics in the following sentences as either **abstract** (a) or **general** (b).

_____ 6. They no longer *love* each other.

_____ 7. Those two are always *affectionate* toward each other.

_____ 8. His *reasoning* leaves a lot to be desired.

_____ 9. Meg's report is very *organized*.

_____ 10. The *plants* thrive during the winter.

_____ 11. They're *beautiful* plants.

_____ 12. She doesn't believe in *evolution*.

_____ 13. Janet has a lot of funny *expressions*.

_____ 14. Her poetry is *expressive* as well.

_____ 15. His words always seem so *vague*.

III. Controlling Word Choice—Abstract and Concrete

Choose the letter of the most concrete word in the following sentences.

_____ 16. It's obvious that he feels a great deal of (love,
a
friendliness, emotion, tenderness) toward her.
b   c   d

_____ 17. Lately, Darcy's mood has been (bad, terrible, obnoxious,
a   b   c
offensive).
d

_____ 18. Working in a job without a future (saddens, frustrates,
a   b
thwarts, disappoints) me.
c   d

_____ 19. His (stupidity, forgetfulness, disorganization,
a   b   c
thoughtlessness) drives me crazy.
d

_____ 20. Having his own room made my little brother feel

(happy, great, independent, satisfied).
a   b   c   d

IV. Controlling Word Choice—General and Specific

Choose the most specific word in the following sentences.

_____ 21. Their (pet, cat, tabby) slowly stalked the bird.
            a   b   c

_____ 22. Susan (walked, moved, strutted) through the room.
            a   b   c

_____ 23. She left her glasses on the (piano, table, furniture).
            a   b   c

_____ 24. My friend Ellen is dating an (artisan, musician, expert).
            a   b   c

_____ 25. The FBI caught that (creep, criminal, arsonist).
            a   b   c

V. Controlling Word Choice—Choosing the Appropriate Word

Choose the word that most appropriately completes the sentences.

a. document
b. itemize
c. cite
d. exemplify
e. quote

_____ 26. Stephen will _____ a case to support his contention.

_____ 27. The pastor will _____ from the Bible at the meeting.

_____ 28. He will _____ the minutes of the meeting.

_____ 29. His attitude seems to _____ that of the church.

_____ 30. He intends to _____ a list of the duties of each committee.

VI. When, Where, Why, How

Indicate what information is missing from the following sentences.

a. When   c. Why
b. Where   d. How

_____ 31. Gypsies travel constantly all over the country in caravans.

_____ 32. Bringing his own wagon, Lazlo gladly joined them when
            they were in town because he enjoyed wandering and
            because they are originally from his home country.

_____ 33. The first gypsies originally came from India by ship
            because wandering had been their practice.

_____ 34. They spoke Romany, the language of the gypsies,
            fluently before they arrived in this country.

_____ 35. They are often suspected when something is missing
            from a town they have just passed through because they
            have a reputation for stealing.

VII. Embedding and Length

Indicate the source of the problems in the following sentences.

a = Needs Embedding
b = Needs Length Variation

_____ 36. My cousin, David, a lawyer, has agreed to take the case. He has handled things from criminal cases to divorce suits. David has enjoyed being a lawyer. He has an interest in becoming a corporate attorney.

_____ 37. They spent two weeks with her sister in Iowa. Then they went to Alabama to see his folks for a week. Then they stopped in Texas where they spent their honeymoon. Then they returned to their home in California.

_____ 38. He has been dating a new girl. Her name is Rita. She's a research assistant at the chemical plant. The plant is conducting research on recombinant DNA.

_____ 39. David found the dog in the deserted town. He tried to find the owner of the dog. He couldn't find anyone who knew about the dog. He decided to take it home with him.

_____ 40. The dog has a lot of personality. It is a mongrel. The dog's name is Benny. Benny knows how to do a lot of tricks. He's a pretty smart dog.

VIII. Openers and Connections

Indicate the source of the problems in the following groups of sentences.

a = Needs an Opener
b = Needs a Connection

_____ 41. The looters plundered the town. They were caught eventually.

_____ 42. The clerk went to the station for information. He was determined to find out what happened.

_____ 43. No one wants to take responsibility for the accident. No one even admits any knowledge of the incident.

_____ 44. Ann's car was stolen. She takes the bus or walks when she needs to go somewhere.

_____ 45. Alan found the missing bank notes. He's a detective. He's very persistent.

IX. Active and Passive Verbs

In the following sentences, choose the one with the active voice.

_____ 46. a. The film was shown to the class.
           b. The instructor showed the film to the class.

_____ 47. a. The invitation pleased me.
           b. I was pleased to receive the invitation.

_____ 48. a. The paramedics took her to the hospital.
           b. She was taken to the hospital by the paramedics.

_____ 49. a. My brother was bitten by a snake.
           b. A snake bit my brother.

_____ 50. a. We were given two hours to take the test.
           b. We had two hours to take the test.

CHAPTER 10

PUNCTUATION, MECHANICS, AND SPELLING

PUNCTUATION

You do not need to be sold on the value of knowing how to punctuate correctly. Many of you fear trying to say what you truly want to say because you do not know how to punctuate well. Punctuation aids the reader, allows the writer variety of expression, and makes for clearer writing.

The Period / .

1. Use a period at the end of sentences, indirect questions, and mild commands.

> American poets are among the best in the world.
> She wondered when the ship would dock.
> Close the door, Don.

2. Use a period after most abbreviations.

> Mrs., Mr., 100 B.C., R.S.V.P., U.S.A., P.M.

No period follows abbreviations for governmental agencies such as NATO, UNESCO, TVA, or FHA or organizations such as PTA or IBM.

Except with an abbreviation, do not use a period with a comma, question mark, exclamation mark, semicolon, or colon.

Has he earned his Ph.D.?

The Question Mark / ?

1. Use a question mark after a direct question.

> Where did you place the money?
> "Did you phone me today?" he asked.

2. Do not use a question mark after an indirect question.

> Bob asked when the car was painted.

The Exclamation Mark / !

Use an exclamation mark very sparingly, but when you do use it, do so after a particularly forceful command or exclamatory phrase.

> Stop!
> Help!
> "Where in the hell have you been!" he screamed.

Exercise 1 Correctly punctuate the following sentences, or mark (c) in the blank if they are already correct.

_____ 1. Hey! Have you read Stephen King's new book!

_____ 2. She asked, "Whether it's really his best work so far?"

_____ 3. I wonder what RSVP means?

_____ 4. My girlfriend told the police that the call came close to 3:00 A M (?).

_____ 5. She said "she'd die (?!) before she would marry him," and now the doctor

gives her only three months to live???!

The Comma / ,

1. Use a comma with the **coordinating conjunctions** *and, but, or, nor, for, so, yet* when they join two sentences.

   > They subscribed to every magazine they could, but they never read any of them.

2. Use a comma after an **introductory phrase** or **subordinate clause**.

   > When they get married, they plan to move to the other side of town.

   Unless leaving out a comma will cause misreading, the comma is optional after a short introductory phrase.

   > After the rain the sun was unusually hot.

3. Use a comma to set off introductory words or a mild exclamation.

   > Yes, I knew you would succeed.
   > However, I shall not buy both of them.

4. Use a comma to set off dates, addresses, and titles.

   > June 19, 1991, in Little Rock, Arkansas
   > Dr. Tom Wilson, dean of instruction

5. Use a comma when a contrasted phrase is used.

   > Emil, not Con, will be at the convention.

6. Use a comma to show an omitted word in a parallel sentence.

> Bob is playing well; Don, hardly at all.

7. If a question comes at the end of a statement, use a comma after the statement.

> The storm is due, isn't it?

8. Use a comma to separate items (words, phrases, or clauses) in a series.

> We ate peanut butter, crackers, tacos, and nachos for lunch.

9. Both beginning phrases and parenthetical elements require a comma.

> The season having passed quickly, we were eager to plant seeds again.

> The letter stated, as you recall, that we could not pay the entire amount.

10. A nonrestrictive clause or phrase is not necessary to the meaning of the sentence and is set off with commas.

> I believed Jim, who said nothing, because he acted so efficiently.

11. Direct quotations are separated by commas from such expressions as "he said," and "they responded."

> "I wonder where we shall eat," he said.

12. Use a comma after the salutation in an informal letter and following the closing phrase of a letter.

> Dear Sally,
> Yours sincerely,

13. Use a comma after items in direct address.

> "Perry, please knock it off."
> "I'm sure, sir, you will agree with me."

14. Commas are used to separate numbers of one thousand or more.

> That old truck has 1,424,836 miles on it.

Although the comma has many correct uses, don't overdo it. Don't, for instance, separate a subject from its verb or set off restrictive elements or separate a noun from its adjective.

Incorrect: Beth and Susan, walked three miles in the rain.
Comma incorrectly separates subject and verb.

Incorrect: Everyone, who took the exam, received a raise.
Commas incorrectly set off a restrictive element, one that should not be set off.

Exercise 2 In the following sentences, place commas where appropriate.

1. After their first night in town things began to settle down a bit.

2. No I haven't told him the news yet.

3. "The last time we heard from him was on July 15 1872" reported Dr. Goldwin department chairman.

4. He did add however that the connection had been full of static.

5. They accused him of defecting but he kept denying it.

6. He asked to speak to Oscar not his young assistant who knew nothing.

7. Glen and Cindy have a good relationship; Dean and Marie none at all.

8. Because we ate so much fudge candy cookies and other goodies over the holidays we each gained five pounds.

9. I've told you many times as you may or may not remember never to lie to me or it's over between us.

10. The women having left the poker game began.

The Semicolon / ;

1. The main use of the semicolon is between two sentences when they are not joined by a coordinating conjunction.

   (Note: A period can be used in this same position; the semicolon shows a closer relationship between the sentences, however.)

   > Television has had a profound effect on the minds of this generation; books continue to hold their own, however, with the bright students.

2. The semicolon is used between sentences when they are connected with a sentence connector, often called a **conjunctive adverb**:

   > *however, nevertheless, consequently, furthermore, otherwise, accordingly, then, moreover, besides,* and so on.

   Punctuation rules can be very detailed; consequently, they should be studied carefully.

3. Use a semicolon with a **coordinating conjunction**—*and, but, or, nor, for, so,* and *yet*—only if the sentences themselves contain other commas.

   > When my grandfather, a Scot, came over on a sailing ship, he brought only his clothes, two books, and a cat; but the cat proved to be the wisest choice.

4. Use a semicolon to separate a series if needed to prevent misreading.

> The group was made up of Jack, a dentist; Warren, a flutist; and Darth, an administrator.

The Colon / :

1. Use a colon in formal situations.
   a. Before a long, formal statement

> The President began his speech: "My fellow Americans, . . ."

   b. After the salutation of a formal letter

> Dear Sir:
> Dear Dr. Shelly:

2. Use a colon to separate hours from minutes, chapter and verse in the Bible, and title from subtitle of a book.

> 6:29 A.M.
> John 3:16
> *A College History: An Introduction*

The Dash / —

If a sentence contains an unusual shift or break, use a dash to indicate the interruption.

> She said—how can I tell you?—she was leaving.

Exercise 3   Properly punctuate the following sentences with commas and a colon, semicolon, or dash. Mark (c) in the blank if the sentences are already correct.

_____ 1. He was born in Japan consequently he speaks no English.

_____ 2. I beg you to reconsider please think it over.

_____ 3. The Bradfords, the ones down the road, are missing two horses, three

   calves, four or five chickens, and a rooster so that conniving coyote must

   have been around last night.

_____ 4. Connie left no trail nevertheless she was nervous.

_____ 5. The section he just read is from Joshua 7 16.

_____ 6. He responded to the urgent call; he just responded too late.

_____ 7. After I received Jack's invitation I excitedly packed my clothes some

   pictures and a few of my favorite books but the books will probably never

   be opened.

_____ 8. I can't go with you because how should I say this? I've got another date.

_____ 9. All sorts of people fly gliders There's Ted a doctor Jim an artist Glen a salesman Nancy a lawyer and Cindy a student.

_____ 10. Their relationship they've been married ten years seems to be falling apart.

Parentheses / ( )

1. Use parentheses to set off material that interrupts the flow of the sentence or that is of little importance.

    > James Rowland (born 1934)
    >
    > Deidre wrote amazing letters (always short ones) to everyone who would read them.

2. Use parentheses to enclose numbers or letters used in a sentence or paragraph.

    > The class discussed (1) grammar, (2) punctuation, and (3) humor.

Quotation Marks / " "

1. Quotation marks are used to enclose all direct quotations, but not indirect quotations.

    > She asked, "When shall we eat?"
    > She asked when they should eat.
    > "When," she asked, "shall we eat?"
    >
    > Lincoln used many parallel constructions in his speeches, such as "of the people, by the people, and for the people."

2. Use a single quotation mark for a quotation within a quotation.

    > The chairperson said, "I'm now going to tell you exactly what the President said. He said, 'I will not run.'"

3. Use a quotation mark with titles of articles, chapters, essays, short stories, short poems, and musical compositions.

4. Use quotation marks around a word used as a word or used in a special sense.

    > Tell me what "sometime" means.

The period and the comma are <u>always</u> enclosed within quotation marks.

The colon and semicolon are <u>never</u> placed inside quotation marks.

Other marks—question mark, dash, exclamation mark—are enclosed within quotation marks if they relate directly to the quoted element, but they are placed outside if they apply to the whole sentence.

Brackets / [ ]

1. Brackets have a limited use, but one use is most helpful: use brackets inside quoted material to correct an error, to explain, or to comment.

    If you find an error in printed material, and you wish the reader to know you found it (or you want to avoid having the reader think you made the error), enclose the word *sic*—Latin for *thus*—following the error.

2. Use brackets to explain what letters stand for.

    His paper was on TWA [Trans World Airlines].

Exercise 4 Properly punctuate the following sentences with parentheses, quotation marks, or brackets. Mark (c) in the blank if the sentences are already correct.

_____ 1. Mrs. Sullivan left the nurses' station if you can call it that and walked down the hallway.

_____ 2. Lincoln said, By the people and for the people.

_____ 3. He said he'd call later, but later may mean next week as far as I can tell.

_____ 4. What time are visiting hours over, she asked.

_____ 5. We the People of the United States, in Order to form a more perfect Union . . .

_____ 6. Stephen King the author of horror fiction is here signing autographs.

_____ 7. Reynolds said, the dolpin sic has an extraordinary method of communication.

_____ 8. William Shakespeare 1564–1616 acted and wrote for a London professional troupe until his retirement in 1613.

_____ 9. She interviewed executives at IBM International Business Machines.

_____ 10. Plaintiff and its assignors deny owing to defendant the sum of three thousand dollars $3,000.00 but claim instead to owe the sum of one hundred fifty dollars $150.00.

Apostrophe / '

1. Use an apostrophe to show possession.

   > the man's suit
   > the student's desk
   > Jack's idea

2. Several endings are possible with nouns and pronouns, so you must carefully select the correct use of the apostrophe.

   a. Add an apostrophe and an *s* for nouns not ending in *s*.

      > cat's meow
      > women's hats

   b. For singular nouns that end with an *s* or *z* sound, form the possessive by adding an apostrophe and *s*. (The former practice was to add only an apostrophe if the singular noun was a *name* of *two or more* syllables.)

Conservative	Modern
Mr. Jones's cars	Mr. Jones's cars
Mr. Hogins' cars	Mr. Hogins's cars

   c. For plural nouns ending with an *s*, simply add an apostrophe.

      > the Hoginses' cars
      > cats' meows

   d. Compound words are sometimes a problem. Add an apostrophe to the last part, the one just before the word it modifies.

      > my brother-in-law's gun

   e. With a series of words, you have a choice whether to make all of them possessive. Place the apostrophe on all the nouns or on only the last one.

      > Flora, Aenea, and Jon's vacation
      > Flora's, Aenea's, and Jon's vacation

3. Apostrophes are used to show where letters (or numbers) have been omitted.

   > he'll, I've, it's, won't, '86

4. Use an apostrophe to show plurals of

   a. figures: 7's, 8's
   b. letters: S's and Y's
   c. words used in a special way:

      > Watch your "if's."

The Hyphen / -

1. Use a hyphen to break a word at a syllable at the end of a line. If you are in doubt, check a dictionary.

    com-pound   sub-tract

2. Compound modifiers used before a noun normally require a hyphen.

    well-rehearsed play
    cease-fire

3. Use a hyphen to spell out a word.

    s-y-s-t-e-m

4. Use a hyphen to separate spelled-out numbers from twenty-one to ninety-nine.

5. Use a hyphen to join the following prefixes with **proper** nouns or adjectives.

anti	anti-American
mid	mid-September
neo	neo-Nazi
non	non-European
pan	pan-American
pro	pro-German
un	un-American

Exercise 5 Properly punctuate the following sentences by adding or removing an apostrophe or hyphen wherever needed.

1. While parked at the curb overnight, Arnies car was hit broadside.

2. He was arrested for non-compliance with the judges orders.

3. A person who is Pan Anglican is one who embraces all of the Anglican Communion.

4. In the 60s people who used material from the flag for clothes were considered dis-respectful and unAmerican.

5. My favorite English teacher always told us to be careful of "ares," "iss," and "weres" in our writing.

6. Once the kittens were asleep, the cat began licking it's paws.

7. Mr. Clarks geography class has frightened students for as long as I can remember.

8. On my brothers twenty first birthday, he went out and got drunk with his friends.

9. If its well prepared, my mother-in-laws recipe for homemade pasta is the best Ive ever had.

10. Andys, Bills, and my project will be complete by mid July.

Exercise 6 Correct the following sentences for all possible punctuation errors.

1. Where in heavens name were you she cried.

2. I want to talk to you Bob not a bunch of people I dont even know

3. Eleanor pleaded if you will just listen Mr Brady to my proposal you may find it worthwhile

4. UNESCO is an acronym for United Nations Educational Scientific and Cultural Organization

5. My friend Paula drives me crazy actually she makes me sick with her prejudices

6. The doctor is still coming isnt he

7. She said she didnt want to see me for a while moreover she asked me not even to call her

8. The clock touched 1 00 A M it was time to get going

9. I wonder why he didnt call but I nevertheless refuse to call him first to find out

10. He wants very much to see me so we can work this out but I get upset when I talk to him besides why should I

11. Mr and Mrs J P Morgan of Fort Collins Colorado won the car by investing only twenty five dollars $25 for a lottery ticket

12. I travel every summer with my mother the journalist my father the reporter and my brother the brat but I wont be able to go with them once I start summer school

13. After we left Missouri on August 11 1983 we began the pre college program in school in San Diego

14. He asked me if I woke up when the alarm rang at 4 00 A M

15. I left school which I enjoyed after the incident with the police

MECHANICS

Like punctuation, mechanics are technical conventions: they have come to us after centuries of usage. Some were invented as mere conveniences for the printer.

Capital Letters

Capital letters are reserved for special words in our language—they are not used the same way in other languages.

Use capital letters only when you have a specific need or reason to do so. Using unnecessary capitals is a sure mark of an inexperienced or careless writer.

1. Capitalize the first word of a sentence.

2. Capitalize the first word of each line of poetry.

3. Use a capital for the first word of a direct quotation within a sentence, unless the quotation is a fragment.

4. Use a capital letter for all nouns referring to God, Christ, the Koran, and the Bible. Also capitalize the names of gods and goddesses of polytheistic religions.

    Venus, Zeus

5. Official titles used before the names of the official are capitalized.

    Mayor Powers
    Queen Elizabeth

    Note: Always use a capital letter for *President*.

6. Capitalize all proper names.

    Americans
    Shakespearean
    Emily Dickinson
    Muriel Davis
    Maine

7. Capitalize all words—except conjunctions, articles, and short prepositions—in works of music, art, literature, magazines, etc.

    The Atlantic Monthly
    The Tempest
    The Fifth Symphony

8. Names of organizations, institutions, businesses, agencies, movements, religions, holidays, and holy days are capitalized.

9. Heavenly bodies are capitalized.

    Mars, Jupiter
    Big Dipper

10. Titles of people and books are capitalized.

> Dr. Guiles
> General Haig
> *Gone with the Wind*

11. Capitalize points of direction when they designate specific regions.

> the South
> *but*
> the north corner

Italics

To show italics in handwriting or while typing, simply underline the words you want in italics.

1. Use italics for titles of books, magazines, plays, movies, and the names given to ships, trains, and planes.

> *A Farewell to Arms*
> *The Ladies Home Journal*

2. You may use italics (sparingly) to show emphasis or to use a word in a special sense.

> The word *like* is overused.

3. Foreign words or phrases are italicized.

> *quid pro quo*

Exercise 7 In the following sentences, place capital letters where they belong and underline any words that should be in italics.

1. hippolytus met with disaster because he refused to recognize aphrodite.

2. his words were, "ask not what your country can do for you; ask what you can do for your country."

3. pet cemetery is reputed to be stephen king's best book yet.

4. one of the most beautiful lakes i've ever seen is lake arrowhead in the san bernardino mountains.

5. when i read ivan ilyich, i almost cried because of his pitiful death.

6. everyone should read don quixote by miguel de cervantes.

7. some people thought that governor brown of california was inept.

8. the war between the north and the south has left scars that are visible even today.

9. attorney general malcom is advising people with heart problems not to take the shuttle to the moon without prior approval from their doctors.

10. if the russians and the americans could get together without their countries' leaders, we could probably end this nonsense about the buildup of nuclear arms.

Abbreviations

When in doubt about abbreviating a word, do not. You will rarely be incorrect if you spell out words unless they are the specific terms of a particular job or discipline.

Be consistent. If you spell out a form in one paragraph, be sure to follow through with spelled-out forms throughout that document.

1. Use abbreviations of these titles and forms of address when they come before a proper name:

> Mr., Mrs., Dr., Ms.

2. Except for very formal settings, titles are abbreviated if the title is followed by a first name or initial plus a surname. However, the title must be spelled out if only a surname is given.

Rev. Mark Trotter	The Reverend Trotter
Hon. Edward Kennedy	The Honorable Mr. Kennedy

3. *Jr.* and *Sr.* following a name are abbreviated.

4. Academic degrees are abbreviated.

> M.A.   Ph.D.

5. Abbreviations of states are acceptable except in the most formal settings.

6. Certain foreign expressions are abbreviated.

> e.g. (for example)
> et al. (and others)
> etc. (and so forth)

Numbers

1. Numbers that can be written in one or two words are generally spelled out.

> Twenty-seven of us left yesterday.

2. Numbers at the beginning of sentences, however, are always spelled out.

3. Numbers are used for dates, measures, data, amounts of money, and time.

> January 26, 1936
> 101 A.D.   22 percent   75 pounds
> 8:40 P.M.   2″ × 4″   6415 Wildwood Drive

4. The numbers between twenty and one hundred are hyphenated.

> twenty-two   forty-three

Exercise 8 In the following sentences, change the proper words to their abbreviated forms and make sure the numbers are correctly handled. Cross out the incorrect forms and write the correct forms in above them.

1. Doctor and Missus Franks are celebrating their 13th wedding anniversary.

2. Where did you plan to earn your Master of Sciences degree?

3. 14 people tried to get into the elevator, and all but 4 made it.

4. Miss Jacobs will be taking my place until June twenty-seven.

5. My mother, who lives in Greeley, Colo., likes baking cakes, cookies, pies, and so forth.

6. She weighs exactly a hundred and twenty one pounds.

7. The doctor can see you at four o'clock P.M.

8. Professor Robert B. Cavero will be lecturing at the university.

9. "Kosher Deli Co., Inc." was printed on the letterhead, but I thought that Kosher Deli Company, Incorporated, had gone out of business.

10. There were four hundred and seventy three people at the reception.

Exercise 9   Mechanics Review Correct the following sentences for all possible mechanics errors.

1. pres. reagan's speech preempted all the regular programming.

2. many people suffer from depression only during certain times for example many get depressed during christmas.

3. jewish people celebrate hanukkah instead of christmas.

4. muriel davis used the norton anthology of world literature in her class called masterpieces of world literature.

5. the scriptures of the mohammedans are called the koran.

6. the punk rock movement is different in many ways from the hippie era.

7. he was a catholic until he became a nichiren shoshu buddhist.

8. my sister, bonnie, will be thirty four on her next birthday in april.

9. the korean language is distantly related to japanese.

10. the tv guide is a weekly magazine telling what's on television.

11. i've never been able to find the big dipper.

12. 29 people took the bus trip to chicago.

13. my dad is william j. way, senior, and my brother is jr.

14. the work of goethe, cervantes, yeats, shelley, and others was included in the collection.

15. president eisenhower was gen. eisenhower before he became president of the united states.

Writers in English have trouble spelling certain words; sometimes simple words trip an otherwise good speller, but for most the same words are consistently difficult. Mark Twain had an answer for misspelling a word that I've found useful (though not always persuasive). "It's a very uncreative mind that can think of only one way to spell a word." No one needs to persuade us that we need to spell correctly. Spelling correctly is associated with "knowing English." That may not be quite fair, but as a convention, nothing is stronger than spelling as a sign of Standard Written English.

Master this first list; these words are misspelled often and seem to stand out even more than other words.

accommodate	believe	occurred	separate
already	consistent	parallel	similar
all right	definite	perform	surprise
a lot	environment	probably	writing
basically	library	receive	

Exercise 10 Correct or mark *correct* above the words in italics in the following sentences.

1. It has *occured* to me that our interests may be running *paralel*.

2. He was *surprised* to see her coming out of the building.

3. *Basicly*, all I have left to read is the last chapter.

4. If he's nothing else, he's *consistant*.

5. He said the party is *definate* for Friday night.

6. He's *probably writing* me a letter right now.

7. We've been studying pollution in our *envirenment*.

8. I *believe* that's my coat you've picked up.

9. They really should have *seperated* those two rowdy boys.

10. *Alot* of people use the school *libary* over the weekend.

Next you need to master this pairs list—words that sound similar or alike but have different meanings.

an/and	affect/effect
accept/except	allusion/illusion
by/buy	capitol/capital
cite/site/sight	complement/compliment
council/counsel	do/due
desert/dessert	hear/here
loose/lose	no/know
personal/personnel	piece/peace
patients/patience	already/all ready
presents/presence	principle/principal
quiet/quite	right/write
sense/since	than/then
there/their/they're	to/too/two
whether/weather	your/you're

Exercise 11 Underline the correct words in the following sentences.

1. She wants to know where to find the (counsel, council) for legal help.

2. The composition we're supposed to (do, due) is (do, due) on Wednesday.

3. This raise in tuition is sure to (effect, affect) all of us.

4. He's developed a sixth (sense, since) (sense, since) the accident.

5. Everyone has (accepted, excepted) the proposal (accept, except) me.

6. His (illusions, allusions) are the result of years of using drugs.

7. Their income is (complimented, complemented) by food stamps and now they have nothing but (compliments, complements) for the government.

8. The (principal, principle) of our school is always harping on what's (write, right) and wrong.

9. We were arguing about the (principals, principles) involved in the case, not the specifics.

10. The overall (effect, affect) is quite impressive.

The third list is one of misspelled words typically found in student papers. Consider checking it when you proofread.

abbreviate	conqueror	gauge	marriage
accelerator	conscience	government	mattress
accept	criticism	grammar	medieval
accommodate	debatable	grandeur	miniature
accumulate	defendant	grievance	mischievous
achievement	definite	guarantee	misspelled
acknowledgment	deity	guerilla	mosquitoes
acquaint	diaphragm	guidance	necessary
acreage	develop	handicapped	nickel
across	dietitian	harass	niece
adolescence	dilettante	hearse	nineteen
amateur	disappoint	height	ninety
analysis	discern	hemorrhage	noticeable
analyze	distribute	heroes	noticing
argument	divine	humorous	nowadays
article	doesn't	hygiene	obedience
athlete	dominant	hypocrisy	occasion
attendance	dully	hysterical	occur
bachelor	echoes	illiterate	occurrence
banister	ecstasy	idiosyncrasy	omission
beautiful	efficiency	immediately	oneself
becoming	eighth	impel	one's self
believe	ellipse	incidentally	opponent
benefited, benefitted	embarrass	independent	opinion
biased	encyclopedia	insistent	original
biscuit	enthusiastic	insofar as	outrageous
brilliant	environment	irrelevant	pamphlet
broccoli	exaggerate	irresistible	parallel
bureaucratic	existence	jeopardy	participle
business	experience	jewelry	pastime
calendar	experiential	judgment	perceive
candidate	extraordinary	judicial	permissible
captain	familiar	khaki	persuade
carburetor	fascinate	knowledge	picnicked
caucus	faucet	knowledgeable	pneumonia
celebrity	February	laboratory	prejudice
changeable	fiend	labyrinthine	privilege
chauffeur	fiery	lavender	procedure
characteristic	financial	liable	psalm
clearance	forehead	library	psychology
colander	foreign	loneliness	quantity
column	foreseeable	magazine	quarantine
committee	forty	maintenance	questionnaire
complexion	friend	maneuver	queue
concede	fulfill, fulfil	manufacturer	quizzes

recede	shriek	thinness	veterinarian
receipt	siege	thorough	view
receiving	similar	traffic	warrant
recognize	sincerely	tragedy	Wednesday
reference	solemn	transcendent	weight
religion	sophomore	tries	weird
restaurant	stomach	truly	whole
rheumatism	straight	Tuesday	worried
rhythm	strength	unanimous	writing
ricochet	stupefy	undoubtedly	written
roommate	subtlety	unforeseen	yacht
sacrilege	superstitious	unnecessary	yeoman
safety	surgeon	until	yield
sandwich	susceptible	usable	your
schedule	tangible	useful	you're
scissors	tasting	vacancy	
seize	technical	valuable	
sentence	temperament	vegetable	
separate	tenderly	vengeance	
sergeant	their	vertical	

Exercise 12 Spell correctly words in italics in the following sentences.
Mark (c) in the blank if they are already correct.

_____ 1. The *lettace* stood draining in the *calendar* in the sink.

_____ 2. His work in *psycology* has *benefitted* all of humanity but he's a little *weird*.

_____ 3. Faster and faster he drove, pushing the *axcelerater* to the floor.

_____ 4. He gets *embarassed* if you tease him about it.

_____ 5. Fred *does'nt* need to hear any more *critisism*; his *conshunse* is already

bothering him.

_____ 6. *Fourty* years ago today we came here on our honeymoon.

_____ 7. My *ninety*-year-old grandmother, *incidently*, lives *accros* the street.

_____ 8. I've had *similiar* experiences before in which a place I've never been will

seem *familar*.

_____ 9. Mr. Bonham had perfect *attendance* on the day of the test.

_____ 10. He's been in *exstasy* since he got the results.

Prefixes

The following prefixes do not affect the spelling of the base word: *un-*, *dis-*, *mis-*.

> unnecessary, unable, unnatural, unnoticed
> dissatisfy, disappoint, dissolve, disable
> misspell, misconduct, misbehave, misshapen

Suffixes

1. A group of troublesome (but easy to learn) words are those ending in *-cede*, *-ceed*, and *-sede*.
   a. only one word ends in *-sede*: **supersede**
   b. three end in *-ceed*: **exceed, proceed, succeed**
   c. the others of this kind end in *-cede*: **precede, secede, recede, intercede**

2. Those words ending in *-able*, *-ible*, *-ance*, and *-ence* you must look up to be sure since no rule applies to all of them. Be aware that words ending in *-able* are more common than those ending in *-ible*.

3. The final (silent) *e* remains in when a suffix that begins with a consonant is added.

   > achievement, arrangement, ninety, movement

   Some exceptions to this rule are:

   > argument, awful, judgment, ninth, probably, truly

4. The final (silent) *e* is dropped when a suffix that begins with a vowel is added.

   > admire, imagine, dining, coming, grievance

5. However, the *e* is kept if:
   a. it helps make *c* or *g* soft: **advantageous, courageous, noticeable**
   b. it prevents mispronunciation: **eyeing, mileage, hoeing, shoeing**
   c. it prevents confusion with another word: **singeing, dyeing**

6. With words of one syllable that end in a **single consonant** preceded by a *single vowel*, double the final consonant before adding a suffix that begins a vowel.

   > dropped, stopping, hottest, spinning

7. If the one-syllable word ends in two consonants, do not double the last one before adding a suffix beginning with a vowel.

   > acting, talking, walking

8. Also, a one-syllable word with two vowels does not double the final consonant.

   > cooling, bearing, foamed, reeling, dealing

9. For words of more than one syllable ending in a consonant, double the final consonant *only if*:

   a. the accent is on the last syllable and
   b. a single vowel precedes the consonant:

   deferred, **regrettable**

Exercise 13 Spell correctly the words in italics in the following sentences. Mark (c) in the blank if they are already correct.

_____ 1. He was stopped for *exceding* the speed limit.

_____ 2. I want to know who is *responsable* for this mess.

_____ 3. Make sure the address is correct so you don't *missend* the letter.

_____ 4. The damage is *negligible*.

_____ 5. Her bluntness really *unerves* me.

_____ 6. This was the *hotest* summer of the year and now the temperature has *droped* fifty degrees.

_____ 7. Steven found *encouragment* in the fact that his dad shared his problem.

_____ 8. We had to *disect* a frog in biology.

_____ 9. Mary resents *dealing* with those people's problems.

_____ 10. There's no way we can *disprove* her story.

Plurals

1. Most nouns form the plural by simply adding *s*.

   towns, bugs, tables, pens

2. Singular nouns that end in *y* form the plural by changing the *y* to *i* and adding *es*.

   babies, ladies, stories

   Note: If the *y* is preceded by a vowel, the words form plural in the normal way—adding an *s*.

   toys

3. Nouns ending in *o* preceded by a consonant form the plural by adding *es*.

   cargoes, heroes, potatoes, tomatoes, vetoes
   Exceptions—autos, pianos, Eskimos

4. If a singular noun ends in *s*, *sh*, *ch*, *x*, or *z*, it forms its plural by adding *es*.

> Joneses, bushes, matches, waxes, churches

5. Remember, *i* before *e* except after *c* or when sounded like *a* as in *neighbor* and *weigh*.

Exceptions to this rule are

either	foreign	seizure
neither	forfeit	sovereign
leisure	height	weird
counterfeit	seige	

Exercise 14 In the space provided write the plural form of the word in parentheses.

1. Those two men over there are (lackey) for the boss. _____

2. My dad waxes the (floor) once a week. _____

3. Men like that have always been my (hero). _____

4. The young woman made some new clothes for her (baby). _____

5. He lurches when he walks since the (accident). _____

6. He has so many broken-down (auto) in his front yard that it looks like a junkyard. _____

7. Our (neighbor) are going to have to do something about that dog's barking all night. _____

8. (Eskimo) must be warm-blooded people. _____

9. We removed all those dead (bush) from the back of the house. _____

10. Nothing bothers me more than the way some (lady) chatter. _____

Exercise 15   Spelling Review In each of these sentences, underline the correct word in parentheses.

1. Dr. Seguno's (presents, presence) intimidates most people.

2. I'm so broke that I'm down to the (nickles, nickels) in my piggy bank.

3. The (preceding, preceeding) message was a special announcement.

4. She can't (hear, here) anything unless you shout.

5. Let's take steps to (disspell, dispel, dispell) that rumor right now.

6. He's been a (bacheler, bachelor) all his life.

7. We had plum pudding for (dessert, desert).

8. The problem isn't big enough to be (unmanageable, unmanagible).

9. His (omision, omission) hurt his alibi rather than helped it.

10. I can't (conceive, concieve) of anything more ridiculous.

REVIEW TEST

I. Punctuation—The Period, the Comma, the Question Mark, and the Exclamation Mark

Indicate whether the following sentences are punctuated correctly (a) or incorrectly (b).

_____ 1. "When will the ship dock" asked Mary Ann.

_____ 2. After the baby was born, their lives were turned upside down.

_____ 3. I wish you would either cooperate with the group, or leave.

_____ 4. The dentist hasn't called has he?

_____ 5. I've always wondered what happened to you?

_____ 6. Where have you been?

_____ 7. Eliot please close that window.

_____ 8. "Why don't you just leave me alone?" she screeched!

_____ 9. No, I haven't heard from Brad since last month.

_____ 10. Dr. Thomas the new dean of admissions is scheduled to arrive on Monday January 3 at 5:00 P.M.

_____ 11. I've heard rumors that I.B.M. is going bankrupt.

_____ 12. Dan will you please be quiet so I can study?

_____ 13. This treachery and deceit must stop!

_____ 14. In Spanish class we've learned the present and the imperfect tenses.

_____ 15. Eliza Bloom was born in 1911 (?) and died in 1954.

_____ 16. Barbara, my sister's friend, teaches jazz dance at the studio.

_____ 17. She saw the car coming but it passed her before she could flag it down.

_____ 18. Neither of us was invited to the wedding nor were we welcome at the reception.

_____ 19. I asked Jamie who only stared into space how he felt.

_____ 20. Steve, not Dale, is my husband.

II. Punctuation—The Comma, the Quotation Mark, the Semicolon, and the Colon

Place in each blank the letter of the best description.

a = Needs one or more commas
b = Needs quotation marks
c = Needs one or more semicolons
d = Needs a colon

_____ 21. I've tried everything to get him to respond but he only stares into space.

_____ 22. Please get the following things at the store thread, glue, paper, and felt-tipped pen.

_____ 23. Merrilee, why, asked Joey, won't you discuss this with me?

_____ 24. She asked, How on earth do you do it?

_____ 25. The mood having passed we wanted to change the subject.

_____ 26. Either behave yourself or you're going to bed early.

_____ 27. She's crazy about the guy I can't stand him.

_____ 28. Her plane is scheduled to arrive at exactly 4 17 this afternoon.

_____ 29. Debbie's brother broke his leg consequently he won't be playing in any more games this season.

_____ 30. My friend Jack, the chemist, my brother Bill, the contractor, and my boyfriend Steve, the mailman, all went to the business convention.

_____ 31. Sam is a big man yet he's as gentle as a lamb.

_____ 32. We were in Oceanside California on February 19 1983.

_____ 33. R. V. Cassill writes, Writing is a way of coming to terms with the world and with oneself.

_____ 34. The traffic woke me at 4 00 this morning.

_____ 35. My father is on a health kick and he has started jogging in the morning.

_____ 36. Her cold was much better nevertheless she stayed in bed another day.

_____ 37. He said I get fooled by the very young ones.

_____ 38. Those who left were lucky those who stayed regretted it.

_____ 39. Tell me what you mean by soon.

_____ 40. My mother a stubborn woman and I argue for hours at a time, and we seldom come to any agreement.

III. Punctuation—The Dash, the Hyphen, Parentheses, and Brackets

Place in each blank the letter of the best description.

a = Use a dash
b = Use a hyphen
c = Use parentheses
d = Use brackets

_____ 41. My uncle works for CBS Columbia Broadcasting System.

_____ 42. It was a well executed performance.

_____ 43. Two hundred and thirty nine people crowded into the stadium.

_____ 44. Your car I don't know quite how to say this your car rolled down the hill and plowed into a truck.

_____ 45. So far this semester we've studied 1 literature, 2 physics, and 3 French.

_____ 46. My dog dislikes mailmen, policemen, and military men anyone who wears a uniform.

_____ 47. We met around mid October.

_____ 48. Niccolo Machiavelli 1469–1527 wrote *The Prince*.

_____ 49. The report said, "All of the item sic were fully insured."

_____ 50. It is hereby ordered that defendant pay to plaintiff the sum of one hundred fifty thousand dollars $150,000.00 on or before December 1984.

IV. Punctuation—The Apostrophe

Indicate whether the following sentences use apostrophes correctly (a) or incorrectly (b).

_____ 51. The jalopy is Cindy's, Flo's, and mine.

_____ 52. My mother's-in-law cooking leaves a lot to be desired.

_____ 53. He told us to watch our P's and Q's.

_____ 54. The dog broke it's leg.

_____ 55. Hell never cooperate with you.

_____ 56. All of my friend's houses are off limits to me since my arrest.

_____ 57. Andrea wants to work at a national women's bank.

_____ 58. The women's meeting has been canceled.

_____ 59. My brother knows all of his multiplication tables except for his 7s and 8s.

_____ 60. It's coats I'm shopping for, not jackets.

VI. Mechanics—Capital Letters and Italics

Indicate whether the capital letters and italics in the following sentences are correct (a) or incorrect (b).

_____ 61. The birds are flying South for the winter.

_____ 62. "I Will Fear No Evil" is a great book by Robert Heinlein.

_____ 63. Cliff just sighted Saturn in his telescope.

_____ 64. They call their yacht princess grace.

_____ 65. You don't even know the meaning of the word friendship.

_____ 66. Hurricane Elly has moved down South.

_____ 67. The result was *quid pro quo.*

_____ 68. He emphatically stated, "those are the men, officer."

_____ 69. I most enjoyed the literature of the renaissance.

_____ 70. The Baptist Religion is the only Religion I have left to try.

VI. Mechanics—Abbreviations and Numbers

Indicate whether the abbreviations and numbers in the following sentences are correct (a) or incorrect (b).

_____ 71. The Honorable Seymour Wishbone will preside.

_____ 72. The Dr. called to change your appointment.

_____ 73. The plank has to measure 14″ × 24″.

_____ 74. I live at fourteen hundred Thirty Ninth Street.

_____ 75. Twenty-three people went on the hike and 22 returned.

_____ 76. He got his Doctor of Philosophy Degree in March.

_____ 77. Forty-three out of a hundred and two people made it.

_____ 78. Mrs. Bradley has 14 children.

_____ 79. 40 percent of the class failed the test.

_____ 80. The date was January thirty-first, nineteen hundred and eighty-four.

VII. Spelling

Choose the correct word to complete each sentence.

a. patients   e. patience
b. capital   f. capitol
c. to   g. too
d. peace   h. piece

_____ 81. That man has an incredible amount of _____ .

_____ 82. Washington, D.C., is our country's _____ .

_____ 83. I'm one of Dr. Willowby's _____ .

_____ 84. All proper nouns begin with letters that are _____ .

_____ 85. My sister wants to come _____ .

_____ 86. All I want is a _____ .

_____ 87. Please let's have a little _____ and quiet.

_____ 88. I don't need _____ .

VIII. Spelling—Prefixes, Suffixes, and Plurals; Commonly Misspelled Words

Choose the letter of the correct word.

_____ 89. He has a (firey, fiery, firy) temper.
                 a   b   c

_____ 90. We're having (broccoli, brocolli) with dinner.
                      a   b

_____ 91. Her scar is barely (noticable, noticeable, noticeible).
                         a   b   c

_____ 92. Brenda's drunken fits are (outragies, outrages, outrageous).
                               a   b   c

_____ 93. It's totally (unecessary, unneccessary, unnecessary) for you to stay.
                     a   b   c

_____ 94. I was just (admireing, admiring) your ring.
                     a   b

_____ 95. It should warm up by (February, Febuary).
                       a   b

_____ 96. Please make yourselves (comfortable, comfortible).
                       a   b

_____ 97. My mother's ideas are absolutely (medeval, medieval).
                       a   b

_____ 98. That Cadillac must get lousy (milage, mileage).
                     a   b

_____ 99. Haley spent all day in (trafic, traffic) court.
                     a   b

_____ 100. The poor man was gripped by a (seisure, seizure).
                       a   b

INDEX